BYRON: THE RECORD OF A QUEST

BYRON:
THE RECORD OF A QUEST

Studies in a Poet's Concept and Treatment of Nature

By Ernest J. Lovell, Jr.

ARCHON BOOKS
HAMDEN, CONNECTICUT
1966

This Book Is For Chris

PREFATORY NOTE

Of the friends who have given their aid and encouragement, I wish especially to thank Elkin C. Wilson, who first led me to the study of Byron; Robert R. Cawley, who gave me his friendship and guidance at Princeton University when I was writing my doctoral dissertation, from which this book grew; and Harry H. Ransom, who exhibited a more than friendly interest in its publication. I should also like here to express my gratitude to The University of Texas Research Institute for providing the necessary funds for publication.

CONTENTS

Chapter I

INTRODUCTION AND CONCLUSIONS

1

*Newtonian Deism and the Retirement Theme
in the Eighteenth Century*

The peace of the Augustans as George Saintsbury described it may or may not have been achieved altogether. The desire for it, however, unquestionably existed. With the opening years of the eighteenth century, one feels, we have not the prelude, merely, to modern civilization; the thing itself is actually present. Like the present period, it was one of the great city; it was an age of social complexity, business rivalry, and an industrialization which was to increase; it was an age of books and culture, political intrigue, literary and religious controversy and jealousy. In short, it was thoroughly "artificial," that is, civilized. And like our own age, it had a strong urge to escape from complexity into simplicity. Then and now, as in the time of Horace, both man and poet sought his relief in the country, in a life of retirement. "Before he can long for the peace and goodness of retirement, the poet must have turbulence and evil to retire from—and no age has offered in its practice so plain and emphatic a challenge to the critic of society and civilization as was offered by the Neo-classic Age."[1]

[1]George G. Williams, "The Beginnings of Nature Poetry in the Eighteenth Century," *Studies in Philology*, XXVII, 585. In the discussion of the historical background of the concept and treatment of nature in the eighteenth century which follows, I have depended heavily upon Williams' article and upon those of Arthur O. Lovejoy, "The Parallel of Deism and Classicism," *Modern Philology*, XXIX, 281–99; Raymond D. Havens, "Romantic Aspects of the Age of Pope," *PMLA*, XXVII, 297–324; May

It has been remarked by Samuel H. Monk,[2] in his study of the ideas of the *Sublime* in eighteenth-century England, that fortunately the time has come when it is no longer necessary to set up a neo-classical straw man, "cold and regular and decorous," merely in order to knock it down. It is now possible to understand the Return to Nature Movement of the Romantic Period not as a revolution but as a slow evolution, its seeds far back in the previous century. For once given the character of the earlier period, properly understood, the degree of interest expressed in the world of external nature seems inevitable. The period was, as is evident, one of rationalistic common sense: it desired a rational life, one governed by the Horatian philosophy of the golden mean. It sought a sensible, contented life and had an obvious wish to avoid extremes, to shun immoderation in any of its forms. Thus many of the neo-classical writers, among them those often regarded as most typical of the age, did upon occasion yearn earnestly for the relief nature might offer from the cares and tribulations of city life. The seeming paradox is that it was exactly those characteristics usually regarded as most typically

---

Dulaney Bush, "Rational Proof of a Deity from the Order of Nature," *ELH*, IX, 288–319; Abbott C. Martin, "The Love of Solitude in Eighteenth Century Poetry," *The South Atlantic Quarterly*, XXIX, 48–59; and C. A. Moore, "The Return to Nature in English Poetry of the Eighteenth Century," *Studies in Philology*, XIV, 243–91. Book-length studies which have proved especially valuable are those of Samuel H. Monk, *The Sublime: A Study of Critical Theories in XVIII-Century England* (New York, 1935); Robert A. Aubin, *Topographical Poetry in XVIII-Century England* (New York, 1936); Elizabeth Wheeler Manwaring, *Italian Landscape in Eighteenth Century England* (New York, 1925); Christopher Hussey, *The Picturesque: Studies in a Point of View* (London, 1927); Basil Willey, *The Eighteenth Century Background* (London, 1940); and Joseph Warren Beach, *The Concept of Nature in Nineteenth-Century English Poetry* (New York, 1936). It has not been thought necessary to indicate particular indebtedness to each of these scholars.

The picturesque and the sublime in the novel have been neglected rather generally.

[2] *The Sublime*, p. 5.

neo-classical which drove men, not only from city to country, but also far along the way toward an actual deification of nature.

In addition, one may recall the fact that England in the seventeenth century had been shaken by civil war and the political upheaval produced by religious quarrel. Englishmen were weary of strife and longed for order and peace. The Augustan age set about to establish it, building on the methods and achievements of the new physical science. "Because reason and nature seemed immutable and unassailable bases for faith, the Augustans made a great synthesis of the two and to the resulting abstraction assigned the attributes of divinity."[3] In religion, the supernatural tended to be displaced by the natural; and reason came forth to offer ample teleological proof of a benevolent Creator in attesting to the wisdom of a well regulated creation, one in which every part was necessary to the perfection of the whole. The cosmology of Newton, with its final solution of the mystery in the Great First Cause, was the foundation stone upon which the Augustans built. The great man himself had written[4] in 1692 to Dr. Bentley that "when I wrote my treatise about our system, I had an eye upon such principles as might work with considering men for the belief of a Deity, and nothing can rejoice me more than to find it useful for that purpose." One of the outcomes was deism, the most typical product, perhaps, of neo-classicism and closely paralleling many of its basic assumptions. Newton, however, did not foresee that his system along with the science which produced it would soon offer indispensable nutriment to a religion and a philosophy that came to be a chief enemy of orthodox Christianity. Nor did he see the thin line separating the idea of a Creator who was

[3]Bush, op. cit., p. 288.
[4]H. Craik, ed., English Prose (London, 1908), III, 313. Quoted by Bush, op. cit., p. 291.

the Great First Cause and continuing Sustainer of the universe, everywhere evident in it, and the idea that pantheistically identified Creator and creation. But their appearance and rapid popularization were not to be long delayed.

Both these tendencies of the neo-classical period—the desire to escape from a life of civilized complexity into one of "natural" simplicity and the desire for order and clarity in intellectual and spiritual spheres, each an aspect of the neo-classical sympathy for the clear and common-sensical—both resulted in a rather large amount of writing, from the literary quarter, in praise of Nature, a word which came to represent, in its many meanings, the dominant idea of the century. And it was but another very short step, from these two tendencies, to the belief which found its ultimate expression in Words-worth, that a life close to nature tends to promote conscious-ness of a supreme cosmic order and to predispose man to sub-limity and goodness. The growing current of writing in praise of nature is sometimes traced from such "precursors" of romanticism as Thomson and Dyer, on to Gray and Collins and Warton, through Cowper and Beattie, until with a glance at Burke on the sublime and another at landscape gardening, one comes to Wordsworth's *Evening Walk* and *Descriptive Sketches*. The picture is falsely incomplete, of course.

It is certainly not the purpose of these introductory remarks to present a complete view of the phenomenon of nature as it appears in the pages of the eighteenth century. Certain pronouncements of the age, however, may be glanced at. One is not overwhelmed, usually, by the enthusiasm of the utter-ances; the restraint of the age and the mask of impersonality typically assumed excludes this. Nor is it contended that utterances in favor of the country life are typical of the period and that those praising life in the city are not. It is well to be reminded, however, that Dr. Johnson[5] noted in 1751, "there is, indeed, scarcely any writer who has not celebrated the happiness of rural privacy." Steele[6] had already observed, in 1711, "to one used to live in a city, the charms of the country are so exquisite, that the mind is lost in a certain transport which raises us above ordinary life, and yet is not strong enough to be inconsistent with tranquillity." And Gay[7] had written,

> You, who the sweets of rural life have known,
> Despise the ungrateful hurry of the town,

and

> With what sublimest joy from noisy town,
> At rural seat, Lucretelus retired.

Such statements, of course, do not necessarily indicate their authors to be dedicated lovers of nature; often they were merely reacting against the city. But that the "beauties" of nature were not wholly overlooked, that they were even recognized as contributing to the tranquillity necessary for contemplation is evident from such a statement as Steele's,[8] that "to stand by a stream, naturally lulls the mind into composure and reverence; to walk in shades, diversifies that pleasure; and a bright sunshine makes a man consider all nature in gladness, and himself the happiest being in it." And Pope has indicated[9] that nature's very reason for existing is to minister unto man's soul:

> What are falling rills and pendant shades,
> The morning bowers, the evening colonnades,
> But soft recesses for th' uneasy mind
> To sigh unheard in. . . .

[5]*Rambler*, No. 135.
[6]*Spectator*, No. 118.
[7]"Rural Sports," ll. 1–2; "Wine," ll. 121–22.
[8]*Tatler*, No. 169.
[9]"A Fragment." Quoted by Williams, *op. cit.*, p. 597.

Pomfret's famous *Choice* (1700) sang this theme and was rewarded with the immense popularity which Johnson glanced at when he called it the composition oftenest perused in the English language. This picture of the Horatian ideal, Johnson explained,[10] "exhibits a system of life adapted to common notions and equal to common expectations; such a state as affords plenty and tranquillity, without exclusion of intellectual pleasures."

The chief force, however, which induced in the Augustans an interest in the external world seems to have been the Newtonian cosmology. Newton appeared to them to provide the proof of the belief,[11] shared by Anglicans along with deists, that "the order, grandeur, beauty, and perfection of the universe, of nature, serve only to demonstrate the greatness, goodness, wisdom, and power of God." Thus Steele writes,[12] "methinks it is a sort of impiety to have no attention to the course of nature." Gay believes that

> Nature's various face informs my sense,
> Of an all-wise powerful providence.

Two of Thomson's earliest poems were "On the Works and Wonders of Almighty Power" and a "Hymn to God's Power," both of them nature poems. The "Hymn" attached to the *Seasons* is entirely given to this theme, and in the *Seasons* themselves[13] it receives frequent treatment:

> Hail, Source of Being, Universal soul
> Of Heaven and earth! Essential presence, hail!
> To Thee I bend the knee; to Thee my thoughts,
> Continual, climb; who, with a master-hand,
> Hast a great whole into perfection touch'd.

[10]*Lives of the English Poets*, ed. Hill (Oxford, 1905), I, 302.
[11]Williams, *op. cit.*, p. 603.
[12]*Guardian*, No. 169.
[13]"Spring," ll. 556–60.

In "A Poem Sacred to the Memory of Sir Isaac Newton" Thomson gave due credit[14] to the physicist in the year of his death, when he pictured him in heaven:

> And what new wonders can ye show your guest!
> Who, while on this dim spot, where mortals toil
> Clouded in dust, from motion's simple laws,
> Could trace the secret hand of Providence,
> Wide-working through this universal frame.
> Have ye not listen'd while he bound the suns
> And planets to their spheres!

And Thomson says of the seasons,[15]

> These, as they change, Almighty Father, these
> Are but the varied God. The rolling year
> Is full of Thee.

Now Newton the scientist had explained the laws which govern the functioning of the universe; Newton the religious metaphysician, however, had attempted to link those laws as closely as possible to the Divine Will. He had done this by refraining from identifying matter and the Divine Spirit, thus avoiding all atheistic implications; but at the same time he had, by means of his concept of the sensorium, placed God everywhere within the universe. This accounts for the seeming pantheism in the passage from Thomson just quoted. The idea of the essence of Deity "wide-working *through*" a universe which is "full" of Him is not very far removed, of course, from the idea expressed by Wordsworth in *Tintern Abbey*. Pope's pantheism[16] is much more explicit than Thomson's, if the word may be applied to the latter poet.

> All are but parts of one stupendous whole,
> Whose body Nature is, and God the soul;

[14]Ll. 12–18.
[15]*Hymn*, ll. 1–3.
[16]*Essay on Man*, I, ix; III, i.

> That, chang'd through all, and yet in all the same;
> Great in the earth, as in th' ethereal frame;
> Warms in the sun, refreshes in the breeze,
> Glows in the stars, and blossoms in the trees,
> Lives through all life, extends through all extent.
> . . . .
> Look round our world; behold the chain of love
> Combining all below and all above.
> See plastic Nature working to this end.

But the more typical expression of the neo-classical age, one feels, kept itself this side of pantheism and aloof from the questionable doctrines of Spinoza, as did Addison in his ode, "The spacious firmament on high," and in the *Spectator*,[17] when he wrote,

> The more extended our reason is, and the more able to grapple with immense objects, the greater still are those discoveries which it makes of wisdom and providence in the work of the creation. A Sir Isaac Newton, who stands up as the miracle of the present age, can look through a whole planetary system; consider it in its weight, number and measure; and draw from it as many demonstrations of infinite power and wisdom, as a more confined understanding is able to deduce from the system of a human body.

It is evident how very closely associated Reason, Newton, God, and the planetary system are in Addison's mind.

2

The Picturesque and Sublime

Addison[18] in 1701 observed of Italy,

> That not a mountain rears its head unsung,
> Renown'd in verse each shady thicket grows,
> And ev'ry stream in heavenly numbers flows.

[17]*Spectator*, No. 543.
[18]*A Letter from Italy*, ll. 14–16.

These lines do not imply, nor do any of the foregoing remarks, that the older attitudes toward the wilder aspects of creation as "deformities" disappeared without a struggle. But the increasing importance attached to the idea that the perfection of the Great Whole revealed the Divine wisdom and that each part was necessary to that perfection obviously demanded a readjusted attitude toward such phenomena as mountains. The defense was taken up early in such works as Ralph Cudworth's *True Intellectual System* (1678), John Keill's *Examination of Dr. Burnet's Theory of the Earth* (1695), William King's *De Origine Mali* (1702; trans. 1729 by Edmund Law with additions), and Sir Richard Blackmore's *Creation* (1712). The arguments offered by these men are primarily pragmatic and utilitarian. The poetic possibilities of mountains, however, were fully appreciated by Shaftesbury.[19] He has shaken off completely the feeling that they were great ruins of a former beauty, the effects of original sin and the destroying Flood.

But, here, midway the mountain, a spacious border of thick wood harbours our wearied travellers, who are now come among the ever green and lofty pines, the firs, and noble cedars, whose towering heads seem endless in the sky, the rest of the trees appearing only as shrubs beside them. And here a different horror seizes our sheltered travellers, when they see the day diminished by the deep shades of the vast wood, which, closing thick above, spreads darkness and eternal night below. The faint and gloomy light looks horrid as the shade itself; and the profound stillness of these places imposes silence upon men, struck with the hoarse echoings of every sound within the spacious caverns of the wood. Here space astonishes; silence itself seems pregnant, whilst an unknown force works on the mind, and dubious objects move the wakeful sense. Mysterious voices are either heard or

[19]Shaftesbury's *Characteristics*, ed. Robertson (London, 1900), II, 123–124. See also Shaftesbury's apostrophe, II, 98, beginning, "O glorious nature!"

fancied, and various forms of deity seem to present themselves and appear more manifest in these sacred silvan scenes, such as of old gave rise to temples, and favoured the religion of the ancient world. Even we ourselves, who in plain characters may read divinity from so many bright parts of the earth, choose rather these obscurer places to spell out that mysterious being, which to our weak eyes appears at best under a veil of cloud.

Shaftesbury's enthusiasm of course represents something of an innovation. Addison could only write,[20] more politely, that "Mount Pausilypso makes a beautiful prospect to those who pass by it" or that "in sailing around Caprea we were entertained with many rude prospects of rocks and precipices." But neither should it be forgotten that, stemming from Denham's *Cooper's Hill* (1642), the development of a distinct genre of "hill-poems" was well on its way by 1726, when Dyer's *Grongar Hill* appeared. Robert A. Aubin lists in his bibliography[21] twenty-eight examples before the turn of the century and sixty-four by 1775. Shaftesbury's influence upon all this is incalculable. By identifying the beautiful, the good, and the true as essentially one, he made esthetic appreciation the distinguishing trait of the eighteenth-century gentleman. To be insensible to the beauty of nature was to be ignorant of the truth and goodness of God. When *La Nouvelle Héloïse* (1761) reached England, the ground had been well prepared.[22] Saint-Preux merely repeats Shaftesbury: "J'ai toujours cru que le bon n'étoit que le beau mis en action, que l'un tenoit intimement à l'autre, et qu'ils avoient tous deux une source commune dans la nature bien ordonnée. Il suit de cette idée que le goût se perfectionne par les mêmes moyens que la sagesse, et qu'une âme bien touchée des charmes de la vertu

[20]*Remarks on Several parts of Italy, Works,* Bohn edition (London, 1856), I, 446, 449.
[21]*Topographical Poetry in XVIII-Century England,* pp. 298–314.
[22]*La Nouvelle Héloïse,* ed. Mornet (Paris, 1925), II, 47.

doit à proportion être aussi sensible à tous les autres genres de beautés." This idea was taken up by Mrs. Radcliffe as well as by numerous novelists before and after her, and made an important basis for characterization, as shall be seen shortly. But the English had anticipated Rousseau in another way. They had early come to regard as most proper for appreciation those parts of creation where the hand of the Creator is least obscured by the hand of man—the rude and "horrid" mountains. Thus John Gilbert Cooper[23] in *The Power of Harmony* (1745), after describing the soft and pleasing aspects of nature, adds,

> Now change the scene,
> Nor less admire those things which view'd apart
> Uncouth appear, or horrid; ridges black
> Of shagged rocks, which hang tremendous o'er
> Some barren heath; the congregated clouds
> Which spread their sable skirts, and wait the wind
> To burst th' embosm'd storm; a leafless wood,
> A mould'ring ruin, lightning-blasted fields,
> Nay, e'en the seat where Desolation reigns
> In brownest horror, by familiar thought
> Connected to this universal frame,
> With equal beauty charms the tasteful soul.

And Thomson[24] had already cried,

> Oh! talk of Him in solitary glooms,
> Where o'er the rock, the scarcely waving pine
> Fills the brown shade with a religious awe,

and alone with nature on the mountain top, he[25] had felt a "sacred terror, a serene delight."

In 1802 in the *Génie du Christianisme* (Part II, Book iv, chapters 1–3), Chateaubriand published what is probably the

[23]Bk. II, 124–35.
[24]"Hymn," ll. 42–44.
[25]"Summer," l. 541.

earliest history of the poetry descriptive of external nature. The first men, he explained, who really understood and loved the divine beauties of nature were the early Christians. The ancients were blinded to nature's charms both by their mythology, which peopled the universe with fauns, nymphs, and satyrs, and by their metaphysics, which offered only the idea of a uniform system, one that he compared to the machinery of an opera. The true God, he went on to say, in returning with the early Christians to His works, imparted His own sublimity to nature. Thus the first recluses,[26] following that delicate and sure religious taste which never deceives, selected always the most striking situations for their monasteries. There is not a hermit who does not know, as well as Claude Lorrain or Le Nôtre, on what rock he ought to form his cell. And so in this manner did the gifts of prophecy and wisdom, mystery and religion, come to fix their abodes in the forests and on the mountain tops, and there finally submit to the rule of taste.

Chateaubriand's book represents, of course, not the beginning of a tradition but a culmination. Long before its publication, Thomson's lines,

>   Whate'er Lorrain light-touched with softening hue,
>   Or savage Rosa dashed, or learned Poussin drew,

had become a cliché useful to the many in discussing landscape. With the wide dissemination of such ideas, the eighteenth-century association of the wilder aspects of nature with Deity often tended to be replaced by more purely esthetic reactions. Thus Walpole[27] in 1739 expressed his enjoyment of the Alps with the exclamation, "precipices, mountains, torrents, wolves, rumblings, Salvator Rosa." And as the century moved on,

---

[26]Part III, book v, chapter 2.

[27]*Correspondence of Gray, Walpole, West and Ashton*, ed. Toynbee (Oxford, 1915), I, 244 and 259.

with the continued use of the Claude glass, with the appearance of Ossian and Rousseau, and the popularity of the Gothic
novels—the "delightful Horrour" experienced by John Dennis
in 1693 before the Alps and the "agreeable kind of Horror"
of Addison a few years later came to be reduced to stock
phrases. Thus William Combe[28] has Dr. Syntax exclaim in
his first *Tour* (1809–11), satirizing the appeal of the sublime,

> Nature, dear Nature is my goddess,
> Whether arrayed in rustic bodice,
> Or when the nicest touch of Art
> Doth to her charms new charms impart:
> But still I, somehow, love her best,
> When she's in ruder mantle drest.

The sublime, however, became merely one aspect of the
picturesque, when it began to be preached by its most famous
expositor, William Gilpin (1724–1804), author of a series
of tours bearing the subtitle, "Relative Chiefly to Picturesque
Beauty." Gilpin, with the possible exception of Mrs. Radcliffe,[29] was probably more influential than any other English-

---

[28]XIV, 1–6.

[29]Mrs. Radcliffe's journals use the same terms to describe both painted
and actual scenes, and glance from one to the other—from the picture on
the wall to the view seen through the window—with a transitionless ease
that assumes the observer is always looking at essentially the same kind
of object. The following passages from her journals lay bare the techniques
which made her novels of such inestimable importance in popularizing
the picturesque. The italics are mine.

"In many of the rooms, the walls, wherever a window occurs, are lined
with dark mahogany, which forms the cases into *frames, as it were, for
the landscape* seen through them . . ." (Anne Radcliffe, *Gaston de
Blondeville. To which is prefixed a Memoir of the Author, with Extracts
from her Journals* [London, 1826], p. 35).

"These objects, with the high line of the Isle of Purbeck, faintly grey
beyond, composed a perfect *picture*, with most harmonious colouring. The
light silver grey of the sea first met the eye, then the dark Alum Rock
projected to meet Hurst Castle, whose towers were *pencilled* in deep grey
beyond, which softened away to the heights of Purbeck, that closed the
perspective" (*ibid.*, p. 48).

man in popularizing the manner of viewing nature as if it were a painting, a manner which prevailed toward the end of the eighteenth century and beyond. The technique had become so popular shortly after the turn of the century that Jane Austen could glance satirically at it in *Northanger Abbey*

"In a shaded corner, near the chimney, a most exquisite Claude, an evening view, perhaps over the Campagna of Rome. The sight of this picture imparted much of the luxurious repose and satisfaction, which we derive from contemplating the finest scenes of Nature. Here was the poet, as well as the painter, touching the imagination, and making you see more than the picture contained. You saw the real light of the sun, you breathed the air of the country, you felt all the circumstances of a luxurious climate on the most serene and beautiful landscape; and, the mind being thus softened, you almost fancied you heard Italian music on the air—the music of Paisiello; and such, doubtless, were the scenes that inspired him. Passed into smaller rooms, and by the same elegant lobbies, to the summer drawing-room, where the bowed window looks down upon a noble sweep of the Thames, with the well-wooded sloping hills of Essex in the distance. The noble simplicity of this long bend of the Thames, and of the whole scene, is very striking. The eye passes abruptly, between the hanging woods of two jutting eminences of the park, to the green level below, which forms in front a perfect bow of several miles. The woods near the house are so planted, as to conceal the entrance and exit of the river upon the plains below, leaving nothing of it visible but that line of perfect grace and grandeur which it marks between the green shores, while the vessels seem to steal upon the scene, appearing and disappearing, on either hand, from behind the woods. The dark verdure of these, the lighter green of the plain beneath, the silver grey of the river that bounds it, the white sails and various shades of the fleeting vessels, ships with clustering top-gallant sails, sloops with the stretching and elegantly swelling sails at their heads and above them, and skiffs, or other boats, with their little sprit-sails, too often bending low:—these, with the hills of Essex bending into bluish distance, form altogether a soothing harmony of tints and objects.—Among other pictures that struck me, (especially the family of Snyders, by Rubens,) was one of Wouvermans, representing the dark gate of a fort, with cavaliers on war-horses, waiting impatiently for admittance, their horses rearing and prancing; upon the high, shadowing walls, shrubs appear against the light sky, and above them is seen a high embankment, with a cannon pointed downwards, and near it a tree, down which a man is hastily descending, as if he had been overlooking a skirmish on the plains below . . ." (*ibid.*, pp. 65–67).

(ch. 14). Catherine had confessed to Henry Tilney her wish to be able to draw:

A lecture on the picturesque immediately followed, in which his instructions were so clear that she soon began to see beauty in everything admired by him; and her attention was so earnest, that he became perfectly satisfied of her having a great deal of natural taste. He talked of foregrounds, distances, and second distances; side-screens and perspectives; lights and shades; and Catherine was so hopeful a scholar, that when they gained the top of Beechen Cliff, she voluntarily rejected the whole city of Bath, as unworthy to make part of a land-scape.

A less known, and more boisterous attack[30] on the picturesque appears in Eaton S. Barrett's novel, *The Heroine* (1813):

"As I walked towards the chapel, my heart dilated at beholding the picturesque scenery. On the left were plantations of tufted turnips, on the right the venerable grandeur of a dilapidated dog-kennel; and every where the eye caught monstrous mountains, and minute daisies; while groups of children and chickens added hilarity to the landscape. Rural beauties dispose the soul for the reception of virtue, and virtue alone is true nobility."

The quite remarkable degree to which the picturesque technique prevailed is witnessed further by the fact that of all the contemporary sources usually consulted for information about Byron, their authors, with few exceptions, reveal themselves to be masters of the art. Jane Austen's exaggerations are seen to be slight. One finds full blown examples in the writings of Lady Blessington, John Cam Hobhouse, Thomas Medwin, William Polidori (Byron's physician), E. E. Williams (friend of Byron and Shelley), Leigh Hunt, Trelawny, Mary Shelley, Claire Clairmont, George Finlay, and J. Hamil-

[30]Eaton Stannard Barrett, *The Heroine* (New York, 1927), ch. x, pp. 85–86.

ton Browne (friends of Byron in Greece). Thus Hobhouse writes of Zitza,[31] a scene which Byron included in *Childe Harold,*

October 12 [1809].—We visited the village of Zitza, which like one of Virgil's goats, hangs literally upon the rocks, and is, perhaps, the most romantic spot in the world. The opposite mountain, clothed with wood and vineyards, and diversified by splashes of crimson-coloured rocks, makes a vivid object in the landscape. To the northward the hills of Sagovi, the mountains of Chimara, with the beautiful plain of the foreground, closes in the landscape, while eastward the windings of the Calamas (Thyamis), enriched by the grand vineyards of the foreground, complete a picture as beautiful as any I know.

It will be noticed that the word *picture* in the last sentence is used as the exact equivalent of *painting.* Lady Blessington[32] uses the word *picture* in the same way: "The prospect from the height above Antibes is one of the finest I have ever seen. Hills covered with wood, whence a spire, village, or château, is seen to peep forth; the blue waters of the Mediterranean spread out in front; and the snow-crowned mountains of the Maritime Alps rearing their heads to the clouds, form a magnificent picture." Mary Shelley[33] reveals herself to be deep in this manner of looking at nature:

We approached it [Provins, France] at sunset. After having gained the summit of a hill, the prospect of the town opened upon us as it lay in the valley below; a rocky hill rose abruptly on one side, on the top of which stood a ruined citadel with extensive walls and towers; lower down, but beyond, was the cathedral, and the whole formed a scene for painting.

[31]*Recollections of a Long Life* (London, 1909–1911), I, 16.

[32]*A Journal of the Conversations of Lord Byron* (London, 1893), p. xxxix.

[33]*Complete Works of Percy Bysshe Shelley*, ed. Ingpen and Peck (London, 1928–1929), VI, 94.

She was equally at home in dealing with the sublime[34] in landscape: "The prospect around, however, was sufficiently sublime to command our attention—never was scene more awfully desolate. The trees in these regions are incredibly large, and stand in scattered clumps over the white wilderness; the vast expanse of snow was chequered only by these gigantic pines, and the poles that marked our road: no river or rock-encircled lawn relieved the eye, by adding the picturesque to the sublime." Polidori's *Diary*[35] abounds with expressions of the picturesque tourist's attitude, although his abbreviated style precludes usually the lengthy and developed word-painting. Typical of his notations is his entry for May 21, 1816.

Set off. Country increases from hills to mountains with great beauty. . . . Went before supper to climb a hill. . . . The scene was very fine: to the right, beautiful; to the left, it had a tendency to sublimity; on one side, hills covered to the tops with trees; on the other, mountains with bald pates. Came down.

Medwin,[36] with greater care, paints in the background of the famous scene for the burning of Shelley's body. The composition is faultless.

In front was a magnificent extent of the blue and windless Mediterranean, with the Isles of Elba and Gorgona,—Lord Byron's yacht at anchor in the offing: *on the other side* an almost boundless extent of sandy wilderness, uncultivated and uninhabited, here and there interspersed in tufts with under-

[34]*Ibid.*, VI, 119. Elsewhere in the *Six Weeks' Tour* we read of "the most romantic spots" (p. 97), "vast and frowning mountains" (p. 98), "beautiful lawns interspersed with picturesque clumps of trees" (p. 100), "wooded islands, where picturesque ruins peeped from behind the foliage" (p. 109), and "scenery [which] perpetually grows more wonderful and sublime" (p. 118).

[35]*The Diary of Dr. John William Polidori*, ed. Rossetti (London, 1911), p. 91. See also pp. 26, 39, 44–5, 73, 81–2, 85–6, 117, 156, 165.

[36]*Journal of the Conversations of Lord Byron* (New York, 1824), pp. 179–184. The italics are mine.

wood curved by the seabreeze, and stunted by the barren and dry nature of the soil in which it grew. *At equal distances along the coast* stood high square towers, for the double purpose of guarding the coast from smuggling, and enforcing the quarantine laws. *This view was bounded* by an immense extent of the Italian Alps, which are here particularly picturesqce [*sic*] from their volcanic and manifold appearances, and which being composed of white marble, give their summits the resemblance of snow.

As a foreground to this picture appeared as extra-ordinary a group. Lord Byron and Trelawny were seen standing over the burning pile, with some of the soldiers of the guard. . . .

Sufficient additional examples of the picturesque technique— that of looking at the external world as if it constituted a picture—will appear in the following pages to prove that Wordsworth was quite accurate[37] when he termed it "a strong infection of the age" and recorded his dislike. It is essentially the despotism of the eye, "most despotic of our senses," which he is attacking. At one period even his own heart, he writes, had been deaf to the Soul of Nature,

> even in pleasure pleas'd
> Unworthily, disliking here, and there,
> Liking, by rules of mimic art transferr'd
> To things above all art. But more, for this,
> Although a strong infection of the age,
> Was never much my habit, giving way
> To a comparison of scene with scene,
> Bent overmuch on superficial things,
> Pampering myself with meagre novelties
> Of colour and proportion, to the moods
> Of time and season, to the moral power
> The affections, and the spirit of the place,
> Less sensible.

Fundamental as this distinction is, it is obscured in particular cases by the degree to which every poet utilizes the poetic

[37]*Prelude*, XI, 152–76 (1805 version).

idiom of his time, and further by the fact that the mood and technique of the picturesque enthusiast may pass over readily into those of the genuinely "romantic" religion of nature. Wordsworth's own religion of nature of course is grounded in the senses, from whose reports he passes on to a sense of something far more deeply interfused. And yet despite the similarities and affinities, Wordsworth recognized the differences between himself and such a poet as Byron, and had him in mind, he confessed, when he wrote the lines "Not in the Lucid Intervals of Life," where he declared that "words, which practiced talent readily affords," do not prove that Nature has actually "touched responsive chords" in the beholder. Keats also recognized a difference, he himself in turn quite different from Wordsworth of course. He wrote[38] to his brother George and his sister-in-law on September 18, 1819:

You speak of Lord Byron and me—There is this great difference between us. He describes what he sees—I describe what I imagine. Mine is the hardest task. You see the immense difference.

And insofar as the romantic mentality partakes of the mystical, Blake has expressed[39] the extreme romantic position. After commenting condescendingly on portrait painting, he continues, ". . . I am become a likeness taker and succeed admirably well; but this is not to be atchiev'd without the original sitting before you for Every touch, all likenesses from memory being necessarily very, very defective; But *Nature and Fancy are Two Things and can Never be join'd; neither ought any one to attempt it, for it is Idolatry and destroys the Soul"* (italics mine). Blake, who observed elsewhere,[40] that "Natural

[38]*Letters,* ed. Forman (Oxford, 1935), II, 452.
[39]*Poetry and Prose of William Blake,* ed. Keynes (Bloomsbury, 1927), p. 1075.
[40]*Ibid.,* p. 1024.

objects always did and now do weaken, deaden and obliterate
Imagination," represents Byron's extreme, mystical opposite.
For Blake,[41]

Mental Things are alone Real; what is call'd Corporeal, No-
body Knows of its Dwelling Place: it is in Fallacy, and its
Existence an Imposture. Where is the Existence Out of Mind
or Thought? . . . I assert for My Self that I do not behold
the outward Creation and that to me it is hindrance and not
Action; it is as the dirt upon my feet, No part of Me. "What,"
it will be Question'd, "When the Sun rises, do you not see
a round disk of fire somewhat like a Guinea?" O no, no, I
see an Innumerable company of the Heavenly host crying,
'Holy, Holy, Holy is the Lord God Almighty.'

Mary Shelley[42] writes somewhat similarly of her husband,
despite the fact that he was a good deal nearer the ground
than Blake: "The eminent German writer, Jean Paul Richter,
says, that 'to describe any scene well, the poet must make the
bosom of a man his *camera obscura,* and look at it through
this.' Shelley pursues this method in all his descriptions; he
always, as he says himself, looks beyond the actual object,
for an internal meaning, typified, illustrated, or caused by the
external appearance."

Enough has been said to fit Byron, in a general way, into
this scale of the senses, with the picturesque toward one end
and Blake with some of the later Romantics at the other.
Byron's general position is obvious. His preoccupation essentially with *seeing* precluded a major emphasis being placed
upon the establishment of any mystical relationship between
man and nature, and, as well, minimized the possibility of
his evolving a genuine philosophy of nature of any kind. Nor
was his purpose, with its emphasis upon accuracy in description and upon the actuality of nature as he perceived it, ever

[41]*Ibid.,* p. 844.
[42]Shelley, *op. cit.,* V, xiii.

that of Wordsworth (Preface of 1800), "to choose incidents and situations from common life, and . . . to throw over them a certain colouring of imagination, whereby ordinary things should be presented to the mind in an unusual aspect," or as expressed by Coleridge (*Biographia Literaria*, chapter XIV), "to give the charm of novelty to things of every day, and to excite a feeling analogous to the supernatural."

3

Byron

It is against the cultural inheritance just outlined that Byron must be considered, for such a one conditioned his variously contradictory reactions to the word and fact of nature. Before examining their fuller implications, however, it may be well here to summarize briefly the major conclusions of this study. Byron was drawn to nature and repulsed by it at different periods in his life, and sometimes these periods were quite inconsistently close to one another in point of time. There were, of course, ideas and qualities within his mind and personality which urged him along directly or indirectly, but never the less strongly, toward a sympathetic acceptance of all that the word *nature* stood for. Among these were his often instinctive rebellion against established institutions, his dream of a life apart from the world, his deism, and his astonishingly easy impressionability, which, when linked with the rather complete absence in him of the philosopher's formal training and cool reasoning temper, left him highly susceptible to the typically romantic influences of the time—influences such as those emanating from Wordsworth, Rousseau, and Shelley. But there were also ideas and qualities within Byron's mind and character which urged him, with even greater force finally, to oppose in one way or another the prevailing attitudes toward nature. These were his Calvinism, his sense of the comic, his real and pretended worldliness, his strong feelings of guilt, his very real unhappiness, and his highly developed sense of fact. The end result of all these ideas, attitudes, and qualities of mind, acting and reacting upon one another and pulling him variously in opposing directions, was a several-sided failure, one which implies certain goals, of course, which Byron was seeking to achieve. There was first the anguished and sometimes hectic search for happiness. It was essentially a religious quest for peace of mind, to be found, he hoped, in the loss of the overwhelming sense of his own wretched identity. Byron tried at times to find it among scenes of great natural beauty, with inevitable unsuccess. The failure of this quest, along with its causes and its effects upon Byron's life, art, and thought, is a central concern of the present study. Occupying him throughout his mature life and assuming many forms, it remained always at bottom a quest for some kind of spiritual cure—a cure for his ennui, discontent, restlessness, and feelings of guilt. His sense of personal guilt worked most strongly against him here. From this failure flowed a second: Byron's inability to formulate for himself an intellectual system satisfactorily relating God, man, and nature. Quite as important, however, in explaining this intellectual failure was Byron's insistent respect for fact, one which is revealed very clearly by a study of his relation to the picturesque tradition. This high regard for fact was fundamentally a basic kind of honesty, and it kept him from throwing out inconvenient evidence which might be prejudicial to a logically unified world-view. But Byron's awareness of the facts finally proved greater than his powers of synthesis. Thus "philosophically," he wavered between the contradictory ideas of a Calvinistic Creator of a universe indifferent or even harmful to man and the benevolently inclined Creator and creation of the deists. His interest in traditional deism, contrary to the opinion sometimes held, was at its height during the last three years of his life. In this area, then, his thought reveals no genuine progression: at the close of his life he had come full circle, and returned to his earliest philosophic position. Yet failures may have their compensations, and all in Byron's concept and treatment of nature is not contradiction which may seem so. For his early "romantic" non-Wordsworthian treatment of nature, which is squarely within the picturesque tradition; his later concept of a nature indifferent or hostile to man, often found in the plays; and even nature viewed in the light of the comic vision—all these derive in their different ways from the same source: Byron's acute sense of fact. One of the consistent threads in Byron, then, running from first to last, is this sympathy for the world of fact, in short—to use an unsatisfactory term—his realism. Thus one of the important causes of Byron's failure to construct an intellectual system also functioned in an important way as a cause of his success as an artist, a poet writing nature poetry which was variously picturesque, realistic, or comic. As time went on, this basic honesty about things and the way people should feel about things led him to realize that the picturesque, although founded on fact, was often inextricably linked with the sentimental, with a kind of self-engendered emotion which was fundamentally false in itself and which viewed the world as it could not be honestly viewed, that is, from a too simple and limited point of view. The result was a net decrease in Byron's sympathetic interest in nature, but more important—it was the comprehensiveness of the comic vision, a view of the universe which, if not integrated, was at least inclusive. It is one quite surprisingly similar to that evident in certain recent verse of the twentieth century. Thus this study indicates that Byron stood much farther outside the Return to Nature Movement than has yet been supposed. The matters of this summary may now be considered in somewhat greater detail, beginning with an introductory examination, from the point of view of this study, of the better-known Byron, the poet who is usually said to be one of the chief figures in the Return to Nature Movement of the Romantic Period.

His most obvious quality, perhaps, is his overwhelming egoism, the basis of his romanticism. It took, of course, the form of personal rebellion—rebellion against the religion which was his from childhood, rebellion against the prevailing romantic tendencies of the literature of his time, rebellion against many aspects of Western civilization as he knew it. He thus turned to civilization's opposite, to nature, as men had done before him.

There was, in addition to this romantic side of Byron, a strain in him, equally strong and native, of common sense and factual-mindedness. These two resulted in the peculiar dual nature of his mind and personality. He represents the clearest instance perhaps in English literature of the "split" personality which managed, at the same time, to remain sane, if it always quite did. The common-sensical part of him produced the satires, gave him his strong ironic sense, and violently rejected anything partaking of the mystical. It also drove him to wish, very strongly, just as it did the Augustans he so loved, for a life quiet and devoid of excess, one of the golden mean. And like the Augustans, he sought it and dreamed about it all his life in the form of a retreat from the world. This too led him in the direction of nature, which always remained for him civilization's great opposite. His scheme of becoming a small planter in South America or the United States represents one of the latest forms which this escapism assumed.

Both these primary elements in him made the assumption of an anti-doctrinaire attitude inevitable. As a rebel he would and did denounce codified systems of thought, religious or secular, because of the very fact that they were systems; as a man of deep affinities with the Augustan age he denounced them because they were elaborate, finely-spun, or unintelligible. In the realm of orthodox Protestant Christianity, which for him meant Calvinism, he was thus drawn doubly to seek another faith. That which he knew repelled him because it was a system established as well as because it was one replete with "mysteries." His frequent recourse was to Newtonian deism, never a more fashionable faith than during his lifetime. This, too, tended to give added spiritual interest to the world of nature for him.

A third characteristic of the man may be considered under the heading of a word to which Byron seems to have given a new meaning in English—*mobility*. It appears in *Don Juan*, XVI, 97. Byron is writing of Adeline, but his note to the stanza clearly indicates that he was thinking of himself. Adeline had been playing so well her role as grand hostess to the visiting country people that Juan began to doubt how much of her was real—

> So well she acted all and every part
> By turns—with that vivacious versatility,
> Which many people take for want of heart.
> They err—'tis merely what is call'd mobility,
> A thing of temperament and not of art,
> Though seeming so, from its supposed facility;
> And false—though true; for surely they're sincerest
> Who are strongly acted on by what is nearest.

In his note Byron refers to the French *mobilité*, and says the quality may be defined as "an excessive susceptibility of immediate impressions—at the same time without *losing* the past." His concluding remark is that it is "a most painful and unhappy attribute." This stanza with its note, one is tempted to think, contains the final word on the poet's personality. It does, certainly, explain and defend much that is in him in

need of explanation and defense—the many-sided contradictions of his life and thought.

The quality did not go unobserved by those who knew him.
Mary Shelley[43] thought that "the feeling of the moment regulated his speech." Madame Albrizzi noted[44] of Byron at Venice
that "what delighted him greatly one day annoyed him the
next." Stanhope[45] remarked that "those only who were personally acquainted with him can be aware of the influence
which every passing event had over his mind, or know the
innumerable modifications under which his character was daily
presenting itself: even his writings took a shade of colouring
from those around him." And Moore[46] makes much of his
"plurality of characters," one passing easily over into the other.
The cause of this "mobility" was undoubtedly a sincerity of
the moment, as the stanza suggests. One of its very important
results was Byron's consistent hatred of what he called cant,
cant in any form, including the cant about nature. Another
very important effect which it had was to induce ideas and
opinions which remained unsettled all his life and were so
until the end. Thus we find Scott[47] remarking of the early
years (1815–16) when he and Byron were seeing one another
that upon the subjects of religion and politics he was not
"inclined to believe that Lord Byron entertained very fixed
opinions." Kennedy,[48] using the same language, wrote of
Byron in 1823 that "in my opinion, the sentiments of his
lordship on religion were not fixed." And Byron, in his let-

---

[43]*The Life of Lord Byron* (London, 1851), p. 567.
[44]*Ibid.*, p. 414.
[45]*Greece in 1823 and 1824* (London, 1825), p. 528.
[46]Moore, *Life*, pp. 643–50.
[47]*Ibid.*, p. 280.
[48]*Conversations on Religion with Lord Byron* (London, 1830), p. 376.

ters to Miss Milbanke in 1814 admitted twice[49] that his religious convictions were by no means settled. This state of Byron's opinions does not seem to have limited itself to religion and politics; unfixed opinions were of the very nature of his mind and serious thought. The present study will illustrate the fact as it is exhibited in the particular strain of Byron's thought here considered. As Byron seems to imply in his note just quoted, his mind was one which grew by accretion rather than by selection and reconciliation. The result,[50] in Leigh Hunt's words, is that Byron "did not know what he was" religiously or philosophically. Goethe's dictum on Byron has become a cliché. After reading all that Byron wrote, one feels strongly that he was simply not equipped intellectually and by temperament to solve the problems which presented themselves to him. Nor is one left with the impression that Byron was a very learned man. The indications seem to be that Bayle's *Dictionary,* which he owned both in the original French and the English translation, was often indispensable to him. This particular indebtedness is worthy of a thorough investigation. Byron's lack of extensive learning was also remarked by his contemporaries. Scott observed[51]

[49]". . . I have not for several years looked into the tract of Locke's which you mention [*Treatise on the Reasonableness of Christianity*]—but I have redde it formerly, though I fear to little purpose since it is forgotten—and have always understood *that* and Butler's Analogy to be the best treatises of the kind. Upon the subject of which it treats, I think I have already said that I have formed no decided opinion; but I should regret any *sceptical bigotry* as equally pernicious with the most credulous intolerance. Of the Scriptures themselves I have ever been a reader and admirer as compositions, particularly the Arab-Job—and parts of Isaiah—and the song of Deborah" (Ethel C. Mayne, *The Life and Letters of Lady Byron* [London, 1929], pp. 86–87).

". . . I will not deny that my own impressions [upon the subject of religion] are by no means settled . . ." (*ibid.,* p. 444).

[50]*Lord Byron and Some of His Contemporaries* (Philadelphia, 1828), p. 114. Kennedy, *op. cit.,* p. xviii, makes the same point.

[51]Moore, *Life,* p. 280.

that Byron's reading before 1816 "did not seem to me to have been very extensive either in poetry or history." Kennedy observed[52] of him in 1823,

The impression which he left on me, judging of his manner merely, was that of a perfectly polished man, with much affability, cheerfulness, vivacity, and benevolence. In the conversations which I had with him, he appeared to shew an acute and cultivated mind, rather than a profound understanding. There was no appearance of extensive science or erudition, nor that coolness and sobriety of judgment, which a learned philosopher might be expected to exhibit. . . . Although he must have looked into a variety of books, and was acquainted with a little on every subject, yet I was not impressed with an idea of the profoundness of his knowledge.

And Moore,[53] in discussing Kennedy's book, concluded, "the truth seems to be, that on neither side were there much stores of theological learning . . . a rapid eye and retentive memory having enabled him [Byron], on this as on most other subjects, to catch, as it were, the salient points on the surface of knowledge. . . . To any regular train of reasoning, even on this his most favourite topic, it was not possible to lead him." And so when Byron writes[54] (1808), "of philosophy, astronomy, and metaphysics, [I have read] more than I can comprehend" or (1819) pondering what to do with the remaining years of his life, "philosophy would be in vain— let us try action," the reader feels himself, before such statements, quite in the presence of literal truth.

Such a mind, then, could not but be influenced greatly by one of more fixed views. As Trelawny said,[55] "a fresh mind, possessing the qualities he lacked, could do anything with him,

[52]*Conversations*, pp. 316–18.
[53]*Life*, pp. 599–600. See also Stanhope, *op. cit.*, p. 540, and Kennedy, *op. cit.*, p. 208, on Byron's conversation.
[54]L. and J., I, 173; *Correspondence*, II, 121.
[55]*Records of Shelley, Byron, and the Author* (London, 1878), I, 132.

for he had not made up his mind on any subject." Words-worth's poetry as expounded by Shelley is usually said to have constituted one of the greatest influences, from the literary quarter, in Byron's life. As Moore[56] pleasantly put it, "from Lord Byron's facility in receiving new impressions, the opinions of his companion were not altogether without some influence on his mind." It is one of the purposes of this study to show how completely foreign to Byron's more usual views this influence was, for its effect was chiefly upon his ideas about nature.

When one considers the man, the age he lived in, and the cultural inheritance of that age, it seems a foregone conclusion that Byron should write a great deal of poetry upon the subject of nature. Of course he did. For in one way or another, it was a prevailing tendency of the Romantic Period to urge itself on in the direction of nature and away from civilization. One may visualize the typical, hypothetical situation in the form of a triangle. At its apex, A, is the individual; at the left corner, B, is organized society and civilization; and at C is civilization's great opposite, nature. There was, within the life of the hypothetical individual, sporadic but strong pressure tending toward the reduction of the line AC to a single point. The achievement of this reduction represents the mystical and romantic experience described by many of the poets of the period—the feeling that the self is fused with the One and consciousness of personal identity lost. It has been described with some justice as the romantic experience. There were, and are, of course, many degrees in between. If one reduces the case of Byron to its very simplest terms, however, terms quite incomplete, it is seen that there were more than a few most important barriers operating against a repeated occurrence of that fusion. Among them were his Calvinistic

[56]*Life*, p. 317.

beliefs and his strong sense of the comic. The existence of both in the same mind sets Byron clearly apart from his eminent contemporaries and removes him from the main stream of the Romantic Movement. His Calvinistic concept of God enabled him, ultimately, to view nature as often destructive and usually non-beneficial to man. And his strong sense of the ridiculous, rendered doubly keen when the ridiculous appeared to touch upon himself, led him on, with the increasing vulgarization of the picturesque by the many English tourists abroad, to satirize most aspects of the Return to Nature Movement and to turn away from it in both his life and poetry. Insofar as the movement had lent itself to an excessive and sentimental glorification of nature and the life close to nature, this is to Byron's credit. He breathed in, along with the air, of course, the Weltschmerz of his age— a state of mind which Goethe described as a "pathological condition" and defined as essentially a conflict between the individual and his environment. But the intellectual milieu which counseled an escape into a cloistered solitude close to nature, he fought—along with his own tendency to move in the same direction—and his chief weapon was his laughter, ironic and common-sensical, sometimes bitter, sometimes vulgar, sometimes turned upon himself. This satire, however, is not to be viewed simply as a late development, without roots, in Byron's career; contemporary conditions merely gave a new impetus to an urge which showed itself as early as *Hours of Idleness.* These two fundamental characteristics distinguished him among the great Romantics.

Another influence which worked effectively to turn Byron against the prevailing romantic concept of nature, and one further complicating his personality, is his conception of his life as a role played before an audience, as so much of it actually was. Thus we find Moore[57] writing of "the perverse

[57]*Life,* p. 422.

fancy he had for falsifying his own character," the Countess Guiccioli[58] saying that in him was "a positive necessity of calumniating himself," Hobhouse noting[59] that "Mrs. Leigh and I talking over Lord Byron agreed that his principal failing was a wish to mystify those persons with whom he lived." Trelawny, Stanhope, Kennedy, Hunt, Lady Blessington—each recorded and saw through the roles he assumed, the painful necessity in him of always cutting a good figure and acting for effect.[60] Indeed, Lady Blessington reports[61] that Byron was quite amused at the thought of the confusion of his future biographers, when they should come to contemplate the many contradictory statements made about him. One of his roles, of course, was the Byron of the black cape and flowing tie, musing under a starlit night far out at sea—the complete romantic poet surrendering himself wholly to the beneficent influences of nature. Another role, quite as familiar, was that of anti-poet, one which grew out of his fierce desire to be considered anything—nobleman, man of the world, man of action, even roué—anything but literary. But Byron's poses were so habitual that they became a part of him. One sometimes wonders that anything else was left of the man. And his many-figured pose of anti-poet undoubtedly affected and reduced, finally, the genuine pleasure which he drew from nature.

The character of man of the world, however, was far from being all deliberate pose. His early years of dandyism

---

[58]*My Recollections of Lord Byron*, trans. Jerningham (London, 1869), II, 96–97.

[59]*Recollections*, III, 44.

[60]See Trelawny, *Recollections of the Last Days of Shelley and Byron* (London, 1906), pp. 44–5, and *Records*, I, 55; Hunt, *Lord Byron and Some of His Contemporaries*, pp. 78, 106; Stanhope, *Greece in 1823 and 1824*, pp. 537–8, 542–3; Kennedy, *Conversations*, p. 426; Lady Blessington, *Conversations*, pp. 20, 39, 95, 98, 103, 114, 117, 311, 323, 351.

[61]Lady Blessington, *Conversations*, pp. 351–52.

never altogether left him. He longed for quiet and retirement, to be sure; but absolute solitude he could not bear, and he who was so much actor needed an audience, a fashionable one. Although he had recorded in *Childe Harold* (III, 90) his experience of "the feeling infinite" that all Nature is One and alive, a feeling which comes with solitude, "where we are *least* alone," this mood could not last forever, and he has also exclaimed[62] "alas! here I am . . ., never *more* alone than when alone." His fits of despondency, too, came upon him most often, as long as he remained in England, when he was secluded at Newstead. Above all men he needed people and a sympathetic society to move in. In 1821 he recalled[63] that he still had a "tinge" of dandyism at the age of twenty-four and that at that time in his life "I liked the Dandies; they were always very civil to *me,* though in general they disliked literary people, and persecuted and mystified [them] damnably." But he noted[64] also in 1821 that "in general, I do not draw well with literary men. . . . Your literary every day man and I never went well in company." Among the exceptions he lists are Scott and Moore: "but then they [were] men of the world." And so one detects sincerity side by side with pose, perhaps even giving rise to the pose, in such a description as George Finlay[65] presents of Byron during his last visit to Greece:

Lord Byron uttered this [a statement upon the character of the Greeks and the Turks] in an unemphatical, and rather affectedly monotonous tone. I afterwards observed, that he adopted this tone not unfrequently, whenever he uttered any thing which diverged from the commonest style of conversation. Whenever he commenced a sentence which showed that

[62]*Correspondence*, II, 130.
[63]L. and J., V, 423.
[64]L. and J., V, 435.
[65]"Reminiscences of Lord Byron" in Stanhope's *Greece in 1823 and 1824*, p. 512.

the subject had engaged his mind, and that his thoughts were sublime, he checked himself, and finished a broken sentence, either with an indifferent smile, or with this annoying tone. I thought he had adopted it to conceal his feelings, when he feared to trust his tongue with the sentiments of his heart. Often, it was evident, he did it to avoid betraying the author, or rather the poet.

Stanhope adds his confirmation of Finlay's observations in a footnote on the same page:

I have observed Lord Byron act thus. He would often suppress noble sentiments that obtruded on his mind, or vainly attempt to turn them into ridicule.

An accepted and popular subject for the expression of "noble sentiments," it may be recalled, was the world of nature; but that sentiment which is often suppressed may atrophy. It was partially so with Byron. This child of the passions, who grew up to fear and dislike the sentimental, came eventually to distrust even the genuine emotion.

The singular position which Byron occupies among the nineteenth century poets of nature is further attested to by a persistent strain of thought which received one of its earliest expressions in the 1812 addition to the original preface of *Childe Harold.* There Byron quietly stated that "even the beauties of nature . . . are lost" on the soul of his hero, and referred in passing to Dr. John Moore's novel *Zeluco* (1789), which delivers the same judgment upon its own villainous title character.

This parallel is far from insignificant. Byron's many later admissions of this kind, which were to be given an increasingly personal application, are only to be understood as one of the forms of expression taken by his feelings of guilt, and represent a clear case of life mirroring literature: for such a statement as the one just quoted had become a commonplace, by 1812, in the novels of the time, and similar statements appear in many which Byron had read before the middle of 1816. Each of these novels makes it very clear that the beneficent influences of nature are denied to all except those of pure heart and virtuous life. These many characters, so excluded from the great natural nurse of benevolence, health, and happiness, are stained all with guilt; they are major or minor villains, often but by no means always in Gothic romances. Byron almost certainly identified himself with them.

Byron's various expressions of this theme—which for the sake of convenience may be called the Zeluco theme—thus represent much more than mere unconscious plagiarism; they constitute a strain of thought far more important for Byron and for those who would understand him than any simple literary influence, as that term is sometimes used. They are, instead, his expressions, in the terms available to him, of his feelings of personal guilt and remorse, the voice of his own accusing conscience. For a reverent and enthusiastic contemplation of the beauties of nature, long before Byron's time, had been associated with the act of worship, both in life and literature. Thus it had become increasingly impossible for an uneasy conscience to take pleasure in contemplating the scenes of nature with any hope of gaining the serenity which was held out to the innocent. There are four separate but closely associated traits which bar one from enjoying or profiting by the healing powers of nature: ennui, melancholy, misanthropy, and out-and-out villainy (only the good are happy); feelings of guilt, gloom, or an aloofness from one's fellow man disqualify equally. From one point of view, of course, the Zeluco theme in Byron may be regarded as simple dramatic propriety: to allow the Byronic hero to learn benevolence or serenity from his life close to nature would be to deprive him of most of his Byronic qualities—violent passions, a sense of sin, and a gloomy haughtiness, cold and aloof. But the poetic expressions of the theme are often too demonstrably personal for the matter to be dismissed so simply; there are also parallels in the prose which cannot be explained away.

If the personal nature of the Zeluco theme then be once admitted, and I believe there can be no reasonable doubt of it, it is possible that new light may be thrown on the purpose of Byron's first travels and on his original choice of the word and idea of *pilgrimage* instead of *tour* or *travels*. The implication may well be that Byron even as early as 1809 was actually going in search of some kind of spiritual cure—a cure for his ennui, discontent, restlessness, and feelings of guilt, whatever their causes may have been or however imperfectly he may have realized the fact at the time. The first cantos of *Childe Harold* make scattered efforts, of course, to depict a medieval religious pilgrim, and less than a year after their publication, in his addition to the preface, Byron clearly intimated the failure of the Childe to effect such a cure. The misanthropic motto from *Le Cosmopolite* also bears this out, with its ironic statement of aversion to life at home overcome by greater aversion to life seen abroad. Thus Byron's lifelong quest for peace of mind, the recovery of Eden's innocence, and his soul's cure may have begun seriously as early as his twentieth year. But it was a quest destined to failure. The sense of doom out of his Calvinistic heritage hung far too heavy upon him. He was a man fated.

In 1814, October 22, Byron wrote to the reforming Annabella of his ruling passion that it "takes its colours, I believe, from the circumstances in which I am placed; there are few which, at one period or other of my life, had not affected me. . . ." Granted this *mobilité*, it is a permissible oversimplification to say, I believe, that Byron saw Clarens and its immediate environs in the summer of 1816 through the eyes of Rousseau (along with those of Wordsworth and Shelley), but viewed the Swiss Alps in the autumn through the eyes of Zeluco, Schedoni, Werther, or any one of a number of other guilt-burdened souls. Byron remembered[66] in 1821 that his mother had compared him before he was twenty to Rousseau and that Madame de Staël used to say the same thing in 1813. Byron himself had made the comparison publicly[67] in 1820. That both men at times felt themselves to be persecuted outcasts is obvious. But that Byron was not Rousseau is also obvious, and once the country of *La Nouvelle Héloïse* and Shelley's exposition of Wordsworth's poetry were left behind, Byron's eyes became those of Manfred and two generations of villains as the novel had described them. The castle and dungeons of Chillon, the wild Salvator Rosa scenery[68] "beyond all description," a rock marking the scene of a murder ("2 brothers—one murdered the other; just the place for it")—this is the setting, "along with something else," which called forth, at the close of the Swiss Journal to Augusta, Byron's anguished and remorseful cry to Mother Nature, and its counterparts in *Manfred*. It is the cry of a man deserted by his God, the voice of Byron damning himself in the terms of his own Christless Christianity.

Byron not only failed to achieve lasting and deep-rooted contentment in his life, he was chronically dissatisfied with it. His discontent and his peculiar, persistent awareness of self, which his heroes are always seeking to lose, he carried with him in his communings with nature just as he did everywhere else. It is almost as if the accumulated, unhappy memories of past days constituted the man. Thus he recalled[69] in 1817, "if I met with any of the race [the English] in the beautiful parts of Switzerland, the most distant glimpse or aspect of them poisoned the whole scene."

[66]L. and J., V, 408–409.
[67]"Reply to Blackwood's *Edinburgh Magazine*," L. and J., IV, 479.
[68]The Swiss Journal for Augusta, L. and J., III, 357.
[69]L. and J., IV, 84.

In answer[70] to the question, "What is the reason that I have been, all my lifetime, more or less *ennuyé?*" he decides that it is "constitutional." Or he writes[71] that he has *"une ame [sic] qui se tourmente."* He remarks[72] that he wakes in the morning "always in very bad spirits—I may say, in actual despair and despondency." He is[73] "not sure that long life is desirable for one of my temper and constitutional depression of Spirits." He recalls[74] that his wife once had told him that at heart he was "the most melancholy of mankind, and often when apparently gayest." He writes Moore[75] of "the growing depression of my spirits" and records among his Detached Thoughts[76] that "I have found increasing upon me (without sufficient cause at times) the depression of Spirits (with few intervals), which I have some reason to believe constitutional or inherited." All these statements were made in the year 1821.

Such being the nature of the man three years before his death, a man who failed to find abiding satisfaction in any of the major departments of his life, it is not to be expected that the relations which he established with nature were of much real consequence in his search for happiness. As Thomas Mulock[77] wrote in his *Answer Given by the Gospel to the Atheism of All Ages* (1819),

Lord Byron's poetry contains glimpses of the great doctrine of human depravity, a deeper insight into which would, under

[70]L. and J., V, 155–6.
[71]L. and J., V, 196. J. Hamilton Browne, who observed Byron with some acuteness in the last year of his life, noted that he was "a most ingenious self-tormentor" ("Voyage from Leghorn to Cephalonia with Lord Byron," *Blackwood's Edinburgh Magazine*, XXXV, 63).
[72]L. and J., V, 198.
[73]L. and J., V, 370.
[74]L. and J., V, 446.
[75]L. and J., V, 387.
[76]L. and J., V, 459–60.
[77]Pp. 43–4. Quoted by E. H. Coleridge, L. and J., IV, 496–97.

the divine guidance, lead him to Jesus. . . . No slight portion of Lord Byron's misery is associated with a sense of isolation. . . . Let Lord Byron, and all other 'wandering out-
laws of their own dark minds,' *search the scriptures*. . . .
Their carnal communings with external nature will never reveal
to them the cause and the cure of their calamities.

To these statements Byron replied in an injured tone[78]—revealing his close affinity with their author—"I never could
understand what they mean by accusing me of irreligion."
The acuteness of Mulock's remarks cannot be denied. If Byron
had found for himself a place of unquestioning faith in a
congenial branch of orthodox Christianity it would undoubtedly have made him a happier, more contented, and different
man. The present study reveals that his "carnal communings
with external nature" did not afford him any deep consolation. Of course the alternative of traditional Christianity
proved equally impossible for him. This fact of his personality and the events of his life contributed in the most important way to his failure to evolve any kind of original system
significantly relating man and nature. For Byron had in no
sense the favorable personal and emotional background to
look back upon and enrich and stimulate his thinking about
nature that Wordsworth had. Professor Havens[79] writes of
Wordsworth in this respect, "The happiest years of his life
had been spent near the mountains and heaths; his most
exalted experiences, his periods of deepest insight were clearly
connected with them; separation from them had meant error,
doubt, despair; and renewed association with them had led
him back

   To those sweet counsels between head and heart
   Whence grew that genuine knowledge, fraught with peace."

[78]L. and J., IV, 416.
[79]*The Mind of a Poet* (Baltimore, 1941), p. 89.

There were very few such associations with the world of nature in the mind of Byron. His childhood years among the mountains of Scotland had been marked by violent disagreements with his mother and by painful, childish awareness of his deformity, which she herself made him aware of; his most exalted experience with nature took place in 1816 in Switzerland, when thoughts of incest blackened the already black memories of social disgrace and his broken marriage. He thus lacked Wordsworth's rich recollections of happiness and contentment, found with nature, upon which to theorize, upon which to erect the structure of a creed. The danger of scholarship lies in the interesting possibility of erecting one for him, out of his scattered and contradictory statements.[80]

The sharp difference between Wordsworth's and Byron's reactions to nature becomes clear when the former poet's hostile reception of Byron's nature poetry is recalled and compared with Goethe's praises of it. Crabb Robinson records,[81]

[80]Several early German studies have done this: J. O. E. Donner's *Lord Byrons Weltanschauung* (1897) and Manfred Eimer's *Byron und der Kosmos* (1912). Donner's study appeared before Prothero's edition of Byron's *Letters and Journals* and so is based on incomplete evidence. The author's bias is indicated by his title. The central thesis of Eimer's study is also that Byron developed a genuine Weltanschauung (p. v), and was a systematic thinker (p. vii). In supporting this thesis Eimer is forced to minimize the influence of Wordsworth upon Byron in 1816, and finds a pantheistic element in Byron's thought as early as 1806. He concludes that what is to be emphasized mainly is the consistency of Byron's development (p. 202), and closes with the remark that Byron penetrated more deeply into the world-mystery than any poet since Milton (p. 203). Contrary to the most obvious evidence, he states that Byron found abiding consolation in nature (p. 201) and that he finally realized an inner peace through his "cosmic" concepts (pp. 200–201). Eimer's chief interest is in Byron's knowledge of science, which he greatly overemphasizes, along with its "quieting" effects on Byron (p. 13).

E. W. Marjarum's *Byron as Skeptic and Believer* (1938), the best recent study of Byron's religious and philosophical thought, falls into none of these errors, and is essential to any investigation of the subject. I have indicated elsewhere the points of difference between this study and mine.

[81]*Diary, Reminiscences, and Correspondence of Henry Crabb Robinson,* ed. Sadler (London, 1869), II, 435.

"it was with reference to the poems of the Old Testament that Goethe praised the views which Byron took of Nature; they were equally profound and poetical. 'He had not,' Goethe said, 'like me, devoted a long life to the study of Nature, and yet in all his works I found but two or three passages I could have wished to alter.' " Professor Beach[81a] seems to offer the explanation: "Goethe is no simple worshiper of nature. As a poet personifying her in her ever-varied aspects, and as a realist in his regard for plain truth, he has many references to nature as a power hostile to man or indifferent to his spiritual aims." There are no such references in Wordsworth's writings. This is the accidental point of contact between Goethe and Byron; this too sets Byron apart from many of his English contemporaries. And in this particular respect, it may be argued, Byron's concept of nature—that is, the totality of his many representations of nature—is more comprehensive than Wordsworth's highly selective truths, and much closer to the attitudes of the present century.

Keats' concrete and highly imaginative world is likewise a thing unknown to Byron. Keats' idea of negative capability, his ability to become himself the sparrow which he sees pecking at gravel before his window and to peck away too—this also was beyond Byron. His strong factual-mindedness, his deep conviction—again shared with Goethe—[82] that "it is by the laborious collection of facts that even a poetical view of nature is to be corrected and authenticated," and these instincts sped on their way by the tradition of the picturesque and the doctrine of *ut pictura poesis*—these excluded the highly or completely imaginative world from Byron. "There should always be some foundation of fact for the most airy fabric, and pure invention is but the talent of a liar," says

[81a]Beach, *op. cit.*, p. 276.
[82]Robinson, *op. cit.*, II, 433–434.

Byron.[83] But Keats writes to his friend Reynolds (February 19, 1818),

Now it appears to me that almost any Man may like the spider spin from his own inwards his own airy Citadel—the points of leaves and twigs on which the spider begins her work are few, and she fills the air with a beautiful circuiting. Man should be content with as few points to tip with the fine Web of his Soul, and weave a tapestry empyrean full of symbols for his spiritual eye, of softness for his spiritual touch, of space for his wandering, of distinctness for his luxury.

This same tendency to factual-mindedness, of course, also sets Byron apart from Shelley in somewhat similar fashion. Yet Shelley's nature poetry, as recent investigation has indicated, takes one of its origins, to a remarkable degree, from the science of the time. Byron's individual debts to particular scientific research are all on the surface and obvious to view; in the realm of his nature poetry they serve principally to substantiate his religious beliefs. But Byron's final debt to science is great: from science stem both his reverent respect for fact and most of his unexamined assumptions about the general nature of the universe.

Perhaps the greatest difference, however, between these three English poets of the Romantic Period and Byron is that each of the three, in his own way, effected an adjustment between himself, the world of nature, and the Deity often found there, which had in it the elements of deep and abiding satisfaction. This Byron never accomplished satisfactorily, although he tried during much of his life. Thus this study is in several ways, intellectual, religious, and psychological, the record of the failure of a quest. If Byron did ever discover his share of peace in this life, it was only when he turned to meaningful activity among men, as in his last trip to Greece, participated in his own element, and refrained from attempting to escape

[83]L. and J., IV, 93.

into natural solitude or to explain to himself the meaning of the universe and its Creator.

When one considers the larger and final question of how great a place the world of nature occupied in Byron's consciousness during the latter years of his life (1821–1824), years which produced about forty-five per cent of all his poetry, it becomes clear that that interest is remarkably less than in any other period. Of course no exactly quantitative results are possible, and it is necessary furthermore to base conclusions upon his writings. It may be said, however, that references to nature in the prose of this period are rare and that picturesque description has almost disappeared. And if the principal plays and poems are classified quantitatively from the particular point of view of this study into groups labelled "negligible," "inconspicuous," and "greater than inconspicuous," most students, I believe, would place in the first group the two Venetian historical plays *Marino Faliero* and *The Two Foscari,* probably *Werner,* the satirical *Age of Bronze, Don Juan,* VI, where the hero spends most of his time in the harem, VII and VIII, when he is at war, IX, at the Russian court, and XII, in London. The second classification would seem to include in it *Sardanapalus,* where many of the allusions to nature are sceptical and antagonistic, *The Vision of Judgment,* with many of its allusions satirical, *The Deformed Transformed,* occupied as much with war as with anything else, *Don Juan,* X, where the principal stanzas on nature represent a parody of the picturesque tour, XI, when Juan is in London, and XIII–XVI at a country estate. There remain for the third classification *Cain, Heaven and Earth,* and *The Island.* Of these three, a beautiful and kindly disposed nature appears only in the last.

It is of interest to note further of *Don Juan* that when Byron comes periodically to state the subject of his poem, as it spins itself out from canto to canto, those statements are always variants of the classical formula. The realm of external nature is never included as a matter that he is concerned with.[84] Thus he writes (VII, 8), " 'fierce loves and faithless wars' . . . I sing," and (XIV, 13–14) "my Muse . . . mostly sings of human things and acts . . . love, war, a tempest . . . a bird's-eye view, too, of that wild Society." Or (XV, 25), "knights and dames I sing, such as the times may furnish," and (XV, 93) "politics, and policy, and piety, are topics which I sometimes introduce . . . because my business is to *dress* society, and stuff with *sage* that very verdant goose." "I . . . play upon the surface of humanity. I write the world, nor care if the world read" (XV, 60). It would seem that Byron had made up his mind upon the proper study of mankind, at least insofar as the poet is concerned. The exuberance, on the other hand, of some of the London stanzas (XI, 7–8, 23–30) loving and satiric at the same moment, recalls the London of Hogarth or of Gay's *Trivia,* although somewhat softened.

Yet the urge to escape the "artificial" civilization which he knew, was a part of him up until the end. In 1812 he had planned[85] to leave England and to "retain a mansion in one of the fairest islands, and retrace, at intervals, the most interesting portions of the East." That strain of escapism never left him completely. J. Hamilton Browne reports[86] him as saying on his last voyage to Greece that, "should his services prove of no avail to Greece," he intended to purchase some "island in the South Sea . . . retire for the remainder

---

[84]Samuel C. Chew's statement supports this judgment of *Don Juan:* "There is more . . . of social satire in the closing episodes, where Byron's attitude toward England is strangely tolerant, as that of a man of the world rather than of a romantic outcast" (*A Literary History of England,* ed. Baugh [New York, 1948], p. 1225).

[85]L. and J., II, 100.

[86]Browne, *op. cit.,* XXXV, 64.

of his life." Trelawny records[87] of the same voyage that
when the vessel passed Sicily, "gliding close by its smooth
hills and sheltered coves, Byron would point to some serene
nook, and exclaim, 'There I could be happy.'" To Lady
Blessington he said,[88] "in the world I am always irritable
and violent; the very noise of the streets of a populous city
affects my nerves: I seemed in a London house 'cabined,
cribbed, confined.'" Yet he also registered[89] during the last
years of his life his earlier boredom in the country at the great
English estates. It was not a life close to nature that he
sought, but a flight from people. His very serious ambitions
of becoming a planter in South America or the United States
represent merely another form of escape. There are more
than a dozen references[90] to such a scheme in his letters and
journals. Byron, of course, had no love for farming or for
the Americas; he wanted to fly from old obligations, from
the artificialities of "this Cicisbean existence," and, as always,
from himself. From any point of view it was flight, but—
significantly—one that he never actually made.

   This tendency received its latest and fullest expression in
The Island, which was written in 1823. Yet the escapism
there given poetic form is troubled. The poem is actually the
record of a conflict in Byron's mind. The mutineers desire
to escape (I, 27–50) from the restraints of shipboard and
the civilization they are returning to into an island paradise
of gushing fruits and promiscuous plenty bestowed by an
untilled nature. That paradise of freedom is described lov-
ingly and at length. But Byron's sympathy with authority
and the principle of civilization as personified by Captain

---

[87]*Recollections*, p. 126.
[88]*Conversations*, p. 305. See also p. 336; contrast pp. 187, 45–6.
[89]L. and J., VI, 187; *Don Juan*, XIII, 101–2.
[90]See L. and J., IV, 356–58, 360, 369, 377, 397–98, 471; *Correspondence*,
II, 122–23, 125, 126, 127, 128, 129, 130 131; L. and J., VI, 90, 110–11,
114–15, note.

Bligh is evident. He is "the gallant chief" (I, 17), "his name was added to the glorious roll of those who search the storm-surrounded Pole" (I, 21–2); he is "bold Bligh" (I, 51). The revolting mutineers, on the other hand, are seeking an "escape from duty's path" (I, 60). The mutiny is described as originating without motive of mistreatment, and after Bligh and his "faithful few" have been forced to leave the vessel it becomes a "moral wreck" (I, 125–28). But as Byron loses himself more and more in his study of life on an island Eden, civilization comes to be contrasted unfavorably with savagery (II, 67–74): it has both the "sordor" usually found within civilization plus all that evil which came as a result of the Fall. "The Old World [is] more degraded than the New." And the girl Neuha (II, 123–44) is "the gentle savage of the wild"—of long descent—"the infant of an infant world, as pure from nature." As Byron abandons himself increasingly to his dream, we read (II,248–71) that the chase, the liberty to roam, healthy slumber earned by sportive toils, the airy joys of social solitudes "did more than Europe's discipline had done, and civilised Civilisation's son!" The peak of this naturalism is reached in II, 370–97, where Byron is imitating himself and Wordsworth[91] again in such lines as, "Live not the stars and mountains? Are the waves without a spirit?" But Byron's moral sense begins to assert itself once more, and we find (II, 312–13) that the hero Torquil's "heart was tamed to that voluptuous state, at once Elysian and effeminate," and that (III, 39) the mutineer's was a "guilt-won paradise." Byron concludes (IV, 259–70) by judging them guilty: "Their life was shame, their epitaph was guilt." Christian's life and soul (IV, 351–2) were

[91]Compare Maturin's *Melmoth* (London, 1892), II, 264–265: "How often does nature thus become an involuntary interpreter between us and our feelings! Is the murmur of the ocean without a meaning?—Is the roll of the thunder without a voice? . . . —Do not they all tell us some mysterious secret, which we have in vain searched our hearts for?"

"misspent." After all, as Byron said,[92] he was "merely trying
to write a poem a little above the usual run of periodical
poesy," but the seeds of indecision in his own mind between
what remained for him the two great extremes of Civilization
and Nature are clearly present. Neither completely satisfied
him. As Lady Blessington said,[93] "Byron wished for that
Utopian state of perfection which experience teaches us it is
impossible to attain,—the simplicity and good faith of savage
life, with the refinement and intelligence of civilization." Thus
the *Juan* mood even carries over into *The Island,* in the character and humorous dialect of Ben Bunting; and although
the two are kept formally separate, the one is an unspoken
commentary on the other.

The life of the child of nature as Byron pictures it,[94] in
the *Juan* stanzas on Daniel Boone (written in 1822), also
contains this failure to give his faith to the ideal. He intro-
duces his remarks on Boone with a stanza which opens with
Cowper's line "God made the country and man made the
town," and proceeds to remark ironically, "so Cowper says—
and I begin to be of his opinion." He had just completed at
this point in the narrative his description of the siege and
bloody capture of Ismail, and is referring back to it. He
then moves on to his stanzas on Boone, which are sincere and
ironic at the same time. Here Byron accepts the obvious
advantages of the life which has left behind it the "great
joys" of civilization, that is, war, and yet he is by no means
duped by the Arcadian dream. He believes and disbelieves at
the same moment.[95] The state of tension set up between the

[92]L. and J., VI, 164.
[93]*Conversations,* p. 367.
[94]*Don Juan,* VIII, 60–68.
[95]Professor Fairchild in *The Noble Savage* (New York, 1928), pp.
242–43, raises the question of the serious intent of the Boone passage and
takes the trouble to refer to a "scholar-friend [who] has insisted in conversation" that the passage is a "parody of the typical back-to-nature

two points of view is something peculiarly modern: it represents, finally—and this is the source of Byron's comic vision— the refusal of his essentially modern consciousness of self to ignore the vast complexity of its experience. Thus Byron, in giving up the struggle to maintain an illusioned view of man and nature and allowing his sense of fact to determine the course of his art and thought, anticipated many a later problem. By his violent rejection of the sentimental we recognize a true contemporary; and as many a modern poet, his fear of sentimentality led him finally toward a distrust of all emotion, however genuine.

The chief outlines of this study may be restated briefly (see the opening paragraph of this section for an introductory and more detailed summary statement). Byron, alone of the great Romantics, was able repeatedly to view nature in a comic light. This was in part a reaction against a prevailing sentimentalized concept of nature. But behind this achievement was a record of conflict on several levels. In Byron's early life he wavered between the idea that God made the country but man made the town, and the blunt opposite of this idea. He came finally to feel himself most at ease among urban surroundings. His earlier devotion to the picturesque tradition, furthermore, although not in itself inconsistent with this realization, prepared the way for a further conflict and failure. Once Byron realized that the tradition was becoming vulgarized and sentimentalized, he

---

gush." Fairchild himself concludes that this opinion seems "extravagant," but goes on to say, "this contrast between natural goodness and civilized viciousness is at bottom seriously ironic," that Boone represents an ideal figure and a device. Byron makes his intention perfectly clear by his use of such stock and sentimental phrases as "wilds of deepest maze" (l. 488), "the rarely trodden wild" (l. 491), Boone's· "darling trees" (l. 506), and "this unsighing people of the woods" (l. 536). The passage was written in 1822, when Byron was in full reaction against the sentimental and the Return to Nature Movement generally.

could only discard it. More important, its limited and fact-bound point of view, appealing primarily to the eye, worked against his achieving any deeply satisfying spiritual experience with nature, a fact illustrated dramatically and clearly by variously contradictory expressions reflecting Byron's experience during the last half of 1816 and the early months of 1817. His feelings of guilt, expressing themselves in the terms made available to him by the novel, seem to have dictated to him the conviction that the beauties of nature are quite lost on the Byronic hero-villain as well as on their author. And philosophically he espoused with equal ease the benevolent Creation of the deists and, on the other hand, the idea of an indifferent or even hostile Nature created by a Calvinistically imagined God whose intentions were by no means always benevolent. The final issue of this history of conflict and contradiction was not in any sense a consistent philosophy of nature. It was, instead, the increased awareness of the comic vision, which enabled Byron to view the world honestly, without oversimplification, in all its immense complexity and so do justice to his own consciousness of it.

Chapter II

BYRON'S LAUGHTER

1

The Comic Vision of Nature

Byron, as even a casual reader can see, must have indeed breathed in, along with the air, the Weltschmerz of his age. But he used his satiric power, to his credit, to combat one of the distinguishing characteristics of this attitude: the sentimental glorification of nature. For this state of mind is the product, essentially, of a conflict between the individual and his environment. Many a poet of the Romantic Period, of course, fled an uncongenial existence, and attempted to exchange his feelings of unrest and dissatisfaction for the tranquillity of a retired life close to nature. Byron's early years exhibit tendencies in this direction, to be sure; but from the first he fought them, and although he found it necessary to do so until the end, he persistently attacked this whole attitude toward life. To examine, therefore, Byron's attitudes toward nature and civilization is to relate a highly important chapter, not only in the life of a poet, but one significant in the history of ideas and important for the present century. Men have never been more painfully aware, perhaps, of the sharp contrast between their ideals and the facts of their environment than they are today. The growing stream of books dedicated to teaching the city man how to live and find peace of mind in the country is a witness to the conflict.

The full extent of Byron's satire upon the attitudes toward nature prevailing during his lifetime has never been adequately defined.[1] The mere presence of this satiric strain of thought sets him clearly apart from his romantic contemporaries and places him again among the descendants of Johnson,[2] who as early as 1750 had satirized the life close to nature, "which is represented [foolishly] as a certain refuge from folly, from anxiety, from passion, and from guilt," the seat of "innocence and tranquillity." The explanation of the presence of this satiric thought in Byron, its growth, and its backgrounds in Byron's reading, life, and personality, will occupy directly or indirectly a large part of the present study.

Byron glanced with a satiric eye upon nature in his earliest verse—in poems written in 1807, 1809, 1810, and 1811. From the latter date, however, up until the autumn of 1817, when *Beppo* was written, all is serious and romantic in his poetry. But from that time on, with the beginning of *Don Juan* in the next year, the satiric stream grows in volume, as one might expect.

It is first to be noticed in *Hours of Idleness,* where Byron twice subjected the pastoral scene to a youthful, boisterous satire, in the lines entitled "The First Kiss of Love" and in "To a Lady Who Presented to the Author a Lock of Hair." In the former piece, his early bias in favor of the "real" may be noticed.

> Your shepherds, your flocks, those fantastical themes,
> Perhaps may amuse, yet they never can move:
> Arcadia displays but a region of dreams.

---

[1]Byron's satiric attitude toward the whole Romantic concept of nature has been neither described nor investigated. Except for scattered references to Wordsworth's nature poetry, Claude M. Fuess, *Lord Byron As A Satirist in Verse* (New York, 1912); P. G. Trueblood, *The Flowering of Byron's Genius: Studies in Byron's Don Juan* (Stanford, 1945); and E. F. Boyd, *Byron's Don Juan* (New Brunswick, 1945) are silent.

[2]*Rambler*, No. 46. See also *Rambler*, No. 42, and *Idler*, No. 71, for further satire of the same kind.

In *English Bards* are to be found the well-known attacks (ll. 235–240) upon Wordsworth's advice, in "The Tables Turned," to leave the study of books for that of nature and (ll. 259–264) upon Coleridge's choice of subject in his "Lines to a Young Ass." Byron also finds place to satirize Bowles's melancholy nature poetry (ll. 327–334 in the first to fourth editions) and his exaggerated use of the pathetic fallacy (l. 360 and note), sneers at a topographical poem on Richmond Hill by Thomas Maurice (ll. 413–414), and glances at the "unmeaning rhyme" of Erasmus Darwin, author of *The Botanic Garden* and *The Temple of Nature* (ll. 891–902). The "rustic . . . soul" of the inspired peasant poet also comes in for an attack, as well as those dilettanti interested in tours and topography (ll. 765–798 and 1032–1034). And finally, there is a humorous account of the shock felt by Nature when Moore and Jeffrey met for the duel which Byron immortalized (ll. 468–475). Each one of these satiric attitudes was to flower magnificently in later years.

A humorous and impious attitude toward nature is evident also in two slight poems[3] written in June, 1810, at the very time that he was composing the first *Childe Harold*. These dates are of particular interest because this juxtaposition of the humorous and romantic was to be repeated in the fall months of 1817, when Byron worked concurrently on *Beppo* and *Childe Harold, IV*.

Hints From Horace, dated from Athens, March 12, 1811, attacks pompous overwriting in landscape description (ll. 21–30), warns away aspirants to eminence in the pastoral form for the reason that none can hope to excel the pastorals of the youthful Pope (ll. 387–392), and contains the inevitable attack upon Wordsworth (ll. 471–478).

---

[3]"Farewell Petition to J. C. H., Esq.," ll. 15–16, and "Oh How I Wish That An Embargo," written atop the Cyanean Symplegades.

The name of poet may be got with ease,

. . . .

Write but like Wordsworth, live beside a lake,
And keep your bushy locks a year from Blake.

The attacks thus far described have been largely concerned
either with the outmoded pastoral or with individuals whom
Byron regarded as nature poets. This kind of purely literary
satire was to continue, but with *Beppo,* Byron was to submit
the very abstraction and idea of nature to satirical treatment.
It was there that he first fully revealed his great comic vision
of nature.

Significant allusions in *Beppo* appear in some half-dozen
stanzas. In several (2, 82), there is a use of nature as a
humorous setting, linking it with sex, such as is seen in the
lines,

> The moment night with dusky mantle covers
> The skies (and the more duskily the better),
> The time less liked by husbands than by lovers
> Begins. . . .

Or, much the same sort of treatment of nature, this time
without the humor of sex, is to be noticed in stanza 41:

> With all its sinful doings, I must say,
> That Italy's a pleasant place to me,
> Who love to see the Sun shine every day,
> And vines (not nail'd to walls) from tree to tree
> Festoon'd, much like the back scene of a play
> Or melodrame, which people flock to see,
> When the first act is ended by a dance
> In vineyards copied from the south of France.

Or, we find the linking of the ludicrous to the beautiful or
the sublime, the technique to be used with such success in
Don Juan, as in the lines from stanza 43, where Byron says
he likes to see the sun rise, but

Not through a misty morning twinkling weak as
A drunken man's dead eye in maudlin sorrow.

And, finally, there is a satirical glance, along with the authors
who are *"all author,"* at the bluestockings who "stare . . .
on the stars from out their attics" (stanza 78). Byron may
possibly have derived hints of all this from Frere's work,[4]
but if so, they fell on fruitful soil.

These tendencies persisted and flourished in *Don Juan,*[5]
which was intended to be more than a little facetious about
everything; Byron had no reason to exempt the cult of nature
or the romantic natural setting. The initial attack in *Don
Juan* (I, 87–94) provides an example of Byron's comic vision
of nature at its most typical best. The first four lines of
stanza 87 have just enough (and no more) of the genuine
pathos of first love to mislead a careless reader, but the last
half of the stanza rings out with Byron's laughter—the source
of it sex, as often. Juan has fallen in love with Julia, and as
yet does not understand what it is that troubles him:

> Silent and pensive, idle, restless, slow,
> His home deserted for the lonely wood,
> Tormented with a wound he could not know,
> His, like all deep grief, plunged in solitude:
> I'm fond myself of solitude or so,
> But then, I beg it may be understood,
> By solitude I mean a sultan's, not
> A hermit's, with a harem for a grot.

[4]Only two cantos of *The Monks and the Giants* had been published at
the time. Stanzas 33 and 51, less possibly 12–16 and 28, may have given
Byron a hint. But Byron had treated nature with a cavalier hand in his
Hours of Idleness period. See above. Frere came out in 1818 with two
more cantos, which contain stanzas quite similar to those of Byron (III,
17–19), but it is quite possible that Frere was influenced by *Beppo*.

[5]A list of such stanzas in *Don Juan* should include the following: I, 87–
88, 90–94, 113, 201; II, 92, 139–140, 144–145, 148, 152; III, 56, 104 (MS);
IV, 75, 110, 112; V, 5, 42, 52; VI, 23–25, 53, 57, 65–68, 75–77; IX, 31
(*cf.* X, 71, 78); X, 1–2; XIII, 36; XIV, 29–30.

Before the section closes seven stanzas later, the theme has been defined: the ridiculous self-deception of those who fly to natural solitude. Young Juan, in Wordsworthian natural surroundings, thinks metaphysical Coleridgian thoughts, utters obscure lines from Campbell's *Gertrude of Wyoming,* and ponders themes which were favorite ones in the poetry of Keats and Shelley. Thus Juan in the ludicrous role of metaphysical and nympholeptic nature poet casts a comic light far beyond his own figure. The implication is that all these spiritually exalted (and obscure) communions with nature have their origins alike in the physical; the Lakers and their tadpoles no more clearly understand what is wrong with them than does Juan, and the "entusy-musy" of the nature poet is thus quite as laughable as the "enthusiasm" of young love's sentimental recourse to nature. The ignorance and self-deception of the one is paralleled by the unintelligibility of the other. Byron concludes the attack with a serio-comic hint that it is unprofitable in the midst of the spiritual and poetic to forget the physical: in poring over the leaves and flowers, listening to the voices in the wind, and thinking on wood nymphs and immortal bowers—Juan found that he had missed his dinner.

The basis of Byron's satiric humor is the unexpected incongruity. Thus he can close a beautiful and colorful description of a rainbow (II, 91–92) with the bathetic lines, that it blended

> . . . every colour into one,
> Just like a black eye in a recent scuffle.

Or in masterfully ironic lines (III, 56), which satirize his own earlier heroes, he attributes to Lambro, the bloodthirsty old pirate and slaver, "a love . . . of scenes sublime, a pleasure in the gentle stream . . . and a joy in flowers." Or, of poor battered Juan on his way to be sold in slavery (IV, 75)—

> The shores of Ilion lay beneath their lee—
> Another time he might have liked to see 'em,
> But now was not much pleased with Cape Sigæum.

And as a final example, a stanza (5) which provides the setting for the first part of the fifth canto.

> The wind swept down the Euxine, and the wave
> Broke foaming o'er the blue Symplegades;
> 'T is a grand sight from off 'the Giant's Grave'
> To watch the progress of those rolling seas
> Between the Bosphorus, as they lash and lave
> Europe and Asia, you being quite at ease;
> There's not a sea the passenger e'er pukes in,
> Turns up more dangerous breakers than the Euxine.

Thus *Don Juan* "strips off the tinsel" from the sentiment of nature along with that of most other sentiments. A contributing reason for this general tendency in Byron's treatment of nature is to be sought in his quarrel with Wordsworth, Coleridge, and Southey—a quarrel quite personal in part, but one rising also from his belief that they along with Keats and the "suburban tadpoles" were responsible for the depreciation of Pope, "who, having no fault, has had REASON made his reproach."[6] There was, as well, the young man reacting against his elders, the man of the world against the provincial, the gentleman poet refusing to accept "the fervour,—the almost religious fervour" of Wordsworth, Coleridge, and those Byron thought of as their followers.[7] But reasons even deeper than these, one feels, provide the ulti-

---

[6]"Reply to Blackwood's *Edinburgh Magazine*," L. and J., IV, 485. See also L. and J., V, 18, 64, 82, 109, 117, for other statements about "your pond poets."

[7]L. and J., IV, 172. See also L. and J., III, 10, IV, 169, 196–197, 225, 238, 486; *Don Juan*, dedicatory stanzas; I, 90–91, 205; III, 94–95, 98, 100.

mate explanation. Byron's consciousness of the growing vulgarization of the picturesque tradition, his own failure to
find any deep or abiding satisfaction in a life close to nature,
his conviction that such a life represented, after all, an effort
to escape, a way deriving in large part from the examples of
Werther, St.-Preux, and the Rousseau of the *Confessions*—
these deep realizations are all that need be named.

2

"This cant about nature"

Byron's growing conviction that appreciation of the natural
world had become a fad of the many—and his increasing
awareness that such a condition offered rich opportunities for
satire or ridicule—had at least two important effects. To a
man of his temperament, which chose regularly the means of
singularity in order to distinguish itself and feared above all
to be detected in the midst of the ridiculous, it may well have
been fatal to the development of a seriously considered
philosophy of nature. This same realization, furthermore,
led him in his life to suppress many evidences of enthusiasm
for nature and in his writing a picturesque or "romantic"
treatment of it.

The earliest evidence of a reaction of this kind, apart
from that in the early verse, is described by Lady Byron.[8]
The scene is a London dinner, October, 1815: "The Misses
were determined to talk, and poetically too, either in honour
of Papa or their Guest; and B. was attacked by ecstasies about
'autumnal tints' in Scotland, which he cruelly answered by
raptures about whiskey. In short, they *yelped* and he *snapped.*"
Byron is here playing his role as man of the world, or some-

[8]E. C. Mayne, *Life of Lady Byron*, p. 194. See, however, *Correspondence*,
I, 29–30, and II, 49, for several other early humorous references to the
"picturesque—*e—e—e—e.*"

thing mysteriously worse. The "avowed libertine" in Maturin's *Wild Irish Boy*[9] (1808) had said to the young hero,

"You pretended a few minutes ago to dislike the wine I
pressed you to take: and now you pretend to luxuriate in
what you call 'the rich and weeping softness of a watery
landscape.' This is all nonsense and self-imposture. Champaigne (when it is good, I mean) has always the same power
of stimulating the spirits, though trees and water have not,
for they have lost their power of stimulating mine long ago.
And it is to be hoped when you come to my . . . experience—you will look upon nature with the same disgust that
I do."

An awareness of the ludicrous quality in the idea of the
"100,000 travellers who broke loose from Great Britain in
all directions" at the end of the war—himself considered perhaps as one of them—this accounts too (along with a dislike
of Sotheby) for the prose sketch[10] which Byron began on
August 19, 1820: "However, by dint of being obliged to get
out [of the carriage] on going up a hill, and of being thrown
out on going down one, they [Mr. and Mrs. Solemnboy and
the six Misses Solemnboy] contrived to see so much of the
country as to acquire a tolerable notion of landscape; and
their letters dated G— were full of past and present description, with very little assistance from Coxe's Guide-book."
The cult of the picturesque was becoming increasingly vulgarized. We read, for example, of Juan and Johnson (V, 42)
that they were plodding on their way

> Through orange bowers, and jasmine, and so forth
> (Of which I might have a good deal to say,
> There being no such profusion in the North
> Of oriental plants, 'et cetera,'
> But that of late your scribblers think it worth

[9]*The Wild Irish Boy* (London, 1808), I, 162–63.
[10]L. and J., IV, 453. In 1818 Sotheby had published his *Farewell to
Italy*, the product of a tour he had made with his family in 1816–1817.

Their while to rear whole hotbeds in *their* works
Because one poet travell'd 'mongst the Turks).

As he wrote in *Don Juan* (V, 52),

> I won't describe; description is my forte,
> But every fool describes in these bright days
> His wondrous journey . . .
> While Nature, tortured twenty thousand ways,
> Resigns herself with exemplary patience
> To guide-books, rhymes, tours, sketches, illustrations.

And so in his "Reply to Blackwood's *Edinburgh Magazine*," dated March 15, 1820, he judges his forte, *"descriptive* poetry, the *lowest* department of the art."

These realizations, strengthened by his dislike for the author who was "all author," his deep distaste for being considered a mere poet,[11] and his abhorrence of sentimentality, explain the description Moore gives[12] of Byron at Venice in the fall of 1819. The realization that "every fool describes in these bright days," which led him in his poetry to the conclusion "I won't describe," also had its effects in his life. Moore writes,

> We set off together in my carriage for Venice; a glorious sunset when we embarked at Fusina in a gondola, and the view of Venice and the distant Alps (some of which had snow on them, reddening with the last light) was magnificent; but my companion's conversation, which, though highly ludicrous and amusing, was anything but romantic, threw my mind and imagination into a mood not at all agreeing with the scene.

When Moore expanded this passage from his diary to fit it into his *Life* of Byron,[13] he revealed that the conversation of Byron which "put at once completely to flight all poetical . . .

[11]See for a typical instance L. and J., IV, 312–13.
[12]Moore, *Memoirs, Journal and Correspondence of Thomas Moore*, ed. Russell (London, 1853), III, 24.
[13]*Life*, p. 411.

associations" was made up of "all that had ever happened, of gay or ridiculous, during our London life together,—his scrapes and my lecturings,—our joint adventures with the Bores and Blues, the two great enemies, as he always called them, of London happiness,—our joyous nights together at Watier's, Kinnaird's, &c."

Several days later Byron evidenced this attitude again. Moore writes[14] that while they were waiting for dinner guests to arrive, "we stood out on the balcony, in order that, before the daylight was quite gone, I might have some glimpses of the scene which the Canal presented. Happening to remark, in looking up at the clouds, which were still bright in the west, that 'what had struck me in Italian sunsets was that peculiar rosy hue—' I had hardly pronounced the word 'rosy,' when Lord Byron, clapping his hand on my mouth, said, with a laugh, 'Come, d—n it, Tom, *don't* be poetical.' " But Byron was to add another dimension to this revelation of himself[15] on Moore's last evening in Venice:

Lord Byron then took me in his gondola, and, the moon being in its fullest splendour, he made the gondoliers row us to such points of view as might enable me to see Venice, at that hour, to advantage. Nothing could be more solemnly beautiful than the whole scene around, and I had, for the first time, the Venice of my dreams before me. All those meaner details which so offend the eye by day were now softened down by the moonlight into a sort of visionary indistinctness. . . . My companion saw that I was moved by it, and though familiar with the scene himself, seemed to give way, for the moment, to the same strain of feeling. . . . This mood, however, was but of the moment; some quick turn of ridicule soon carried him off into a totally different vein, and . . . at the door of his own palazzo, we parted, laughing, as we had met. . . .

[14]*Ibid.*, p. 412.
[15]*Ibid.*, p. 422.

In the light of these attitudes, we may expect to find Byron, during the last few years of his life, from 1821 on, continuing to glance with a satirical eye,[16] as he had done as early as his *Hours of Idleness* days, at the sentimental lover's recourse to nature. Nor is it surprising to discover him continuing to treat[17] a sacred world of nature with impiety and irreverence, making a self-conscious and humorous use of nature similes, maliciously mixing the incongruous with the sublime and the sentimental, introducing the vulgarly unpoetical along with the very serious. The attacks upon the Lakers and those Byron classified among their followers are present, and appear with unabated frequency and vigour. He unerringly selects for ridicule[18] Wordsworth's notorious lines,

> I measured it from side to side:
> 'Tis three feet long, and two feet wide,

compares him again with Joanna Southcott and Emanuel Swedenborg, terms him[19] "the great Metaquizzical poet," speaks[20] of the "filthy trash of Epics, Excursions, etc., etc.," damns,[21] among others, Campbell, Southey, Wordsworth, Coleridge, and Bowles because "these men . . . never lived either in *high life,* nor in *solitude:* there is no medium for the knowledge of the *busy* or the *still* world," and decides[22] Keats "was spoilt by Cockneyfying and Suburbing." Of himself,[23] "the fact is (as I perceive), that I wrote a great deal better

---

[16]*Heaven and Earth,* ii, 160–67, 196–97; *Don Juan,* XVI, 13–15. Such passages represent not satire of Byron's earlier poetry but, one would think, of the man himself.

[17]See *The Vision of Judgment,* 2, 16, 27, 61.

[18]L. and J., VI, 381.

[19]L. and J., V, 226.

[20]L. and J., V, 600.

[21]L. and J., V, 362–3.

[22]L. and J., V, 269. See L. and J., V, 277, "the Cockney-and-Water washing-tub Schools"; V, 337, "the Suburban School."

[23]L. and J., V, 222.

in 1811, than I have ever done since." He is referring to his *Hints from Horace.* The observation was made in January, 1821.

Indicative of Byron's continued and even heightened awareness, during the remaining years of his life, of the mob of tourists who also scribbled are his reference[24] to Jane Waldie's *Sketches descriptive of Italy* as "one of the hundred tours lately published," his having[25] the Bluestockings ask Juan in England "whether in his travels he saw Ilion?" his reference[26] to the "years before the peace, ere all the world had travelled," to[27] "gazing tourists" staring at a scene from "hackney'd height" (one cannot but recall here the many church steeples and towers Byron himself had climbed in order to view landscapes), his mock appeal[28] concerning the English to Mrs. Elizabeth Fry, the Newgate reformer, to "cure them of tours," his mention[29] of the "Anglo-invasion" of France and[30] of the "travelling English . . . these tourists," his description[31] of Switzerland as "the most romantic region of the world" but ruined by "English visitors," his satiric reference[32] to "those ladies who like cuts, and landscapes, and all that," and his several expressions[33] of contempt for travel books.

An immediate and obvious result of Byron's awareness of this deluge of descriptive tours and poems, and the consequent repression of sentiment, is a succession of statements, several already quoted, in which he refuses to describe. How much descriptive poetry Byron did *not* write as a result may

[24]*Poetical Works,* IV, 471, note to *Marino Faliero.*
[25]*Don Juan,* XI, 50.
[26]*Poetical Works,* VI, 586, note to *Don Juan.*
[27]*The Age of Bronze,* l. 182.
[28]*Don Juan,* X, 86.
[29]L. and J., V, 311.
[30]L. and J., V, 311, note.
[31]L. and J., V, 365.
[32]L. and J., V, 271.
[33]L. and J., V, 307, 373, 375.

only be conjectured. Its virtual disappearance from the poetry
written in 1821–1824 has already been commented upon. It
is significant, though, when Juan is to make his trip from
Ismail to the Russian court at St. Petersburg, that Byron dis-
poses of the journey in a single stanza (IX, 42), deliberately
rejecting the tradition of the picturesque tour.

> I left Don Juan with his horses baiting—
> Now we'll get o'er the ground at a great rate.
> I shall not be particular in stating
> His journey, we've so many tours of late:
> Suppose him then at Petersburgh. . . .

In the next canto Byron writes, "I won't describe,—that is,
if I can help description" (X, 28), and when, later, Juan
has to make his trip across Europe from Russia to England
(X, 58–63), the half-dozen stanzas are a parody of picturesque
description and deliberately "unpoetical," little more than a
roll call of famous cities and a list of natural resources. It
is one of Byron's finest, most subtle attacks. Juan "journey'd
on through Poland and through Warsaw, famous for mines
of salt and yokes of iron" (58), "through Prussia Proper . . .
whose vaunt [is] some veins of iron, lead, or copper" (60),
"thence through Berlin, Dresden, and the like" (61),

> . . . on through Manheim, Bonn,
> Which Drachenfels frowns over like a spectre
> Of the good feudal times forever gone,
> On which I have not time just now to lecture, (62)

and "thence to Holland's Hague and Helvoetsluys, that
waterland of Dutchmen and of ditches" (63)—this, and Juan
is at the Channel ready to cross over into England. Once in
England, on his way from Dover to London, Juan travels
(X, 76) through "a paradise of hops and high production."
Byron concludes with the lines,

I could say more, but do not choose to encroach
Upon the Guide-book's privilege. (XI, 23)

Thus we come to Byron's final judgment[34] passed upon his country that "in these days the grand *primum mobile* of England is *cant* . . . multiplied through all the varieties of life," his exclamation,[35] "away, then, with this cant about nature," his statement,[36] "I hate cant of any kind, and the cant of the love of nature as much as any other," and the curious picture presented of Byron in 1823 by Lady Blessington. She records[37] that

One of our first rides with Lord Byron was to Nervi, a village on the sea-coast, most romantically situated, and each turn of the road presenting various and beautiful prospects. They were all familiar to him, and he failed not to point them out, but in very sober terms, never allowing anything like enthusiasm in his expressions, though many of the views might have excited it.

She writes elsewhere[38] in her *Journal,*

I observed that when, in our rides, we came to any fine point of view, Byron paused, and looked at it . . . [but] he rarely praised what so evidently pleased him, and he became silent and abstracted for some time after. . . .

Byron explained[39] to Lady Blessington that he was laying up the scene in his memory for future use just "as artists filled their sketch-books with studies from Nature, to be made use of on after-occasions," and that he did not want to exhaust his admiration in effusive expressions. In regard to this explanation, several facts may be recalled. Lady Blessington was an author, a lady author and famous bluestocking; she was a tourist, an expert with the picturesque technique; she

[34]L. and J., V, 542.
[35]L. and J., V, 557.
[36]Blessington, *op. cit.*, p. L.
[37]*Ibid.*, p. 48.
[38]*Ibid.*, p. 119.
[39]*Ibid.*, p. 120.

was from Byron's own circle in London, quite able to return and talk about him there to his old friends; he almost certainly knew that she was taking notes on their conversations. The probability is rather strong that he did not give her the true explanation. Early in their friendship he had said[40] to her regarding his apparent insensibility to natural scenery, "I suppose you expected me to explode into some enthusiastic exclamations on the sea, the scenery, etc., such as poets indulge in, or rather, are supposed to indulge in." Now this and the two other instances recorded by Lady Blessington are clearly examples of the same kind of reaction which Moore recorded when he visited Byron in 1819. Trelawny seems to offer the key to the accounts of both Moore and Lady Blessington. He noted[41] that whenever any of Byron's London acquaintances paid him a visit, Byron suspected that their purpose was to observe and at once assumed his character of man of the world and anti-poet. This is what he obviously did with Moore and, as far as he was able, with Lady Blessington. But Lady Blessington seems finally to have captured Byron. We may well believe that as her beauty and intelligence exerted greater and greater effect upon him, he condescended against his usual practice to reveal to her, however false a revelation it might be, the "romantic" poet whom she was wishing so obviously to discover, a Byron who solemnly and deliberately stored up images of natural scenery in his memory for future use. That Byron's explanation did not convince even Lady Blessington, however, who was so willing to be convinced, is evident from the last statement[42] she made upon the subject: she concluded that it was "one of the strangest anomalies" that "fine scenery seemed to produce little effect on his feelings." She had evidently forgotten an earlier evening spent with Byron, one that quite corresponds

[40]*Ibid.*, xlix–l.
[41]Trelawny, *Records*, I, 80.
[42]Blessington, *op. cit.*, p. 239.

with Moore's last evening with him in Venice. Early in her book[43] she had devoted several poetic pages to a description of a moonlit night when they had sat on a balcony overlooking the harbor at Genoa, "every object . . . tinged with . . . silvery lustre." The scene had "formed a picture that description falls far short of," and evoked "a delicious melancholy." Suddenly the different crews in the ships below them began to sing "national hymns and barcaroles"—there needed only "God Save the King" from an English crew to touch off the "delicious melancholy" already felt as a result of the night and the view. It came, and "Byron was no less touched than the rest." He is reported to have said,

Why, positively, we are all quite sentimental this evening, and I—I who have sworn against sentimentality, find the old leaven still in my nature, and quite ready to make a fool of me. "Tell it not in Gath"—that is to say, breathe it not in London, or to English ears polite, or never again shall I be able to *enact* the stoic philosopher. Come, come; this will never do. We must forswear moonlight [and] fine views. . . .

The validity of the total impression of Byron which Lady Blessington gives is borne out by the remaining evidence relating to his life during 1821–1824, though she and Moore are the only two authorities who relate this side of him at length to a love of nature. Thus the Countess Guiccioli notices[44] that "books with affected sentiment of any kind, imaginary itineraries, made him very impatient. High-sounding phrases jarred on his ears." Medwin quotes[45] Byron as saying, "I remember Keats somewhere says that 'flowers would not blow, leaves bud,' &c. if man and woman did not kiss. How sentimental!" Hobhouse writes[46] that although Byron found

[43] *Ibid.*, pp. 55–58.
[44] Guiccioli, *op. cit.*, II, 416.
[45] Medwin, *op. cit.*, p. 171.
[46] John Cam Hobhouse, "Lord Byron in Greece," *The Westminster Review*, II, 227.

"sincere delight" in the "glories of the material world," "he was far above any affectation of poetical ecstacy." Galt, writing upon the subject of Hunt and Byron growing tired of one another at Albaro, states[47] without giving his source, "it is certain that he laughed at his [Hunt's] affected admiration of landscapes." And Moore observes,[48] "the anxiety with which, at all periods of his life, but particularly at the present [1823 in Greece], he sought to repel the notion that, except when under the actual inspiration of writing, he was at all influenced by poetical associations, very frequently displayed itself."

This excessive desire to conceal the poet, which was linked in Byron's mind with sentimental effusions over the beauties of nature, joining with his realization that the picturesque had become vulgarized, could not fail to affect sooner or later the actual pleasure which Byron was able to realize from nature. His rejection of the sentimental cant about nature was in part the act of a sentimentalist trying to protect himself from the easy emotion, but the violence of his reaction almost certainly carried over into a distrust of the genuine emotion evoked by a natural scene. Byron came to fear them both. He who talks, furthermore, of the cant about nature and writes nature poetry at the same time places himself in a difficult position. Byron could not but be aware of the glass house in which he lived. All this must certainly be considered in attempting to explain the seemingly sudden development of Byron's comic vision of nature, and the remarkably few references in the poetry of his last years to a nature either picturesque or benevolently inclined. There was also in the mind of Byron the memory of earlier experiences and attitudes which helped to make inevitable, finally, his satiric treatment of nature. These shall be considered next.

[47]Galt, *op. cit.*, p. 257.
[48]Moore, *Life*, p. 608.

Chapter III

TOWN VERSUS COUNTRY

1

Byron's Early Dilemma

When one examines Byron's most typical reaction to the external world of nature during the important, formative years before his meeting with Shelley in 1816, the keynote struck is one of indecision and relative failure—indecision before the two distinct poles of his generation, nature and civilization; relative failure and inability to offer up his whole faith, growing out of this indecision, when he attempted to establish the deepest and most meaningful relations with nature. Byron was driven on in the attempt by strong elements of his character, personality, and cultural heritage. The amount of poetry which he wrote on the subject of nature points to the fact. But there were elements almost equally strong which led him from his earliest years, in the opposite direction, away from any kind of deification of nature and from the romantic and mystic experience of complete self-surrender in a rapt contemplation of the beauties of nature, with the resultant loss of the self in the One. For there was, as has been recognized, a general antagonism in Byron's mind, evident from the very first, to anything hinting of the mystical or the incomprehensible, a tendency which has usually been identified with or related to his affinities with the neoclassical spirit. To this kinship must be assigned his early delight[1] in life, high and low, "as it really is" and his ex-

---

[1] L. and J., II, 378.

pressed preference[2] for a life of action "to all the speculations of those mere dreamers of another existence (I don't
mean religiously but fancifully)." "Let us make the most of
life," he writes,[3] "and leave dreams to Emanuel Swedenborg."
In his poetic theory and criticism, clarity and common sense
are primary principles. They led him at various times in his
life to denounce[4] Wordsworth, Coleridge, Hunt, Southey,
Keats, and Rousseau for obscurity, mysticism, unintelligibility,
or madness, and to champion Johnson as "the noblest critical
mind which our country has produced" and Pope as "the
best of poets," whose poetry he has "ever loved and hon-
oured . . . with my whole soul." Thus he termed[5] " 'imagination' and 'invention,' the two commonest of qualities: an
Irish peasant with a little whiskey in his head will imagine
more than would furnish forth a modern poem." He regarded[6] his own age as "the age of the decline of English
poetry." But this side of Byron is too well known to require
extensive treatment here. What must be borne in mind, however, is that these judgments were not mere expressions of
perversity or arbitrarily assumed. They had their solid foun-
dations deep in Byron's thought and personality.

And yet despite this general distrust of the imagination
and of the mystical and despite this general emphasis upon
the dictates of common sense, there were other and powerful
forces within him which drew him, quite early in his life,
toward nature. The remarkable fact about Byron, however,
is not that he wrote nature poetry in some quantity or that

[2]L. and J., II, 345; III, 405. Byron's rejection of the spectator attitude
toward life, coupled with his conception of the gentleman poet, led him
repeatedly to depreciate the profession of writer and drew him finally to
Greece. See L. and J., II, 338; III, 263, 405; IV, 84, 238.

[3]L. and J., II, 36.

[4]L. and J., I, 193; II, 75; III, 226, 239; IV, 172, 238, 486; V, 117, 161, 564.

[5]L. and J., V, 554.

[6]L. and J., IV, 485. See also IV, 277; V, 82, 165, 587, 591; VI, 67.

he sometimes attributed to nature qualities which the man of the present century recognizes as remote from his immediate experience; but that he subordinated this interest in nature to the extent that he actually did. For he was early the great rebel against society and had written[7] "I hate civilization"; dissatisfaction with the "artificial" society which he knew was one of his habitual moods and, being born with the cultural heritage which was his, it was inevitable that he should turn to nature. Thus the Byronic heroes of 1813–1814 explicitly prefer a life outside cities and condemn the effects following from existence in them. Selim in the *Bride of Abydos* expresses the view[8] that his life on the sea and his tent ashore are "more than cities" to him, and that[9] "Luxury" and "Corruption" come "when cities cage us in." Conrad, the Corsair,[10] had been "warp'd by the world," there "doom'd by his very virtues for a dupe." And like Conrad, Lara too[11] had a heart "not by nature hard"; "his early dreams of good outstripp'd the truth." Thus[12] Byron and these youthfully disillusioned heroes often stand "a stranger in this breathing world." In similar fashion, Byron himself had written[13] to Augusta in 1808, "my intercourse with the world [has] hardened my heart"; "it has now become as hard as a Highlander's heelpiece."

The hardened heart of these years was the product in large part of Byron's sense of isolation. That sense of being isolated and alone in the world, a hermit in the midst of crowds and lost in the desert of London, forms a recurring theme in the

[7]*Correspondence*, I, 226.
[8]*The Bride of Abydos*, II, 390–91.
[9]*Ibid.*, II, 436–43.
[10]*The Corsair*, I, 249–56.
[11]*Lara*, I, 304, 323.
[12]*Ibid.*, I, 315.
[13]L. and J., I, 204, 203.

Hours of Idleness collection and the early miscellaneous verse.[14] The feeling in Byron is an obvious and often-chronicled characteristic. Viewed in the special light of this study, however, it constituted a major temptation for him to attempt identification of himself in some manner with that which was outside and alien to man, in short, to transfer a part of his sympathies to nature—a generous part. Man and his civilization were despicable. On the other side of the coin was an admirable world of nature, and the two sides were opposites. Childe Harold repeatedly contrasts the wickedness or baseness of man and the goodness of nature. Thus he asks,[15] "Why, Nature, waste thy wonders on such men?" referring to the "poor, paltry slaves" of Portugal, "yet born 'midst noblest scenes"; and laments[16] in passing over the "romantic hills" of that same nation, "Oh, that such hills upheld a freeborn race!" Of Greece he writes,[17]

> Strange—that where Nature loved to trace,
> As if for Gods, a dwelling place,
>
> .   .   .   .
>
> There man, enamour'd of distress,
> Should mar it into wilderness.

And in the land of the East,[18] "all, save the spirit of man, is divine."

And so Byron, expressing the dictates of his personality in the form that his century made available to him, viewed nature from the time of his adolescence as a refuge for a

[14]See "Childish Recollections," ll. 209–42; "Lines Addressed to the Rev. J. T. Becher, On His Advising the Author to Mix More with Society"; "Stanzas to a Lady on Leaving England," ll. 19–42; "If Sometimes in the Haunts of Men."

[15]I, 18; see also I, 15.

[16]I, 30.

[17]*The Giaour*, ll. 46–51; cf. ll. 103–14, 142–60.

[18]*The Bride of Abydos*, I, 15. It should be noted that even though in these passages Nature is praised in terms extravagantly honorific, it is never implied that the desirable condition for man is the state of nature.

troubled mind or as a place of sympathetic escape. As early
as *Hours of Idleness*[19] the often expressed theme occurs. The
misanthrope of the first line quoted below is the product and
result of "love's last adieu," the title as well as the refrain
of the poem, which was written in 1806.

> From cities to caves of the forest he flew:
> There, raving, he howls his complaint to the wind;
> The mountains reverberate love's last adieu!

Or,[20] in only slightly more refined form:

> Fain would I fly the haunts of men—
> I seek to shun, not hate mankind;
> My breast requires the sullen glen,
> Whose gloom may suit a darken'd mind.

Childe Harold's "Good Night"[21] is in much the same tone:

> Welcome, welcome, ye dark blue waves!
> And when you fail my sight,
> Welcome, ye deserts, and ye caves!

Finally, this same sentiment receives its most finished expression before 1816 in the second canto of *Childe Harold* (stanzas
25, 26, and 37).

> To sit on rocks, to muse o'er flood and fell,
> To slowly trace the forest's shady scene,
> Where things that own not man's dominion dwell,
> And mortal foot hath ne'er or rarely been;
> To climb the trackless mountain all unseen,
> With the wild flock that never needs a fold;
> Alone o'er steeps and foaming falls to lean,
> This is not solitude; 'tis but to hold
> Converse with Nature's charms, and view her stores
>   unroll'd.

[19]"Love's Last Adieu," ll. 21–4.
[20]"I Would I Were A Careless Child," ll. 49–52.
[21]I, ll. 194–96.

But 'midst the crowd, the shock of men,
To hear, to see, to feel, and to possess,
And roam along, the world's tired denizen,
With none who bless us, none whom we can bless;
Minions of splendour shrinking from distress!
None that, with kindred consciousness endued,
If we were not would seem to smile the less,
Of all that flatter'd, follow'd, sought, and sued;
This is to be alone; this, this is solitude!

   .   .   .   .

Dear Nature is the kindest mother still,
Though always changing, in her aspect mild;
From her bare bosom let me take my fill,
Her never-wean'd, though not her favour'd child.
Oh! she is fairest in her features wild,
Where nothing polish'd dares pollute her path:
To me by day or night she ever smiled,
Though I have mark'd her when none other hath,
And sought her more and more, and loved her best in
    wrath.

I have quoted these passages at length to emphasize the
origins of the final stanza quoted and thus to highlight, by
means of its genealogy, the essential difference between such
a stanza, common enough in Byron, and the true Wordsworthian note, with which it is easily confused.[22] Indeed, one
begins to suspect the depth and meaningfulness of even these
last lines when it is noticed that stanzas 25–26 grow out of
several others on a love now past and that stanza 37 is preceded by six stanzas on "sweet Florence" (Mrs. Spencer
Smith), with whom Byron carried on a shallow and half-
hearted affair in Malta. With such emotional associations
and surroundings, it is impossible to feel that these utterances express any genuine religion of nature. Although it is
unprofitable to argue from the false or hollow note in Byron's
rhetoric to actual insincerity in the poet, the lines quoted

[22]See the note to this passage in the E. H. Coleridge edition.

reflect literary tradition much more clearly than any deeply significant and original personal experience. The tone is quite close to lines[23] in Beattie's *Minstrel,* for example:

> In truth he was a strange and wayward wight,
> Fond of each gentle, and each dreadful scene.
> In darkness, and in storm, he found delight.

Or,[24]

> And oft the craggy cliff he lov'd to climb,
> When all in mist the world below was lost,
> What dreadful pleasure! there to stand sublime.

This is the familiar Byron. Quite as numerous, however, and equally convincing are statements of the opposite point of view: that the busy scenes of human life and activity are the proper refuge for a poet's troubled mind. Thus,[25] once the rural scene was sweet and Nature seemed to smile, but now (1807) "in thoughtless throngs and empty noise" he combats best his "bosom's sadness"; or comparing himself in 1808 to the fallen Adam expelled from Paradise he finds[26] "in busier scenes relief." Back at Newstead in 1811 after his first tour, he resolves[27] that he will "whine no more, nor seek again an eastern shore."

[23]*The Minstrel,* I, 190–92. The relative shallowness of Byron's reactions to natural beauty during these years is also to be seen in his "Stanzas Composed During a Thunder Storm," ll. 31–72 and "Stanzas Written in Passing the Ambracian Gulf," ll. 9–20. In each the memory of "sweet Florence" is the principal vision evoked. Byron took repeated early notice of the fact that particular scenes lost their power of pleasing once the love affair with which they were associated had dissolved. See "To Emma," especially ll. 31–32; "Fragment Written Shortly After the Marriage of Miss Chaworth," ll. 5–8; and "Translation of Romaic Song," ll. 13–16, 33–36. Selim in *The Bride of Abydos,* I, 57–64, although a professed nature lover, remarks that "to view alone the fairest scenes . . . were irksome. . . . I love not solitude."

[24]*Ibid.,* I, 181–83.

[25]"To a Lady," ll. 33–40.

[26]"To a Lady On Being Asked My Reason for Quitting England in the Spring," ll. 1–9.

[27]"Epistle to a Friend," ll. 41–4.

The world befits a busy brain,—
I'll hie me to its haunts again.

Or he finds relief[28] from love melancholy in "busy life again," and to combat his sense of isolation in the world[29] he clings to "IDA'S social band." Typical of the attitudes of this period of his life are the statements,[30] directed from the solitude of Newstead, that

I am growing *nervous* (how you will laugh!)—but it is true,—really, wretchedly, ridiculously, fine-ladically *nervous*. Your climate kills me; I can neither read, write, nor amuse myself, or anyone else. My days are listless, and my nights restless. . . . I don't know that I sha'n't end with insanity, for I find a want of method in arranging my thoughts that perplexes me strangely. . . . I must try the hartshorn of your company; and a session of Parliament would suit me well,—anything to cure me of conjugating the accursed verb *"ennuyer."*

London, he admits,[31] "is a damned place to be sure, but the only one in the world . . . for fun: though I have seen parts of the globe that I like better, still upon the whole it is the completest either to help one in feeling oneself—alive— or forgetting that one is so." Knowledge of London[32] is even a necessary part of a poet's education: ". . . half of these Scotch and Lake troubadours, are spoilt by living in little circles and petty societies. London and the world is the only place to take the conceit out of a man—in the milling phrase."

The only conclusion possible in view of such shifting opinions is that Byron simply had not made up his mind upon the basic question of the beneficial effects of a life with nature. That "God made the country and man made the town" was an idea which he admitted, even in principle, only partially

28"One Struggle More, And I Am Free," l. 4.
29"Childish Recollections," l. 242.
30L. and J., II, 54–5.
31L. and J., III, 270.
32L. and J., III, 119.

and with reservations. Virtue had announced herself a country gentlewoman, rural, refined, and sentimental, twenty years before Byron was born; but he, as is well known, was more than often interested in ladies of another stamp.

2

Byron's Life in Town and Country, Chiefly Before 1816

Byron's reaction to the actuality of life in the country, as he first experienced it in the village of Southwell, he has described at some length over several years and without any of the indecision which marks those of his utterances already noticed. He completely rejected his Southwell existence. The evidence is chronicled with such completeness and with such violence as to take on something of the humorous, as he lived out his long months there. He was first in Southwell during the Easter holidays of 1804. His original reference[33] to his life there is expressed in terms of some moderation. "I am as you may imagine a little dull here . . . my resources of amusement are Books." But a week[34] later his feelings had reached a pitch which they were ever to retain whenever the subject of life at Southwell came up. He is writing to his sister.

You tell me that you are tired of London. I am rather surprised to hear that, for I thought the Gaieties of the Metropolis were particularly pleasing to *young ladies.* For my part I detest it; the smoke and the noise feel particularly unpleasant; but however it is preferable to this horrid place, where I am oppressed with *ennui,* and have no amusement of any kind. . . . There are very few books of any kind that are either instructive or amusing, no society but old parsons and old Maids;—I shoot a Good deal; but, thank

[33]L. and J., I, 23.
[34]L. and J., I, 25–6.

God, I have not so far lost my reason as to make shooting my only amusement. There are indeed some of my neighbours whose only pleasures consist in field sports, but in other respects they are only one degree removed from the brute creation. . . . I sincerely wish for the company of a few friends. . . . I am an absolute Hermit; in a short time my Gravity which is increased by my solitude will qualify me for an Archbishoprick. . . . Your letters and those of one of my Harrow friends form my only resources for driving away *dull care.* For Godsake write me a letter as long as may fill *twenty sheets.* . . .

Or, on April 9, he refers[35] to his "drooping spirits" and "the Gloom which envelopes me in this uncomfortable place." Back there in the following summer,[36] it is "this accursed place, which is the region of dullness itself, and more stupid than the banks of Lethe. . . . I wander about hating everything I behold, and if I remained here a few months longer, I should become, what with *envy, spleen and all uncharitableness,* a complete *misanthrope.* . . ." In December[37] he writes to his mother's solicitor John Hanson, pleading for "the pleasure of spending the Holidays at your House [in London] . . . at Southwell I should have nothing in the World to do, but play at cards and listen to the edifying Conversation of old Maids." It would be tedious to note his many expressions of disgust[38] with rural life at Southwell. From June of 1806 to June of 1807 he was forced to live there with his mother as a measure of economy because of the extravagances of his first year at Cambridge. In April, 1807, he is still issuing[39] the old charges: "You speak of the *Charms* of Southwell; the *Place* I *abhor* . . . this *Crater* of Dullness,"

[35]L. and J., I, 26–7.
[36]L. and J., I, 31.
[37]L. and J., I, 52–3.
[38]See L. and J., I, 58, 60, 73, 78.
[39]L. and J., I, 126.

"this damned place."[40] In August, 1806, he had run away
from home. He was at that time approaching the age of nineteen years.

In estimating any of Byron's expressed views or feelings,
the particular and immediate situations of his life must be
taken into account. His inability to live amicably with his
mother clearly influenced his opinions of existence in Southwell, but the fact is equally clear that country life impressed
itself upon his consciousness only unpleasantly and that he
was wholly unaware of the beauties of his natural surroundings. For the region itself was pleasant enough. The town
was described[41] in 1813 as "seated on a gentle eminence,
embosomed in trees, and in the centre of an amphitheatre of
swelling hills, on a fertile soil, well wooded, and their bases
washed by the little river Greet. . . ." We learn further[42]
that "the ruins [of the Archbishop's Palace, which adjoin
Southwell Cathedral] are still extensive . . . and being deeply
overshadowed with ivy, and embosomed in trees, they add
much to the romantic beauty of Southwell."

And yet in addition to the "romantic beauty" of Southwell
Byron was also situated on the very edge of Sherwood Forest,
which offered rich opportunities for the nature enthusiast,
were one there, whether in the mode of the picturesque tourist
or the contemplations of the deist. I select several passages[43]
from the eighteen-page description by the authors of *The
Beauties of England and Wales* (1813):

It is a matter of serious regret, in the picturesque point of
view, that none of our landscape painters have ever thought
of studying in this forest; for it cannot be denied by those

[40]L. and J., I, 127. See also L. and J., I, 131, 133, 135, 136, 142, 146.
[41]The Rev. J. Hodgson and F. C. Laird, *The Beauties of England and
Wales* (London, 1813), XII, part I, 254–5.
[42]*Ibid.*, XII, part I, 266.
[43]*Ibid.*, XII, part I, 51, 54–5.

who have actually traversed it, that it would afford many specimens of landscape, new to the English school, and of which no good likeness can be found among the Italian painters. Its style is totally different from the rocks and woods of Claude Lorrain, or the savage scenery of Salvator Rosa; but it has a wildness peculiar to itself, varying with the hours of the day and with all the atmospheric changes to which England is so subject, so that in fact there is scarcely a ferny heath, a knoll, or glade, that does not present some novelty to the lover of picturesque beauty. Having traversed its woodland haunts in every direction, under all the changes of an autumnal season, and midst all the varieties accompanying the aerial landscape at early dawn, during the glare of open day, and whilst the dewy hand of evening is slowly drawing her sober tinted mantle of grey over the receding thickets, and all nature sinks into repose, the editor of these sheets feels. . . . The whole of which is finely contrasted on the eastern bounds, by the rich scenes of cultivation and enclosure [these separated Byron from the actual Forest] extending from Haughton park to Southwell and where in general the ground is sufficiently broken to add the picturesque to the beautiful.

The 1834 editor of William Gilpin's *Remarks on Forest Scenery and Other Woodland Views*, which was first published in 1791 and which underwent many later editions, quotes with approval[44] from this volume:

The author of the Account of Sherwood Forest in *The Beauties of England and Wales*, says, that "if this forest does not possess all that the landscape gardener would call beautiful, it has in itself every variety of sylvan scenery, consisting of pasture, tracts of woody country intermixed with pasturage, and in many places with cultivated enclosures. These intermingled scenes are again divided from other intermixtures of the same kind by wild heaths, which are sometimes bounded by a naked line of horizon, at others skirted with wood; and this intermixture of wood and pasturage, with large separa-

[44]William Gilpin, *Remarks on Forest Scenery and Other Woodland Views*, ed. Lauder (Edinburgh, 1834), II, 35.

tions of heath, gives a variety to many tracts of Sherwood Forest, which could not be expected in a boundless continuance of woody scenery alone. The forest heath, too, becomes a most interesting scene to the admirer of Nature, when bounded, as it generally is in this forest, by woods in various directions, and interspersed here and there with lately planted clumps, which almost imperceptibly unite its woody boundaries with the wide foreground of heath and gravel. . . . In some places, too, the most pleasing ideas of animated Nature break in upon the desert scene, from the woodman's cottage, or groups of cattle, or the starting deer. . . ."

It becomes obvious that Southwell with its surrounding country was a place of recognized picturesque beauty during the period. Byron, it is equally obvious, was insensible to these beauties. The nature poetry which he wrote before his tour of 1809–1811 must be read in the light of these attitudes.

When one considers the personality and the opinions already described, it is hardly to be imagined that Byron originally undertook his first tour with any very "romantic" notions about experiencing the beauties of nature. Indeed, when he left England in 1809 his conception of the aims and purposes of his trip bore most of the characteristics of the Grand Tour of the previous century. Although he was inevitably to assume the point of view of the picturesque tourist once he had begun,[45] a point of view certainly nourished by Hobhouse, his original attitude toward travel was overwhelmingly humanistic. Thus,[46] as early as 1806 he writes to his mother that

[45]See below, chapter IV.

[46]L. and J., I, 95–6. See Dr. Johnson on travel, Boswell's *Life*, ed. Hill (Oxford, 1887), I, 499; and the purposes of the Grand Tour as summarized and illustrated from contemporary documents in *Johnson's England*, ed. Turberville (Oxford, 1933), I, 156–57. But the prevailing attitude of the preceding century is well known. At various other times during these years Byron entertained ideas of making a tour of the Hebrides and the Highlands in order to collect Erse traditions and poems to be later published as "*The Highland Harp*, or some title equally *picturesque*" (L. and J., I, 143–4); while in Athens he proposed a merry tour to Wales or

Improvement at an English University to a Man of Rank
is, you know, impossible, and the very Idea *ridiculous.* Now
I sincerely desire to finish my Education . . . & wish to pass
a couple of years abroad, where I am certain of employing
my time to far more advantage and at much less expense,
than at our English Seminaries. 'Tis true I cannot enter
France; but Germany and the Courts of Berlin, Vienna &
Petersburgh are still open. . . . I presume you will all agree,
and if you do not, I will, if possible, get away without your
Consent, though I should admire it more in the regular manner & with a Tutor of your furnishing.

Early in 1808 he is thinking of a tour abroad which he seems
to have conceived of as differing from the usual one only in
its extensiveness.[47] Late in that same year he plans[48] to sail
for India:

    . . . I can easily get letters from government to the am-
bassadors, consuls, etc., and also to the governors at Calcutta
and Madras. . . . If I do not travel now, I never shall, and
all men should one day or other. . . . When I return I may
possibly become a politician. A few years' knowledge of other
countries than our own will not incapacitate me for that part.
If we see no nation but our own, we do not give mankind a
fair chance;—it is from *experience,* not books, we ought to
judge of them. There is nothing like inspection, and trusting
to our own senses.

His purpose[49] is "to study India and Asiatic policy and manners. . . . If I return, my judgment will be more mature,
and I shall still be young enough for politics." He left Fal-

---

Scotland (*Correspondence,* I, 30); as early as 1805 he was contemplating
a tour of the Highlands for the express purpose of escaping his mother
(L. and J., I, 75); and in 1807 he had decided to go to sea for four or
five months with a cousin, a Captain Bettesworth, "probably to the Mediterranean, or to the West Indies, or—to the devil" (L. and J., I, 146). The
inconspicuousness of the idea of nature in these passages is apparent.

  [47]L. and J., I, 176.
  [48]L. and J., I, 194–5.
  [49]L. and J., I, 199–200.

mouth[50] with letters of introduction "in plenty," collected others[51] as he went along, and came to regard court dress[52] as "indispensable in travelling." After travelling for a year and a half[53] he is still convinced that the purpose of travel is to study mankind and to rub off provincial prejudice:

. . . I am so convinced of the advantages of looking at mankind instead of reading about them, and the bitter effects of staying at home with all the narrow prejudices of an islander, that I think there should be a law amongst us, to set our young men abroad, for a term, among the few allies our wars have left us.

Here [at Athens] I see and have conversed with French, Italians, Germans, Danes, Greeks, Turks, Americans, etc., etc., etc.; and without losing sight of my own, I can judge of the countries and manners of others. Where I see the superiority of England (which, by the by, we are a good deal mistaken about in many things), I am pleased, and where I find her inferior, I am at least enlightened. Now, I might have stayed, smoked in your towns, or fogged in your country, a century, without being sure of this, and without acquiring any thing more useful or amusing at home.

He undoubtedly travelled with the ideal in mind[54] of making himself a "citizen of the world," able to feel[55] that "all climates and nations are equally interesting." Although such a purpose of itself need not exclude an enthusiasm for nature, it did for Byron, certainly, temper severely his enthusiasm for nature and reduce its importance in his mind.

Byron's actual choice of residence, however, once he had reached the age which made choice possible, must be accepted as his final comment on the town versus country question

[50]L. and J., I, 224.
[51]L. and J., I, 241.
[52]L. and J., I, 241.
[53]L. and J., I, 309. See also *Correspondence*, I, 29.
[54]L. and J., I, 310. See also L. and J., I, 123.
[55]L. and J., VI, 452.

generally. His biography reveals the facts. Immediately following the long year at Southwell, he spent the summer in London; during his last year at Cambridge he spent an immoderate amount of time in London, even for those lax days; the summer of 1808 before settling for the first time at Newstead he spent in London; he was in London for a total of six weeks or more in the first quarter of 1809 and there again for six weeks before leaving on June 11, 1809, for Falmouth to embark. During the fifty-seven months between Byron's return from his tour and his departure from London on April 23, 1816, he was absent from the city, for all reasons, only sixteen months at the most, or something more than a quarter of the total time. Of these, five months were spent pursuing Lady Oxford and three on his honeymoon before he and Lady Byron settled at 13 Piccadilly Terrace. There is no conclusion possible except that during these years Byron was essentially a man of the city.

There were periods of time, of course, which were spent at Newstead, the longest being between September, 1808, and April, 1809, but this was punctuated with two visits to London. And there were numerous visits outside London. Several of these require particular notice here.

In November and December, 1812, and again in January, 1813, he visited at Eywood, the estate of Lord and Lady Oxford near Presteign on the border of Wales and Herefordshire. In later years[56] he was to recall Lady Oxford's "autumnal charms" and compare her beauty to that of a "landscape by Claude Lorrain." It was in many respects the happiest attachment that Byron ever formed with a woman. She was forty at the time. The point of interest here, however, is Byron's enthusiastic reaction to his natural surroundings and to life in the country during these visits. "The country round this

[56]L. and J., II, 164, note 3.

place," he writes,[57] "is wild and beautiful, consequently very delightful." "This country is very much to my taste; and I have taken a seat of Ld Oxford's (Kinsham Court, about five miles off, in a *delightful* situation) for next year."[58] "I am still here—only sad at the prospect of going; reading, laughing, and playing at blindman's-buff with y^e *children:* a month has slipped away in this and such-like innocent recreations; my eye is well, and my person *fatter. . . .*"[59] ". . . I have not been guilty of once *yawning* in the eternity of two months under the same roof—a phenomenon in my history. We go on admirably in y^e *country;* but how town may suit us I cannot foresee."[60] "I shall be very *qualmish* at the thoughts of returning to town—it is an accursed abode for people who wish to be quiet."[61] Back again at Eywood in April, 1813, he writes,"[62] "We have had very few fine days, and these I have passed on the water and in the woods, scrambling and splashing about with the children, or by myself. I always feel happier here or at Newstead than elsewhere, and all my plagues are at least 150 miles off. . . ." All this time, of course, Byron was making love to Lady Oxford.

With these statements ("our mutual wish is *quiet*"), it is interesting to compare the record of another sojourn in a secluded spot—his visit to his father-in-law's house during his honeymoon at Seaham, then only a fishing village. Exactly

[57]*Correspondence*, I, 98.
[58]*Ibid.*, I, 100.
[59]*Ibid.*, I, 110.
[60]*Ibid.*, I, 124.
[61]*Ibid.*, I, 128.
[62]*Ibid.*, I, 145. But contrast what is probably Byron's loftiest altitude of boredom (L. and J., II, 54-5), dated from that very Newstead; and L. and J., II, 32, "I feel very restless where I am, and shall probably ship off for Greece again; what nonsense it is to talk of Soul, when a cloud makes it *melancholy. . . .*"

a month after his marriage he writes[63] to Moore, who had been recently in London:

I wish you would respond, for I am here *oblitusque meorum obliviscendus et illis.* Pray tell me what is going on in the way of intriguery, and how the w——s and rogues of the upper Beggar's Opera go on—or rather go off—in or after marriage; or who are going to break any particular commandment. Upon this dreary coast, we have nothing but county meetings and shipwrecks. . . .

A month later he gives voice again[64] to his boredom. "I am in such a state of sameness and stagnation, and so totally occupied in consuming the fruits—and sauntering—and playing dull games at cards—and yawning—and trying to read old Annual Registers and the daily papers—and gathering shells on the shore—and watching the growth of stunted gooseberry bushes in the garden—that I have neither time nor sense to say more than Yours ever."

The first fact to notice, probably, is the one that Lady Oxford's attractions for Byron were of greater force than those of the former Miss Milbanke. In any event it is clear that Byron carried his own happy or wretched identity with him always, never able to escape it within natural scenes of any description.

When one recalls the places of residence selected by Byron after he had thrown off the influence of Shelley following the latter's departure from Lake Leman in 1816, the list sounds like a roll call of famous Italian towns and cities. Never did Byron ever choose the kind of retired spot which

[63]L. and J., III, 176.
[64]L. and J., III, 182.

Rousseau[65] or Wordsworth favored: he established himself always within a city or its immediate environs. The simple and obvious facts of his life may be briefly summarized.

After Shelley had left, Byron lingered at Diodati only a few months. On October 6, 1816, he started by way of Milan and Verona for Venice, where he settled early in November. Here he lived for the next three years—at first in apartments in the Frezzeria, and after January, 1818, in the central block of the Mocenigo palace on the Grand Canal. About the middle of April, 1817, he visited Rome with Hobhouse, where he stayed for three weeks, and arrived back at Venice on May 28. Shortly after his return he took a villa at La Mira on the Brenta about seven miles inland, but retained his apartments on the Grand Canal. When Moore visited Byron, he was given these apartments and Byron lived at La Mira; but Byron made the trip into Venice almost every day, without any very great inconvenience. The charms of Venice were always within easy reach. La Mira, though, was no hermitage: it was here, and at Fiesso, and the Dolo, in villas overlooking the Brenta, that wealthy Venice sought to escape the summer's heat. Beckford[66] in his *Dreams, Waking Thoughts and Incidents* described Mira in a letter dated 1780 as "a village of palaces, whose courts and gardens, as magnificent as statues, terraces, and vases can make them, compose a grand, though far from a rural, prospect. Not being greatly delighted with such scenery, we stayed no longer than our dinner required. . . ." Byron, at the close of 1819 in pursuit of Guiccioli, finally left Venice and settled at Ravenna in his own

[65]Rousseau writes (*Confessions*, trans. Mallory [New York, 1928], p. 628), "It was on the ninth of August, 1756, that I left cities, never to reside in them again: for I do not call a residence the few days I afterwards remained in Paris, London, or other cities, always on the wing, or contrary to my inclinations."

[66]*The Travel-Diaries of William Beckford*, ed. Chapman (Cambridge, 1928), I, 111.

apartments in the Palazzo Guiccioli. He left Ravenna on October 28, 1821, for Pisa, where he took up his quarters in the Palazzo Lanfranchi. At the end of September, 1822, he established himself at Genoa in the suburb of Albaro, where he remained until he sailed for Greece in July of the next year. These facts of Byron's life are their own commentary. They prove that Byron was essentially a city dweller, one who felt himself most at ease among urban surroundings and who did not find what he sought in a life close to nature. They go far toward explaining why he failed to develop a satisfactory philosophy or religion of nature, and was able finally to satirize the entire Return to Nature Movement.

Chapter IV

BYRON AND THE PICTURESQUE
TRADITION

1

Poetic Practice

When Wordsworth was making his objections to Byron's "natural piety," he probably recognized in Byron the mere lover of the picturesque, a role that seemed to suit Byron well, and one representing a stage that he himself had gone through and left behind. This essential preoccupation with seeing and the determination to make a highly accurate and almost literal transcription of the natural scene before him, set Byron apart from all the other great Romantic poets.

All things considered, it was inevitable that the man Byron was—undecided and highly impressionable intellectually; highly sensitive to the fashionable; possessed of sympathies with the factual, the mundane, and even the vulgar; unsympathetic to most systems of thought and to all mysticisms, simply because they were developed systems or mystical—it was inevitable that he should serve an apprenticeship of some years to the "rational, and agreeable amusement"[1] of the typical picturesque tourist.

It is the intent of this chapter to examine Byron's habit of looking at a natural scene as if it were a painting, that is, in the manner prescribed by the picturesque tradition, and to explain, in terms of that tradition, another element in the

---

[1]William Gilpin, *Three Essays: On Picturesque Beauty; On Picturesque Travel; And On Sketching Landscape; To Which Is Added A Poem, On Landscape Painting* (London, 1792), p. 47. See also p. 41.

failure of Byron's naturalism: for Byron's regular habit of viewing a natural scene with the relative detachment of the picturesque tourist reduced the possibility of his repeatedly achieving any deeply satisfying spiritual experience, and the failure to do so is an important element in his further failure to develop a genuine philosophy of nature, or even to adopt that of Wordsworth with any consistency. This deeply ingrained habit also helps to clarify—once Byron had begun to be conscious of the growing vulgarization of the picturesque tradition—his comments upon the "cant of the love of nature"[2] and to explain why his strong sense of the ridiculous was brought to bear so devastatingly upon the entire complex of ideas and attitudes which constitutes the Return to Nature Movement of the Romantic Period.

It is obvious to any reader of Byron's poetry, and it has been remarked by most commentators, that Byron was a lover of wild nature. Joseph Warren Beach in his *Concept of Nature in Nineteenth-Century English Poetry*[3] selects him as the typical exponent and example of this preference. But there is something more than rebel spirit calling to wild nature: there is a close kinship between this poetry and the principles and attitudes of the picturesque painter and traveller, a kinship which becomes clear only when the one is examined in the light of the other.

Of all the several masters of the picturesque, William Gilpin has perhaps as much value as any other when one attempts to estimate the accepted and conventional points of view of the tradition during the lifetime of Byron. For three decades Gilpin was the vigorous champion of the picturesque element in nature (that which pleases the eye from some quality capable of being illustrated in a painting); he was in some ways original but was essentially the product of an important eighteenth-century tradition, to which he gave a developed

[2]Blessington, *op. cit.*, p. L.
[3]Beach, *op. cit.*, pp. 34–36.

esthetic; and he was perhaps the most influential, during later years, of the many writers on the subject. His statements thus have an authoritative value.[4]

In 1792 he summarized his principles in a small book entitled *Three Essays: On Picturesque Beauty; On Picturesque Travel; And On Sketching Landscape: To Which Is Added A Poem, On Landscape Painting.* His point of view throughout is that of the painter. His purpose, he explains,[5] is to expound "the *distinguishing characteristic* . . . of *such beautiful objects,* as are suited to the pencil." This single distinguishing characteristic of picturesque beauty is not the "smoothness" which Burke gives emphasis to; the *"neat* and *smooth* . . . disqualify the object"* for the picturesque eye. Instead it is the quality of roughness or ruggedness which distinguishes the picturesque from the merely beautiful and hence the unsuitable for pictorial representation.[6] "In landscape universally the rougher objects are admired."[7] Thus "an elegant piece of garden-ground make[s] no figure on canvas."[8] The sublime, however, is included in the picturesque, although the tradition does not restrict its tribute to scenes of awe-evoking grandeur.[9] It is the quality of roughness which makes all the difference.

This quality of roughness, obviously, is one easily "observable in . . . the rude summit, and craggy sides of a mountain," as Gilpin points out. Although this statement hardly provides the full explanation of Byron's fondness for mountains, it certainly may be accepted, once the extent of Byron's interest in the picturesque is realized, as a contributing element: the parallel requires no elaboration. It is to be noticed, however,

[4]See William D. Templeman, *The Life and Work of William Gilpin* (Urbana, Illinois, 1939), pp. 225–306.
[5]Gilpin, *op. cit.,* pp. iii–iv.
[6]*Ibid.,* pp. 5–7.
[7]*Ibid.,* p. 17.
[8]*Ibid.,* p. 8.
[9]*Ibid.,* pp. 42–43.

that Byron often chooses his epithets for their power to convey just this idea of roughness, selecting such words as "hoary,"[10] "rude," "shaggy," "craggy," or "steepy." Lands generally are "rugged."[11] Gilpin's doctrine seems to be indicated also in Byron's expressed preference for the Alps rather than the Apennines because there "the pine sits on more shaggy summits" and in his implication that the "shaggy shade" of the pine is equally as characteristic of the Alps as are the rocks and snow.

A second distinguishing quality of the picturesque school is its fondness for the somber shades and for shadows, and a strong dislike of bright color,[12] which "is to the picturesque eye, what a discord of harsh notes is to a musical ear." Nature's "variety of semitints . . . have a general chastizing effect; and keep the several tints of landscape within proper bounds, which a glare of deep colours cannot do." Gilpin himself actually developed a series of a half-dozen or more washes to be applied over the whole as well as the parts of a painting in order to subdue the colors to a dark brownish tint. Quite in keeping with this aspect of the tradition is the fact that dusk and actual night are the favored hours in Byron's romantic poetry.[13] This is especially true of *Childe Harold* and the Oriental tales. Byron's curious use, furthermore, of the

[10]"Childish Recollections," l. 121; *Childe Harold*, I, 14, 19, 32. See Gilpin, *op. cit.*, p. 7.

[11]*Childe Harold*, II, 46. See also *Childe Harold*, IV, 73, and *The Prophecy of Dante*, II, 63.

[12]Gilpin, *op. cit.*, p. 83. Elizabeth Wheeler Manwaring, *Italian Landscape in Eighteenth Century England* (New York, 1925), p. 16, reports that this "admiration for dark pictures held from the time of Dryden's lines to Kneller [1694], which prophesy that Time's ready pencil shall 'Mellow the Colours and imbrown the Teint,' to the days of Constable, who rebelled when advised by Sir George Beaumont to adopt the colour of an old Cremona violin for the prevailing tone of his pictures."

[13]Gilpin also recommended, once the painting was completed, that the harmony of the whole should be tested by examining it at "the twilight hour" (Gilpin, *op. cit.*, "On Painting Landscape, A Poem," ll. 490–510).

word *brown* or one of its related forms points directly to
the picturesque school. Thus mountains are "imbrown'd,"[14]
forests are "brown," and foliage, leaves, and the ridge of a
hill are this color. It is his usual epithet for landscape seen
in the moonlight, as E. H. Coleridge points out.[15] And indicative of the picturesque painter's distaste for glaring and even
bright light are the lines[16] describing the light of the rising
moon which,

> . . . hallowing tree and tower,
> Sheds beauty and deep softness o'er the whole

of the scene. In the same way the Coliseum "will not bear the
brightness of the day," and demands a light which "shines
serene but doth not glare,"[17] in order that the scene may be
"soften'd down."[18]

The two ideas of roughness and duskiness are combined in
such a brief but skillfully composed landscape as the one
attempted in the following lines[19] from *Childe Harold,* II, 51,

[14]*Childe Harold,* I, 19; II, 22, 70; *Parisina,* 1. 10; *The Siege of Corinth,*
l. 242. See also *Childe Harold,* II, 48, 51, and *The Siege of Corinth,* l. 71.

[15]Note to *Childe Harold,* II, 22.

[16]*Don Juan,* I, 114. Compare Gilpin, *op. cit.,* "On Painting Landscape,
A Poem," ll. 504–508, who writes that during the twilight hour,

> Free from each garish ray: Thine eye will there
> Be undisturb'd by *parts;* there will the *whole*
> Be view'd collectively; the distance there
> Will from its foreground pleasingly retire,
> As distance ought, with true decreasing tone,

and (ll. 153–155) "with blending tints / [Be] soften'd so, as wakes a
frequent doubt / Where each begins, where ends. . . ."

[17]*Childe Harold,* IV, 143–144.

[18]*Manfred,* III, iv, 293.

[19]In these lines the idea of roughness, of course, is conveyed by the
word "volcanic." But it is also conveyed by the state of motion of each
of the objects in the distant "living valley": Gilpin (*op. cit.,* pp. 20, 22)
explained that light and shade also produce the effect of roughness in
objects, when they are "sometimes turning to the light in one way, and
sometimes in another." This is as true of the flowing streams in Byron's
lines as of the waving trees and playing flocks, for even a smooth lake
"appears broken by shades of various kinds; by the undulations of the

descriptive of mountains in Albania:

> Dusky and huge, enlarging on the sight,
> Nature's volcanic amphitheatre,
> Chimæra's alps extend from left to right:
> Beneath, a living valley seems to stir;
> Flocks play, trees wave, streams flow, the mountain-fir
> Nodding above. . . .

A third point that Gilpin makes much of is variety in a view: it must be variegated in both form and tint. Indeed, John Entick's dictionary in 1797 defined the very word *picturesque* as variegated, or like a picture.[20] Thus Byron writes[21] of the "variegated maze of mount and glen," states that all the aspects of nature, "mix'd in one mighty scene, with varied beauty glow," and remarks[22] that Greece is "Nature's varied favourite." Similarly, he praises[23] the Rhine region as "a blending of all beauties" and elsewhere[24] as "the perfection of *mixed* beauty." Gilpin[25] had used the latter term to define that type of beauty which partakes "both of the *beautiful* and the *picturesque*."

> More mighty scenes may rise—more glaring shine
> But none unite in one enchanted gaze[26]

---

water. . . ." The scarcity of adjectives in the description of the "living landscape" parallels Gilpin's doctrine that only the "general idea" of a tree or a figure should be attempted: "a few slight touches are sufficient" (*ibid.*, pp. 77–8). "The mountain fir / Nodding above" the high, prominent foreground illustrates another of Gilpin's teachings: "The foreground must always be considerable. . . . It is the very basis, and foundation of the whole. . . . Some part of the foreground should be the highest part of the picture. In rocky, and mountainous views this is easy, and has generally a good effect. And sometimes even when a country is more level, a tree on the foreground, carried higher than the rest of the landscape, answers the end" (*ibid.*, "Notes on the Foregoing Poem," p. 27).

[20]Quoted by Manwaring, *op. cit.*, p. 168.
[21]*Childe Harold*, I, 18–19.
[22]*Ibid.*, II, 85.
[23]*Ibid.*, III, 46.
[24]*Correspondence*, II, 9.
[25]Gilpin, *op. cit.*, p. 11.
[26]*Childe Harold*, III, 60. MS reading.

all the varieties of scenic beauty, the "fair, and soft," "the negligently grand," and the "precipice's gloom."

Finally, it is to be noticed that Gilpin emphasizes the fact that this variety of parts must be united or harmonized into a whole, and that this harmony is achieved by means of the atmosphere:[27] "The sky gives the ruling tint to the landscape; and the hue of the whole . . . must be harmonious."[28] Thus Byron[29] writes,

> Rock, river, forest, mountain, all abound,
> And bluest skies that harmonise the whole.

During the years 1821–1824, however, the picturesque elements almost disappear from Byron's poetry: extended and wholly serious picturesque description appears only in *The Island,* which represents in several ways to be indicated a curious throwback to earlier techniques and attitudes.[30]

Before 1821,[31] however, it is "a most living landscape"[32] that Byron usually describes, as in "The Dream," and not a high vision of a spiritualized nature. Of a passage in this poem, Sir Walter Scott could write,[33] "This is true *keeping*— an Eastern picture perfect in its foreground, and distance, and sky." Or Mary Shelley, with the scene actually before her, could write[34] of *Childe Harold,* III, "The part of the Rhine down which we now glided, is that so beautifully described by Lord Byron. . . . We read these verses with delight, as they

[27]Gilpin, *op. cit.,* pp. 19, 44.

[28]Gilpin, *op. cit.,* "Contents of the Following Poem" on landscape painting, p. iv.

[29]*Childe Harold,* II, 48.

[30]See especially I, 1–16; III, 19–26, 59–72, 85–86, 91–94, 165–180; IV, 9–26, of *The Island.* The opening lines are an instance of the introductory backdrop technique used in most of the Oriental tales.

[31]See the final paragraph of the present chapter.

[32]"The Dream," l. 32.

[33]Quoted in Byron's *Poetical Works,* IV, 37, note 2.

[34]Shelley, *op. cit.,* VI, 109.

conjured before us these lovely scenes with the truth and vividness of painting. . . ." John Galt, who had been over most of the route travelled by Childe Harold, writes[35] that the details of the poem "are the observations of an actual traveller. Had they been given in prose, they could not have been less imbued with fiction." "Childe Harold's Pilgrimage is the most faithful descriptive poem which has been written since the Odyssey. . . ."[36] And Medwin reports[37] that Byron himself referred to *Childe Harold* as a *"voyage pittoresque."*

The purpose of these remarks, of course, is not necessarily to imply that Byron had studied Gilpin's essays, although this is quite possible. The point to be made absolutely clear, however, is that when Byron wrote the word *scene*,[38] he ordinarily meant quite literally that, and something very different from what a Shelley or a Wordsworth or a Keats meant. When one finds a man like Gilpin, who expressly excludes the moral and the religious element as extraneous to the picturesque,[39] talking about learning "to read Nature's works,"[40] it is well to wonder what Byron meant when he wrote[41] of holding "converse with Nature's charms." Byron's observation[42] in *Childe Harold* that "ne city's towers pollute the lovely view" is essentially one with Gilpin's remark[43] that the picturesque traveller "is disgusted with the formal separations of property—with houses,

[35]John Galt, *The Life of Lord Byron* (New York, 1830), p. 86.

[36]*Ibid.*, p. 126. See also pp. 125, 148, 199, 255.

[37]Medwin, *op. cit.*, p. 112.

[38]Note, for example, in the stanzas on the Rhine in *Childe Harold*, III, 55–60, his use of the word *scene*, which appears three times.

[39]Gilpin, *op. cit.*, pp. 46–47.

[40]*Ibid.*, "Notes" on his poem on landscape painting, p. 26.

[41]*Childe Harold*, II, 25.

[42]*Ibid.*, II, 52.

[43]Gilpin, *op. cit.*, p. 57. Gilpin also wrote (*ibid.*, p. 46) that "among all the objects of art, the picturesque eye is perhaps most inquisitive after the elegant relics of ancient architecture; the ruined tower, the Gothic arch, the remains of castles, and abbeys." It has not been thought necessary to assemble evidence of this well-known interest of Byron's.

and towns, the haunts of men, which have much oftener a
bad effect in landscape, than a good one." Except when he was
directly under the influence of Shelley and Wordsworth,
Byron's Book of Nature was written principally in an esthetic,
not a spiritual language. Its appeal was primarily to the eye.[44]

2

Poetic Theory

Quite as significant, however, as Byron's poetic practice,
in determining his relation to the picturesque tradition, are his
theories—his many efforts to formulate the purpose and methods of descriptive poetry. Here the great emphasis which he
gave to foundation upon fact (rejecting the wholly imaginative description), to "accurate" representation (but rejecting
microscopic particularity), and to the necessity of viewing the
scene before writing (believing, however, that nature must
often be selected and improved, although undue liberties are
not to be taken)—this emphasis identifies him directly with
the basic assumptions of the picturesque tradition, as well as
with the earlier theory which fathered it and which Gilpin
accepted[45] and built upon.

The picturesque position may be summarized again from
Three Essays. Painting[46] "is an art *strictly imitative,*" Gilpin

[44]If any doubt can remain on this matter, the following passages may
be added to a list already too long: "To Emma," ll. 13–20, 25–31;
"Lachin Y Gair," ll. 1–3 ("Away, ye gay landscapes"), 33–40 (England!
thy beauties are tame and domestic"); "Childish Recollections," ll. 121–26
("Fair Ida's bower adorns the landscape round"); "Fragment from the
'Monk of Athos,'" ll. 1–11; *Childe Harold,* I, 15 ("What goodly prospects
o'er the hills expand"), 18ff. ("What hand can pencil guide, or pen, to
follow half on which the eye dilates"), 30 ("romantic hills . . . whereon
to gaze the eye with joyance fills"), 60; *Childe Harold,* II, 22, 48–49
("Nature's sheen to see"), 51–52 ("the lovely view"), 54 ("the wearied
eye reposes gladly" on a smooth vale).

[45]Gilpin, *op. cit.,* pp. 8–9, 65, 88, "Notes on the Foregoing Poem," p. 44.

[46]*Ibid.,* p. 29.

writes. He is not concerned[47] with *"imaginary sketching."* "This essay is meant chiefly to assist the picturesque traveller in taking *views from nature."*[48]

> Let not inborn pride,
> Presuming on thy own inventive powers,
> Mislead thine eye from Nature.[49]

"The *marvellous* disgusts the sober imagination; which is gratified only with the pure characters of nature."[50] Although for Gilpin, "Nature is the archetype,"[51] which keeps the sketch of the picturesque traveller "within proper bounds"[52] of representational accuracy, he "descends not to the minutiae of objects."[53] "The province of the picturesque eye is to *survey nature;* not to *anatomize matter. . . .* It examines *parts,* but never descends to *particles."*[54]

"The characteristic features of a scene . . . and the leading ideas must be fixed on the spot: if left to the memory they soon evaporate."[55] "Written references, made on the spot," are especially necessary if there is the possibility of confusing the several distances in a landscape: "The traveller should be accurate in this point, as the spirit of his view depends much on the proper observation of distances."[56] Thus the picturesque sketch is founded upon fact and in its significant features is faithful to the original. Yet nature is to be depicted "in her best attire";[57] it may be necessary to limit oneself to a

[47]*Ibid.,* p. 62.
[48]*Loc. cit.*
[49]*Ibid.,* "On Landscape Painting. A Poem," ll. 27–29.
[50]*Ibid.,* p. 53.
[51]*Loc. cit.*
[52]*Ibid.,* p. 67.
[53]*Ibid.,* p. 86.
[54]*Ibid.,* p. 26.
[55]*Ibid.,* pp. 64–65.
[56]*Loc. cit.*
[57]*Ibid.,* pp. 75, 63, 70.

portion of a too extensive landscape, to choose the best point of view, to reject unpicturesque and inharmonious objects, or even to rearrange the parts. "Nature is most defective in composition. . . . Liberties however with truth must be taken with caution."[58]

Byron's theories of descriptive poetry parallel Gilpin's ideas on sketching with some exactness. More than any other of his eminent contemporaries, Byron emphasized the quality of accuracy and the sense of actuality in description,[59] that is, "truth to nature"—as he interpreted that doctrine. A convenient contrast with Shelley, as often, offers itself and helps to clarify Byron's position. After having "traversed all Rousseau's ground, with the *Héloise* before me," Byron continues[60] that he is "struck, to a degree, with the force and *accuracy* of his descriptions and the beauty of their reality." Shelley writes[61] of the same tour, on the other hand, that Rousseau's scenes "were created indeed by . . . a mind so powerfully bright as to cast a shade of falsehood on the records that are called reality." With Byron, the interest in accuracy and correctness of description amounted almost to a passion. Thus he somewhat maliciously plans to take notes on the spot[62] for Leigh Hunt, "who will be glad to hear of the scenery of his

[58]*Ibid.*, pp. 67–68.

[59]From the first Byron took great pride in the accuracy of his descriptions and in the fact that he had "sketched" on the spot. For early indications not noticed below, see the Preface to *Childe Harold*, I–II, of February, 1812; *Childe Harold*, I, 60–62; *The Bride of Abydos*, II, 28–38; L. and J., II, 283, 303, 388; III, 229, 239–41, 254. See also L. and J., I, 234; *Correspondence*, I, 27–28.

[60]L. and J., III, 335 (italics mine).

[61]Shelley, *op. cit.*, IX, 173.

[62]L. and J., IV, 104.

Poem," *The Story of Rimini*. Instead of writing to Hunt, however, he wrote[63] to Hobhouse:

Hunt made a devil of a mistake about—
"Old Ravenna's clear shewn towers and bay."
There has been no bay nor sea within five miles since long before the time of the Exarchs, and as to *"clear shewn,"* the town lies so low that you must be close upon it before it is seen at all, and then there is no comprehensive view unless you climb the steeple.

He is greatly pleased[64] to discover that John André de Luc, who "was *with Rousseau* at *Chillon*," finds that his "description is perfectly correct." He writes indignantly[65] to Murray on two occasions about the publisher's mistake in printing a note to *Childe Harold*, III, concerning the topography around the château of Clarens: "it is quite impossible that I should have so bungled." In answer to the charges that *Manfred* is indebted to Marlowe and Goethe, he defends[66] first and most jealously the first-hand character of his descriptions: "I have the whole scene of *Manfred* before me, as if it was but yesterday, and could point it out, spot by spot, torrent and all." Twice he refers[67] to the "correctness" of his depiction of the storm in the second canto of *Don Juan:* "*There's* a gale of wind for you! all nautical and true to the vocabulary." The original *Childe Harold,* he notes carefully in his preface, "was written, for the most part, amidst the scenes which it attempts

[63]*Correspondence*, II, 119. Byron used almost the same words in writing to Lady Byron: "He (Hunt) has made a sad mistake about 'old Ravenna's *clear-shewn* towers and *bay*' the city lies so low that you must be close upon it before it is 'shewn' at all, and the Sea had retired *four miles* at least, long before Francesca was born, and as far back as the Exarchs and Emperors" (Ralph Milbanke, *Astarte* [London, 1921], p. 292).

[64]L. and J., IV, 100.

[65]L. and J., IV, 116–117. See also IV, 168.

[66]L. and J., IV, 174.

[67]L. and J., IV, 305, 366.

to describe. . . . Thus much . . . for the correctness of the descriptions."

To achieve this accuracy and "correctness," Byron felt that he must view the actual scene, confessing[68] that he could better describe what he had seen than he could "invent." Thus, back in England in 1811, he writes[69] that in order to continue *Childe Harold,* "I must return to Greece and Asia; I must have a warm sun, and a blue sky; I cannot describe scenes so dear to me by a sea-coal fire. I had projected an additional canto when I was in the Troad and Constantinople, and if I saw them again, it would go. . . ." To this statement Rousseau's *Confessions* (Book IV) has provided the perfect contrast:

It is very singular that my imagination never rises so high as when my situation is least agreeable or cheerful. When everything smiles around me, I am least amused; my heart cannot confine itself to realities, cannot embellish, but must create. Real objects strike me as they really are, my imagination can only decorate ideal ones. If I would paint the spring, it must be while surrounded with walls. . . .

But Byron, in denying the authorship of an imitation of *Childe Harold* called *Lord Byron's Pilgrimage to the Holy Land,*[70] finds place to say, "How the devil should I write about *Jerusalem,* never having yet been there?" Medwin reports[71] his stating, "Moore did not like my saying that I could never attempt to describe the . . . scenery of a country that I had not visited." And the Countess Guiccioli writes of him[72] that "Lord Byron did not admit the possibility of describing a site that had not been seen. . . ."

[68]L. and J., II, 66.
[69]L. and J., II, 27–28.
[70]L. and J., IV, 22.
[71]Medwin, *op. cit.,* p. 172.
[72]Guiccioli, *op. cit.,* II, 406.

Along with this passion for correctness and for writing only after having viewed the scene, there is a succession of statements in his letters professing inability to describe.[73] Attached to one[74] of them is his explanation.

> But I can't describe, because my first impressions are always strong and confused, and my Memory *selects* and reduces them to order, like distance in the landscape, and blends them better, although they may be less distinct. There must be a sense or two more than we have, as mortals, which I suppose the Devil has (or t'other); for where there is much to be grasped we are always at a loss, and yet feel that we ought to have a higher and more extended comprehension.

This statement is more valuable for the light it throws on what Byron thought he was trying to do in description—his aims and ideals in art—than as an account of his mental processes. The Aristotelian *mimesis,* certainly enough, is in the back of his mind, but present in the meaning of the slavish "imitation" or "copy" given the term by the eighteenth-century translators, commentators, and critics, and related here by Byron to the copying of external nature. Hence his realization that the "imitation" of the natural scene must always fall miserably below the model. This idea, it may be, also tended to increase the emphasis he placed on accuracy and truth to the actuality in description, thinking thereby to approach that much "closer" to the original. His misunderstanding of the Aristotelian term, however, leads clearly to the explanation[75] of his relative failure, as it did in Gilpin's mind,

---

[73]L. and J., III, 335; IV, 119, 122.

[74]L. and J., IV, 119–120.

[75]L. and J., IV, 107. Compare Gilpin, *op. cit.,* pp. 57–58: "The more refined our taste grows from the *study of nature,* the more insipid are the *works of art.* Few of it's [*sic*] efforts please. The idea of the great original is so strong, that the copy must be very pure, if it do not disgust. But . . . let our taste be ever so refined, her [nature's] works, on which it is formed (at least when we consider them as *objects,*) must always go beyond it; and furnish fresh sources both of pleasure and amusement."

to appreciate the visual arts, and of his placing them and nature together, as if they both gave rise to the same kind of experience within the observer.

Depend upon it, of all the arts, it [painting] is the most artificial and unnatural, and that by which the nonsense of mankind is the most imposed upon. I never yet saw the picture—or the statue—which came within a league of my conception or expectation; but I have seen many mountains, and Seas, and Rivers, and views. . . .

Elsewhere[76] he takes exactly the same position concerning poetry: the poet is the "most artificial, perhaps, of all artists in his very essence," that is, least true to nature, reproducing her least faithfully. External nature, then offers esthetic satisfaction because it is one stage closer to the Ideal than the painting or poem which attempts to reproduce it. This same misconception of the Aristotelian idea led on historically (as it also did in Byron's mind) to a semi-identification with Horace's *ut pictura poesis,* each concept strengthening the force of the other and both helping to make possible such opinions as those held by Gilpin—and by Byron.

Despite the virtual disappearance of picturesque description from Byron's poetry of 1821–1824, Byron continued to express the idea in his theory that poetry strives to produce the effects of painting. Thus he praises[77] Pope's lines on Sporus by saying, "Look at . . . the *imagination:* there is hardly a line from which a *painting* might not be made, and *is.*" In arguing that a ship confers additional poetic interest upon the sea, he draws a parallel betwen poetry and painting and makes the assumption[78] that the aims of both arts are the same: "Did any painter ever paint the sea *only.* . . ? . . . . In the poem of *The Shipwreck,* is it the storm or the ship which most inter-

[76]L. and J., V, 550.
[77]L. and J., V, 260.
[78]L. and J., V, 544.

ests?" Or again, in taking the position that the natural scene must be improved upon, he draws a parallel between the landscape artist and the poet.[79] He exclaims in *Don Juan,* following a description of Gulbeyaz in her grief over Juan,

> Would that I were a painter! to be grouping
> All that a poet drags into detail!
> Oh that my words were colours! but their tints
> May serve perhaps as outlines or slight hints.   (VI, 109)

It has been observed already that Byron recognized the inability of poetic descriptions to achieve the visual effect of painting,[80] yet he seems never to have made a place in his theory for any other kind of ideal. Instead he continues to lament, during the last years of his life, the deficiency of poetry in this respect. Following a description of Gulbeyaz's boudoir, he pulls himself up short with the statement,

[79]L. and J., V, 549–50.

[80]This realization, perhaps, should also be taken into account in the explanation of the disappearance of picturesque description from Byron's poetry. Gilpin (*op. cit.*, p. 72) also felt a difficulty: "The art of painting, in it's [*sic*] highest perfection, cannot give the richness of nature. When we examine any natural form, we find the multiplicity of it's [*sic*] parts beyond the highest finishing. . . ." But he thought (*ibid.*, p. 88) it possible to convey "ideas more distinctly in an ordinary [landscape] sketch, than in the best language."

Mrs. Radcliffe interrupts the descriptive pages of her *Journey Through Holland and Germany* (London, 1795), II, 265–266, in order to say the same thing: "It is difficult to spread varied pictures of such scenes before the imagination. A repetition of the same images of rock, wood, and water, and the same epithets of grand, vast and sublime, which necessarily occur, must appear tautologous, on paper, though their archetypes in nature, ever varying in outline, or arrangement, exhibit new visions to the eye, and produce new shades of effect on the mind. It is difficult also, where these delightful differences have been experienced, to forbear dwelling on the remembrance, and attempting to sketch the peculiarities, which occasioned them. The scenery at the head of Ullswater is especially productive of such difficulties, where a wish to present the picture, and a consciousness of the impossibility of doing so, except by the pencil, meet and oppose each other."

> . . . but all descriptions garble
> The true effect, and so we had better not
> Be too minute; an outline is the best,—
> A lively reader's fancy does the rest. (VI, 98)

And he complains (XIV, 40) that "the soft ideal" (*i.e.,* the actual scene) is "seldom shown,"

> And ne'er to be described; for to the dolour
> Of bards and prosers, words are void of colour.

In the Pope-Bowles controversy,[81] however, Byron placed a major and extreme emphasis on the idealistic element in picturesque theory:

In landscape painting, the great artist does not give you a literal copy of a country, but he invents and composes one. Nature, in her natural aspect, does not furnish him with such existing scenes as he requires. [The artist painting a particular scene must] heighten its beauties . . . shadow its deformities. . . . Nature is not lavish of her beauties; they are . . . to be selected with care.

Here Byron's position reflects the confusion in earlier theory which arose from the desire to be "true to nature" and to depict, at the same time, a nature "improved." With the second sentence of this quotation it is interesting to compare one[82] which Byron had made earlier: "I never yet saw the picture—or the statue—which came within a league of my conception or expectation; but I have seen many mountains, and Seas, and Rivers, and views. . . ." And with the first and final statements we may compare another earlier one,[83] in which he gives as the explanation of his inability to describe satisfactorily the fact that his "memory *selects* and reduces [his

[81]L. and J., V, 549–50.
[82]L. and J., IV, 107.
[83]L. and J., IV, 119.

impressions] to order," the resulting selection and order being false to the actuality! Actually the picturesque position may be justly summed up as one demanding a basis in actuality and accuracy but allowing an element of idealization, or "improvement" upon the model. Byron, as it suited him, gave varying degrees of emphasis to each of these principles, and perhaps was a little confused between them. Thus he wrote in reply to Bowles[84] (italics mine),

Of sculpture in general, it may be observed, that it is more poetical than nature itself, inasmuch as it represents and bodies forth that ideal beauty and sublimity which is never to be found in actual Nature. *This at least is the general opinion. But . . . I differ from that opinion. . . .*

It is a meandering and qualifying-upon-qualification kind of discussion which finally leads him back to Gilpin's position, but if it means anything very clearly it means confusion. The explanation seems to be contained within a statement made by Professor C. T. Goode,[85] although not elaborated upon or explained, that Byron "equates truth with fact, although he is a little confused in his usage." Byron's entire predilection in favor of accuracy in description and foundation upon fact, his proud assertions that he never described a scene without having seen it, his belief that the poet was "the most artificial, perhaps, of all artists," that is, least true to Nature, reproducing her least faithfully—all these tendencies contradict the extreme idealist position.

The literal-minded fashion in which Byron reasoned upon the aims and methods of description, on the other hand, is as much in evidence during these years (1821–1824) as it was in the preceding. To the instances already noted in this

[84]L. and J., V, 549.
[85]Clement Tyson Goode, *Byron As Critic* (Weimar, 1923), p. 93. Professor Goode refers to *Don Juan*, XI, 37.

chapter, there may be added his continued pride[86] in the shipwreck scene of *Don Juan,* II, because it is based on *"actual* facts," his indignation[87] over an error made by Murray's printer in a topographical note to the fifth canto of *Don Juan,* his contemplation[88] of a fifth and sixth canto of *Childe Harold* only after he has "studied the Country" around Naples, his reduction[89] of imagination and invention to "the two commonest of qualities," his several attacks[90] upon the "undersect" of the Lakers, the "Cockney School," because its members attempted to write about nature which in London they could not be familiar with.

> 'Tis the part
> Of a true poet to escape from fiction
> Whene'er he can; for there is little art
> In leaving verse more free from the restriction
> Of truth than prose, unless to suit the mart
> For what is sometimes called poetic diction,
> And that outrageous appetite for lies.[91]

Thus he confides to his diary (January 11, 1821)[92] that in spite of Jacob Bryant's *Dissertation* assaulting the authenticity of the events and places described by Homer, "I still venerated the grand original as the truth of *history* (in the material *facts*) and of *place.* Otherwise, it would have given me no delight."

[86]L. and J., V, 346. See also L. and J., VI, 387.

[87]L. and J., V, 354.

[88]L. and J., VI, 157.

[89]L. and J., V, 554.

[90]L. and J., V, 586–88, 590, 544. See also Byron's note to *The Island,* IV, 153, *Poetic Works,* V, 631, defending the accuracy of his own description. Medwin (*Conversations,* p. 107) records Byron as saying "I can never write but on the spot." George Finlay ("Reminiscences of Lord Byron," p. 523, in L. F. C. Stanhope's *Greece in 1823 and 1824* [London, 1825]) records that Byron made frequent attacks upon the accuracy of one of Sir William Gell's books, "chiefly directed against the drawings, and particularly the view of the bay."

[91]*Don Juan,* VII, 86.

[92]L. and J., V, 166.

And he goes on in the same entry to explain that "the secret of Tom Campbell's defense of *inaccuracy* in costume and description is, that his *Gertrude* [*of Wyoming*] has no more locality in common with Pennsylvania than with Penmanmaur. It is notoriously full of grossly false scenery, as all Americans declare." These statements were written less than a month before the date of Byron's first "Letter" on Bowles (February 7, 1821) and should be sufficient in themselves to indicate that Byron's most firmly believed theories did not permit him with conviction to attack the picturesque position. But Bowles had provided the perfect provocation.[93] He had taken quite the same position in regard to Pope that Byron had expressed in the privacy of his diary concerning *Gertrude of Wyoming*. In his "Invariable Principles of Poetry" Bowles had preferred Cowper to Pope as a descriptive poet—the wrong man for the right reason—"because he is the most accurate describer of the works of *external nature*, and for that reason is superior, as a *descriptive poet*." This was Byron's invitation to emphasize, in the controversy, a nature heightened, improved, and selected. It was convenient for him, at the time, temporarily to forget the doctrine closest to his heart: as Gilpin phrased it (and Dr. Johnson would have agreed), although "Nature is most defective in composition . . ., liberties however with truth [*i.e.*, the actual scene] must be taken with caution." With both Byron and Gilpin the question was one of emphasis.

Although Byron placed this great emphasis, in his theory, on fact, accuracy, and the visual element, like Gilpin and Dr. Johnson he instinctively turned away[94] from "a stick-picker's detail of a wood, with all its petty minutiæ of this, that, and the other," quoting an anecdote, purportedly from the dramatist Sheridan, in which he derides a description of a phoenix

[93]L. and J., V, 528.
[94]L. and J., V, 557.

which was like that a poulterer might make, with every feather described. Similarly he ridicules[95] "Cowper's Dutch delineation of a wood, drawn up, like a seedsman's catalogue," and calls attention[96] to "his laboured minutiæ of the Wood or the Shrubbery." Nature is never to be represented *"exactly* as she appears";[97] the gentleman poet always keeps a gentlemanly distance, and never botanizes.

[95]L. and J., V, 556–57.

[96]L. and J., V, 565.

[97]L. and J., V, 549. The phrase is echoed on the following page with the same uncomplimentary connotations: "Nature, exactly, simply, barely, Nature will make no great artist."

It is perhaps hardly necessary to point out how exactly Byron's opinions parallel those of Dr. Johnson; however, as there are sometimes verbal echoes I shall list some of the more striking similarities. For the sake of convenience I have quoted from J. E. Brown's very useful *Critical Opinions of Samuel Johnson* (Princeton, 1926).

Poetry parallels painting: they are "two arts which pursue the same end, by the operation of the same mental faculties . . ." (p. 197). However, description falls short of the reality. "Description only excites curiosity: seeing satisfies it. . . . Description is always fallacious . . ." (p. 61). Nevertheless, it is necessary to view the scene before describing it: Warton "justly ridicules those who think they can form just ideas of valleys, mountains, and rivers, in a garret of the Strand. For this reason I cannot regret with this author, that Pope laid aside his design of writing American pastorals; for as he must have painted scenes which he never saw, and manners which he never knew, his performance . . . would have exhibited no representation of nature or of life" (p. 60). Imlac the poet remarks, "I could never describe what I had not seen . . ." (p. 197). The principle of selection, however, is equally necessary for the poet describing nature: "It is justly considered as the greatest excellency of art, to imitate nature; but it is necessary to distinguish those parts of nature, which are more proper for imitation . . ." (p. 110). ". . . The poet's art is selection, and he ought to shew the beauties without the grossness of country life" (p. 187). It is an "established maxim, that the poet has the right to select his images, and is no more obliged to shew the sea in a storm, than the land under an inundation; but may display all the pleasures, and conceal the dangers of the water, as he may lay his shepherd under a shady beach, without giving him an ague, or letting a wild animal loose upon him" (p. 232). But the microscopic eye is not that of the poet: "The business of a poet, said Imlac, is to examine, not the individual, but the species; to remark general properties and large appearances; he does not number the streaks of the tulip,

In spite of all this analysis of the theory of descriptive poetry, however, Byron continued to place it as a type near the bottom of the scale. Here he is with Pope,[98] who had written of the days when "pure Description held the place of Sense," and again with Gilpin,[99] who had no very high opinion either of picturesque travel or landscape sketching. Whatever Byron's motives, and they were undoubtedly complex, it is[100] "mere descriptive poetry . . . never esteemed a high order"; "descriptive poetry has been ranked as among the lowest branches of the art, and description as a mere ornament";[101] "the *lowest* department of the art";[102] "the highest of all poetry is ethical poetry. . . . It requires more mind, more wisdom, more power, than all the 'forests' that ever were 'walked for their description'. . . .'The proper study of mankind is man.' "[103] Critical opinions such as these help to explain why Byron turned against one of the major literary currents of his time.

---

or describe the different shades in the verdure of the forest. He is to exhibit in his portraits of nature such prominent and striking features, as recall the original to every mind; and must neglect the minuter discriminations . . ." (p. 198). Johnson remarked in his own person, "Great thoughts are always general, and consist . . . in descriptions not descending to minuteness. . . . The metaphysical poets could no more represent by their . . . laboured particularities the prospects of nature . . . than he who dissects a sun-beam with a prism can exhibit the wide effulgence of a summer noon" (p. 117). "Thus all the power of description is destroyed by a scrupulous enumeration . . ." (p. 117).

[98]*Prologue to the Satires,* l. 148.

[99]Gilpin, *op. cit.,* pp. 41, 46–47, 85–86. Gilpin (p. 34) prints a letter from Sir Joshua Reynolds to him (April 19, 1791) in which Reynolds suggests that the term *picturesque* is "applicable to the excellences of the inferior schools, rather than to the higher."

[100]L. and J., V, 544.

[101]L. and J., V, 553.

[102]L. and J., IV, 493.

[103]L. and J., V, 554. To the same effect is Byron's statement, "But this [the visual quality of Pope's lines on Sporus] is nothing in comparison with his higher passages in the *Essay on Man*" (L. and J., V, 260).

3

Byron as Picturesque Tourist

Even more significant, however, than Byron's theories or his use of the picturesque technique and vocabulary, in explaining the failure of his naturalism, are the rather consistently commonplace and conventional expressions, principally in the letters and journals, of the typical attitudes of the tourist.[104] In these statements is to be found a more intimate view of Byron the man and of the fundamental qualities of Byron's mind than is to be discovered either in the descriptive poetry or in the critical theory.

Although Byron left England in 1809 on his original travels with an attitude toward them reminiscent of the Grand Tour of the previous century, that is, with the primary purpose of observing men and their civilizations, he was not immune to what Wordsworth called "a strong infection of the age,"[105] a comparison of scene with scene, or to that judging of nature, satirized by Jane Austin,[106] as if a particular view were a painting. Indeed, such an attitude is not occasional with him but habitual. As a traveller, he was until his last three and a half years, essentially a collector and comparer of landscape views. At least as early as 1805 he exhibits the perceptions and emotions of the full-blown picturesque tourist and admirer of

[104]This is not to deny that Byron's remarks are often enthusiastic or that they usually have the interest which the Byronic personality gives to most of the activities it engages in.

[105]*Prelude*, XI, 152–76 (1805).

[106]*Northanger Abbey*, Chapter XIV. Gilpin (*op. cit.*, pp. 42, 49) wrote that the chief object of picturesque travel is picturesque beauty: "This great object we pursue through the scenery of nature; and examine it by the rules of painting." "Or we compare the objects before us with other objects of the same kind:—or perhaps we compare them with the imitations of art."

the sublime.[107] His first travels, of course, offered him endless opportunities. Thus[108] the village of Cintra in Portugal,

contains beauties of every description, natural and artificial. Palaces and gardens rising in the midst of rocks, cataracts, and precipices; convents on stupendous heights—a distant view of the sea and the Tagus. . . . It unites in itself all the wildness of the western highlands, with the verdure of the south of France.

He writes[109] from Albania that Zitza has "the most beautiful situation" he ever beheld, "always excepting Cintra, in Portugal." On his journey through the mountains to Yanina in Albania he finds[110] the country "of the most picturesque beauty." "Greece, particularly in the vicinity of Athens, is delightful;—cloudless skies and lovely landscapes."[111] Or he can assume the pose of the picturesque tourist turned blasé, and write,[112] "all countries are much the same in my eyes. I smoke, and stare at mountains, and twirl my mustachios very independently." With a thoroughly professional air he can remark[113] that the natural beauties of Greece "are nothing to parts of Illyria and Epirus, where places without a name, and rivers not laid down in maps, may, one day, when more known, be justly esteemed superior subjects, for the pencil and the pen, to the dry ditch of the Ilissus and the bogs of Bœotia." Or,[114] "I know of no Turkish scenery to equal this" around Constantinople, "which . . . cannot be compared with Athens and its

[107]L. and J., I, 77.

[108]L. and J., I, 237. As far as it is known, Byron never saw "the verdure of the south of France," or any part of that country.

[109]L. and J., I, 249. Earlier he had thought "Cadiz, sweet Cadiz!" to be "the first spot in the creation" (L. and J., I, 234).

[110]L. and J., I, 249.

[111]L. and J., I, 258.

[112]L. and J., I, 268. See also L. and J., I, 306, "my appetite for travelling [is] pretty well satiated."

[113]L. and J., I, 264.

[114]L. and J., I, 292.

neighbourhood." Again, still in the manner of the connoisseur, describing the ride along the land side of Constantinople by the walls of the city, he writes,[115] "I have seen the ruins of Athens, of Ephesus, and Delphi. I have traversed great part of Turkey, and many other parts of Europe, and some of Asia; but I never beheld a work of nature or art which yielded an impression like the prospect on each side from the Seven Towers to the end of the Golden Horn."

His tour abroad on the way to Geneva in 1816 evoked reactions which are largely repetitions of these of earlier years. Significantly, he has taken to climbing church steeples in order to gain a better view of the prospects of the Low Countries,[116] and characteristically the "tame beauty" of the countryside attracted and repulsed him[117] at the same time. It exhibits "little for description," "it is a perpetuity of plain . . . but it is a country of great apparent comfort, and of singular . . . beauty," and he evidently took pleasure in seeing the succession of "highly cultivated farms . . . sprinkled with very neat and clean cottages." Still judging, still comparing, with the exactness of the connoisseur, he observes[118] that "the plain at Waterloo is a fine one—but not much after Marathon and Troy. . . . From Bonn to Coblentz, and Coblentz again to Bingen and Mayence, nothing can exceed the prospects at every point; not even any of our old scenes; though this is in a different style."

Even after the momentous meeting with Shelley in 1816 and the study of Wordsworth's poetry, he continues to evidence the tourist's mind, comparing scene with scene and classifying them as first, second, or third best. In this fashion (September 30,

[115]L. and J., I, 282. See also *Correspondence*, I, 29–30.

[116]*Correspondence*, II, 4, 5.

[117]L. and J., III, 332–333. Compare Gilpin, *op. cit.*, Dedication to William Lock, iii: "From scenes indeed of the *picturesque* kind we exclude the appendages of tillage. . . ."

[118]*Correspondence*, II, 6.

1816), Byron thus declares "many of the scenes [in the Bernese Alps] finer than Chamouni,"[119] on his way out of Switzerland to Italy he views "one of the finest torrents in Switzerland,"[120] and the Borromean Islands, seen on the way into Italy, too, "are fine, but too artificial."[121] It is of interest from a chronological point of view that Byron was able to view nature essentially as scenery even upon the very occasion which gave rise to his most visionary poetry. He writes to Hobhouse, June 23, 1816, during his trip around Lake Leman with Shelley, that "Tomorrow we go to Meillerei, and Clarens, and Vevey, with Rousseau in hand, to see his scenery. . .; the views have hitherto been very fine. . . ."[122] The adjective *fine* rings through his letters like a bell, in each of its degrees. From Verona he proudly writes[123] to Moore that he has seen "the finest parts of Switzerland, the Rhine, the Rhone, and the Swiss and Italian lakes. . . ." Virgil's Lago di Garda is a "fine stormy lake."[124] Still the picturesque tourist, he recalls[125] that the Wengen is not the highest but offers the "best point of view—much finer than Mont-Blanc and Chamouni, or the Simplon." He writes[126] to Moore, "I sha'n't go to Naples. It is but the second best sea-view, and I have seen the first and third, viz. Constantinople and Lisbon, (by the way, the last is but a river-view; however, they reckon it after Stamboul and Naples, and before Genoa)." To conclude with several final instances of this particular attitude, for a complete record of all Byron's expressions of it is not necessary, he writes[127] to Murray,

[119]L. and J., III, 369. See L. and J., III, 366 for another statement of this same judgment.
[120]L. and J., III, 373.
[121]L. and J., III, 375.
[122]*Correspondence*, II, 12.
[123]L. and J., III, 382.
[124]L. and J., IV, 1.
[125]L. and J., IV, 80.
[126]L. and J., IV, 101.

soon after arriving at Venice, that he has ascended the highest tower in Venice in order to see the city "and its view." Richard B. Hoppner[128] states of Byron that he "took great interest in any observations, which as a dabbler in the arts, I ventured to make upon the effects of light and shadow, or the changes produced in the colour of objects by every variation in the atmosphere."

Byron's references to the sublime in nature also regularly express the conventional reaction, that of the pleasing fear evoked in the beholder. Thus he refers to "horrid" crags,[129] "hanging rocks, that shock yet please the soul,"[130] rocks which are in "horror set," "charming the eye with dread," "horribly beautiful,"[131] and quotes in his note Addison's description of the scene (the waterfalls at Terni) as one of "horror and confusion." Or on the Alps he sees "horrid snow, and rock,"[132] and from the sight of a storm at sea derives "a pleasing fear."[133] The earliest reference to this kind of reaction[134] Byron made in 1805; I have discovered only three[135] made after 1820.

Although the events of Byron's life conspired with his ideas and his attitudes greatly to reduce expressions of the typical tourist's mind, during 1821–24, nevertheless, there are still indications, though scanty, to show that he continued to look at nature in this way, seeking out striking views, regarding nature

[127]L. and J., IV, 105. For a later expression of this attitude (March 25, 1821), see L. and J., V, 587, where Byron states that England "is, in general, far from a picturesque country. The case is different with Scotland, Wales, and Ireland; and I except also the Lake Counties and Derbyshire, together with Eton, Windsor, and my own dear Harrow on the Hill and some spots near the coast."

[128]Moore, *Life*, p. 417.

[129]*Childe Harold*, I, 19, 32.

[130]*Childe Harold*, II, 48.

[131]*Childe Harold*, IV, 69, 71–72 and note.

[132]*The Prophecy of Dante*, II, 63.

[133]*Childe Harold*, IV, 184.

[134]L. and J., I, 77.

[135]L. and J., V, 190; *Heaven and Earth*, iii, 266–272; *Don Juan*, XIV, 5–6.

as a superior kind of picture or as an interesting spectacle. Nearly all of the little evidence which there is has its origin either in the trip to Greece or in the tour of Ithaca which he made from Metaxata, and, significantly, most of it appears not in Byron's own prose, but in the contemporary accounts of these final years written by others. Thus Gamba records[136] Byron's saying to him of the storm which caused their ship to turn back to the port of Genoa, "You have lost one of the most magnificent sights I ever beheld. . . . I have always looked upon a storm as one of the sublimest spectacles in nature." Of this same voyage Hobhouse[137] writes that Byron "had never seen any of the volcanic mountains, and for this purpose the vessel deviated from its regular course in order to pass the island of Stromboli." J. Hamilton Browne records[138] that "Byron sat up nearly all night watching Stromboli: it was, however, overcast, and emitted no flame." The same writer also notes[139] that as the vessel approached Porto Ercole and Piombino, "the splendid scenery . . . was much admired by Lord Byron" and that "he was always on deck to view the magnificent spectacle of the sun setting." Trelawny writes[140] that Byron and his party of ten or twelve, once upon the island of Ithaca, climbed to the summit of a high mountain, in genuine tourist fashion, in order to look at "a magnificent view of the Ionian Sea, Greece, and many islands." Upon another day of the tour of Ithaca, Byron and his party planned a "picnic"—so termed by Browne[141]—at the fountain and

[136]*A Narrative of Lord Byron's Last Journey to Greece*, p. 12.

[137]"Lord Byron in Greece," *The Westminster Review*, II, 227.

[138]Browne, *op. cit.*, XXXV, 61. Compare Trelawny, *Recollections of the Last Days of Shelley and Byron*, p. 125, who states Byron said, "If I live another year, you will see this scene in a fifth canto of *Childe Harold*," thus implying that Byron witnessed the volcanic eruption.

[139]*Ibid.*, XXXV, 61.

[140]*Recollections*, p. 137.

[141]Browne, *op. cit.*, XXXVI, 393.

grotto of Arethusa: "The path, winding at first amid vine-yards and olive grounds, soon became rugged and difficult of ascent, sweeping along the brow of richly wooded banks, descending abruptly to the sea. . . . Byron narrowly escaped a grave accident, his head coming in contact with a branch, whilst he was intently gazing on the splendid sea-view, of which an occasional glimpse was caught through the wide-spreading foliage." On this same day,[142] once arrived at their destination, the party discovered that

The view from the mouth of the grotto, embracing the vast sea prospect, the Æchirades, the entrance to the gulf of Cor-inth, or Lepanto, with the distant purple mountains of Epirus and Ætolia, lifting their lofty peaks into the clouds, was su-perb; and ascending the hill at the back of the cavern, Sancta Maura, the ancient Leucadia, with its dependencies, was dis-tinctly descried, together with Cephalonia, apparently close at hand; Zante, and the coast of the Peloponnesus, trending far away to the south-east. A more lovely situation could scarcely be imagined. Lord Byron's spirits were buoyant and elastic; as usual, on such occasions, he overflowed with an inexhausti-ble fund of anecdote, replete with brilliant wit and humor; and I never remember to have passed so delightful a day.

In Byron's own prose, evidences of the attitudes of the tourist are few indeed. He records[143] in his journal that he has "made the tour" of Ithaca and that "the fountain of Arethusa . . . alone would be worth the voyage; but the rest of the Island is not inferior in attractions to the admirers of Nature." The only reference[144] made to this tour in his letters is in one to Hobhouse: "I made a tour over the hills here [Metaxata] in our old style, and then crossed over to Ithaca, which as a pend-ant to the Troad, a former Greek traveller would like to see.

[142]Browne, op. cit., XXXVI, 393.
[143]L. and J., VI, 242.
[144]Correspondence, II, 274. I have discovered no other reference any-where to the "tour over the hills here in our old style."

I was much gratified by both; and we have, moreover, been treated in the kindest manner by all the authorities. . . ." I have discovered only two attempts at visualized picturesque description in Byron's prose.[145] In the poetry, extended and wholly serious picturesque description appears as a significant element only in *The Island*,[146] his contribution to "periodical poesy." Thus had Byron's interest dwindled. The picturesque tradition, whose point of view was too limited to support a philosophy of nature and too shallow to provide a basis for deeply satisfying spiritual experience, wilted in the light of the comic vision.

[145]L. and J., V, 206; VI, 249.

[146]See especially I, 1–16; III, 19–26, 59–72, 85–86, 91–94, 165–180; IV, 9–26, of *The Island*. The opening lines are an instance of the introductory backdrop technique used in most of the Oriental tales.

Chapter V

THE WORDSWORTHIAN NOTE AND THE BYRONIC HERO

1

The Great Principle of the Universe

The present section, concerned largely with the important and critical months of Byron's stay in Switzerland in the summer of 1816, has a twofold purpose: (1) to indicate that Byron's "Wordsworthian" communions with nature failed to convince him that love, as he expressed it at the time, is the "great principle" of the universe; and (2) to emphasize the fact that the pantheistic and "mystical" passages in Byron's poetry are the product of a limited literary influence—the expression neither of deeply satisfying spiritual experience nor of settled intellectual conviction, but of his *mobilité,* acted upon by others and reflecting views wholly foreign to his more usual thoughts and feelings. In short, for one of the most important elements of his "romanticism," Byron turned not to himself but to Shelley, Wordsworth, and Rousseau; and without them *Childe Harold*, III, could not have been written.[1]

Before examining in detail Byron's Swiss sojourn, however, it is necessary to recall briefly certain attitudes characteristic of an earlier period of his life. His most typical attitude toward nature before his meeting with Shelley in 1816 may

---

[1]This introductory section of necessity must rehearse certain well-known facts. The best recent study of the subject is in E. W. Marjarum's *Byron as Skeptic and Believer*, pp. 47–65 (Princeton, 1938). Marjarum's study, however, fails to emphasize sufficiently either the contradictions implicit in the poetry which Byron wrote in 1816 or the purely literary character of the pantheistic element. He does not consider the Zeluco theme, the chief concern of the present chapter.

justly be summed up as a variously expressed mixture of in-difference, conventional deism, and the enthusiasm of the tourist in search of the picturesque. And yet despite the truth of this, there seems to be evidence that Byron was aware, be-fore 1816, that nature had something more to offer than he had found and that he may have been striving, without quite clearly realizing it, to discover a deeper experience. One of the strongest forces apart from his cultural inheritance which would drive him early in this direction, and did, was the fact that Byron was extremely ill-fitted for living with people from day to day. Close and constant association with individuals simply exhausted him. Thus he wrote[1a] after Hobhouse—one of his closest friends—had left him for England in June, 1810,

I am very well, and neither more nor less happy than I usually am; except that I am very glad to be once more alone, for I was sick of my companion,—not that he was a bad one, but because my nature leads me to solitude, and that every day adds to this disposition. If I chose, here are many men who would wish to join me—one wants me to go to Egypt, another to Asia, of which I have seen enough. The greater part of Greece is already my own, so that I shall only go over my old ground, and look upon my old seas and mountains, the only acquaintances I ever found improve upon me.

His repeated early resolutions in favor of a life of solitude and quiet stem directly and almost exclusively from this desire to escape from people.[2] Books and his writing, he usually in-dicated, would be his customary preoccupations in his solitude. Nature is referred to only incidentally, if at all. And yet such a state of mind, in the early years of the nineteenth century, would inevitably seek solace in nature, as his often did in one way or another. Of course he regularly became bored with his

[1a]L. and J., I, 295. See also I, 286, 289–91.

[2]See L. and J., I, 203, 204–5, 310, 312, 316, 333; II, 100. I have not attempted to make this list complete.

own company. A further stimulus too was his seeking after a faith, sceptical as he was of traditional Christianity, even though this led him no farther than a rather cold, rationalistic, and traditional form of deism. But whatever causes prompted him in this direction, and they were certainly several, he wrote two passages,[3] one in 1813, the other in 1815, which seem to have a note of "mystical" longing within them. The two passages constitute the whole of Byron's expressions, before 1816, of any kind of mystical union with nature. Although they do not describe the experience shortly to be considered—the feeling of complete oneness with nature—they were not produced by a picturesque tourist, nor do they employ the language of Wordsworth, which he was to use in every future expression of a related kind.

> . . . my tongue can not impart
> My almost drunkenness of heart,
> When first this liberated eye
> Survey'd Earth, Ocean, Sun, and Sky,
> As if my spirit pierced them through,
> And all their inmost wonders knew!

> . . . blue the sky
> Spreads like an ocean hung on high,
> Bespangled with those isles of light,
> So wildly, spiritually bright;—
> Who ever gazed upon them shining
> And turn'd to earth without repining,
> Nor wish'd for wings to flee away,
> And mix with their eternal ray?

[3]*The Bride of Abydos*, II, 343–48, and *The Siege of Corinth*, ll. 244–51. Two other passages, which appear doubtful to me, may be examined: *Childe Harold*, II, 4, where the phrase "mingled with the skies" appears and line 369 in "The Episode of Nisus and Euryalus," "Ye starry spheres! thou conscious Heaven!" In the first passage Byron seems to have in mind nothing more than the usual belief in personal immortality. The second is not to be interpreted literally; Nisus has a few lines earlier offered up a prayer to Diana in "Luna's orb." The poem is a paraphrase of the Aeneid.

The poet of these passages was eminently prepared for the guidance of a Shelley.

The experience characterized by self-abandonment to a rapt contemplation of nature, carrying with it the loss of the sense of personal identity, temporarily mingled with the great Whole, has been described with some justice as the romantic experience.[4] Evidence of some such experience may be discovered in many of the Romantic poets. Rousseau[5] gave it one of its earliest and most complete expressions in 1762.

Bientôt de la surface de la terre j'élevois mes idées à tous les êtres de la nature, au système universel des choses, à l'Etre incompréhensible qui embrasse tout. Alors, l'esprit perdu dans cette immensité, je ne pensois pas, je ne raisonnois pas, je ne philosophois pas: je me sentois, avec une sorte de volupté, accablé du poids de cet univers, je me livrois avec ravissement à la confusion de ces grandes idées, j'aimois à me perdre en imagination dans l'espace; mon cœur resserré dans les bornes des êtres s'y trouvoit trop à l'étroit, j'étouffois dans l'univers, j'aurois voulu m'élancer dans l'infini. Je crois que, si j'eusse dévoilé tous les mystères de la nature, je me serois senti dans une situation moins délicieuse que cette étourdissante extase, à laquelle mon esprit se livroit sans retenue, et qui, dans l'agitation de mes transports, me faisoit écrier quelquefois: O grand Etre! O grand Etre! sans pouvoir dire ni penser rien de plus.

Werther[6] gave voice to the experience in 1774 (in English in 1779):

When the mist is rising from the lovely valley and the sun is high above the impenetrable shade of my wood, so that only now and then a ray steals into the inner sanctuary and I lie in the tall grass by the falling brook, and discover a thousand

---

[4]L. A. Bisson, "Rousseau and the Romantic Experience," *Modern Language Review*, XXXVII, 46.

[5]*Lettres à M. de Malesherbes*, ed. Rudler (London. 1928), pp. 43–4.

[6]William Rose's translation (London, 1929), pp. 2–3, 24–25, letters dated May 10 and June 21.

different grasses on the surface of the earth; when I feel nearer
to my heart the teeming little world among the blades, the
innumerable, unfathomable creatures in the shape of worms
and insects, and when I feel the presence of the Almighty
Spirit Who created us all in his image, the breath of the All-
loving One who sustains us as we float in illimitable bliss—
Oh! friend, when the world then grows dim before my eyes
and earth and sky are absorbed into my soul like the form of
a beloved, I am often consumed with longing and think, ah!
would that I could express it, would that I could breathe on
to paper that which lives so warm and full within me, so that
it might become the mirror of my soul as my soul is the mirror
of the eternal God! My friend—but it is beyond my power,
and I succumb to the splendour of what lies before me.

. . . . Oh! distant vistas are like the distant future! A vast
darkling whole lies before our soul, our emotions merge into
it, like our gaze, and we yearn to surrender our entire being,
to be filled with all the rapture of a single great glorious
feeling.

Byron has recorded this same rapture in the well known
stanzas in the third canto of *Childe Harold*.

> I live not in myself, but I become
> Portion of that around me. . . .[7]

> Are not the mountains, waves, and skies, a part
> Of me and of my soul, as I of them?[8]

The experience, furthermore, as Byron described it, is a cleans-
ing one which offers a kind of spiritual rebirth, "spurning the
clay-cold bonds which round our being cling."[9] This "feeling
infinite"[10] is

> A truth, which through our being then doth melt
> And purifies from self. . . .

[7]*Childe Harold*, III, 72.
[8]*Ibid.*, III, 75.
[9]*Ibid.*, III, 73.
[10]*Ibid.*, III, 90.

The universe with which the individual can be thus in harmony must necessarily be one highly benevolent to man. Thus we find Byron explaining in a note[11] that "love in its most extended and sublime capacity . . . is the great principle of the universe . . . of which, though knowing ourselves a part, we lose our individuality, and mingle in the beauty of the whole." In short, the experience thus described is a regenerative one arising out of the mystic fusion of the individual with a universe whose governing and pervading principle is love. If these stanzas originate in Byron's actual experience, he did certainly achieve at some time during his stay in Switzerland the quest which was his throughout all of his life: to throw off that humanity which plagued him and to achieve a self-oblivion free of both ennui and despair.

Byron's debt to Wordsworth and Shelley, however, for leading him down these paths of thought was recognized from the first. Medwin states[12] that Byron told him that "Shelley, when I was in Switzerland, used to dose me with Wordsworth physic even to nausea. . . . He had once a feeling of Nature, which he carried almost to a deification of it:—that's why Shelley liked his poetry." The Countess Guiccioli records[13] that Byron "was wont to say in laughter" that he "received many large doses of Wordsworth from Shelley." Trelawny concurs in these statements,[14] and Wordsworth himself more than once pointed out the indebtedness. Moore writes[15] in his diary under the date of October 27, 1820, that Wordsworth

[11]*Poetry*, II, 304–5.
[12]Medwin, *op. cit.*, p. 135.
[13]Guiccioli, *op. cit.*, I, 160.
[14]Trelawny, *Recollections*, p. 95.
[15]Moore, *Memoirs*, III, 161. Byron's debt to Wordsworth and Shelley has been investigated by Heinrich Gillardon, *Shelleys Einwirkung auf Byron* (Karlsruhe, 1898) and by F. H. Pughe, *Studien über Byron und Wordsworth* (Heidelberg, 1902). The parallels offered in E. H. Coleridge's edition of the *Poetry* are sufficient to establish the fact of the indebtedness.

Spoke of Byron's plagiarisms from him; the whole third canto of "Childe Harold" founded on his style and sentiments. The feeling of natural objects which is there expressed, not caught by B. from nature herself, but from him (Wordsworth), and spoiled in the transmission. "Tintern Abbey" the source of it all. . . .

The facts of particular interest here, however, are three: poetry with this "Wordsworthian" note appears after Byron's departure from Switzerland only twice, at widely separated intervals—once in *Childe Harold*, IV, and once in *The Island;* the only statement in prose of the experience of losing the sense of personal identity in a universe whose great principle is love is that just quoted, written in 1816, and it is found in Byron's note to *Childe Harold*, III, stanza 99, on Clarens[16] and refers directly to *La Nouvelle Héloïse;* and finally, there are a great many indications of a positive kind which show clearly that Byron failed to establish satisfactory relations between himself and the natural world, and was himself aware of that failure. A considered view of all the evidence indicates that for Byron this "mystical" experience depended for its existence upon the country of Rousseau's novel and the presence of Shelley—was consequently short-lived—and that the two poetic expressions of the experience written after 1816 (in *Childe Harold*, IV, and *The Island*) represent nothing more nor less than Byron recalling his own earlier productions. The similarities of phrase and idea between the early and late passages are too exact for it to be otherwise. A comparison of the passages in question makes the fact evident. The italics throughout are mine.

[16]Byron was a close student of *Julie, ou La Nouvelle Héloïse* and the *Confessions*, and reread both while writing *Childe Harold*, III. See L. and J., III, 335; IV, 100; *Poetry*, II, 303–304. Rousseau should certainly share the honors with Wordsworth for inspiring Byron's momentary outburst of natural piety. It is probable, however, that neither man alone could have called forth Byron's stanzas.

Childe Harold, III, 75:

> Are not the mountains, waves, and skies, a part
> Of me and of my soul, as I of them?

The Island, II, 384–88:

>   . . . the intense
> Reply of hers [Nature's] to our intelligence!
> Live not the stars and mountains? Are the waves
> Without a spirit?

Childe Harold, III, 72:

>   . . . the soul can flee,
> And with the sky, the peak, the heaving plain
> Of ocean, or the stars, *mingle,* and not in vain.

Childe Harold, IV, 178:

> I love not Man the less, but Nature more,
> From these our interviews, in which I steal
> From all I may be or have been before,
> To *mingle* with the Universe. . . .

Childe Harold, III, 73:

> And thus I am absorb'd, and this is life:
>
> . . . .
>
> *Spurning the clay-cold bonds* which round our being
>   cling.

The Island, II, 389–92:

> [The stars, waves, and mountains] woo and clasp
>   us to their spheres,
> *Dissolve this clog and clod of clay* before
> Its hour, and *merge* our soul in the great shore.
> Strip off this fond and false identity!—

It will be noticed that the same pattern is expressed or implied in each of the three poems: (1) there is some kind of
interview or communion with nature; (2) nature is possessed

of some kind of intelligence or sentience: (3) with nature the poet mingles or merges himself; and (4) in so doing he loses his awareness of self.

Byron's comments on the two later poems, furthermore, also substantiate the view that he was describing neither actual psychic experience nor settled intellectual conviction. Of *Childe Harold*, IV, he said,[17] it is "not a continuation of the Third. I have parted company with Shelley and Wordsworth." And of *The Island* he had a low opinion: as he put it,[18] he was "merely trying to write a poem a little above the usual run of periodical poesy." The only conclusion possible is that the post–1816 passages are of purely literary origin, and reflect neither deeply felt personal experience nor seriously considered belief.

Although the 1816 instances of the Wordsworthian-Rousseauistic note are clearly the product of Byron's *mobilité*, "an excessive susceptibility of immediate impressions"—as he defined it—these "impressions" of the summer of 1816, too, of course, were in large part literary. This fact is further borne out by two poems whose dates of composition reveal the remarkable contradictions that Byron could contain within himself. The poem "Darkness" (many of the images in which have been traced to the novel *The Last Man*, 1806) is dated from Diodati, July, 1816, and is thus concurrent with *Childe Harold*, III. There Byron's theme is an extinguished sun, an earth without light or warmth, stars which "did wander darkling in the eternal space," and the resultant destruction of humanity. It is an extremely powerful poem. There is no mention of deity in it. The same month produced "Prometheus," however, and in that poem there are the lines (18–23), to be later echoed in *Cain* and in *Heaven and Earth*,[19]

---

[17]*Poetry*, II, 311. The comic treatment of nature in *Beppo* is concurrent, of course, with the pantheistic stanzas in *Childe Harold*, IV.

[18]L. and J., VI, 164.

[19]See *Poetry*, IV, 50, note 1.

And the inexorable Heaven,
And the deaf tyranny of Fate,
The ruling principle of Hate,
Which for its pleasure doth create
The things it may annihilate,
Refused thee even the boon to die.

These lines nominally refer to Zeus, of course. But their autobiographical significance, relating them to Byron's own concept
of God, seems to be indicated by two facts: the extraordinary
number of times which allusions to the Promethean story occur
in Byron's poetry[20] and the lines in *Manfred*,[21] admittedly
sublimated autobiography, in which the hero declares, just
as Byron had declared of Prometheus,

There is a power upon me which withholds,
And makes it my fatality to live.

Of the man who could thus seriously write, in all probability
during the same month, that "love . . . is, the great principle
of the universe" and then speak of "the ruling principle of
Hate" elsewhere, it is difficult to know what to say. Reduced
to its very simplest form, an acceptable explanation would
seem to be that the one statement represents the wish, the
other the fact, as it appeared to Byron's deepest consciousness.
For the autobiographical value of the lines from "Prometheus"
is established beyond any doubt by further evidence in *Manfred,* the first two acts of which were composed between
September 17 and October 5, 1816. In that poem a Nature
awful and harmful to man is also clearly depicted and related
to a "ruling principle of Hate."

[20]E. H. Coleridge, *Poetry*, IV, 48–49, note 3, lists four instances and
quotes Byron's statement that "The *Prometheus*, if not exactly in my plan
[of *Manfred*], has always been so much in my head, that I can easily
conceive its influence over all or anything that I have written."
[21]I, ii, 284–285.

It is enough to notice here that of the seven Spirits of Nature which Manfred calls up in the opening scene, all but the first, third, and sixth are expressly stated to have functions harmful to mankind. They represent the "mind and principle" of the elements, "spirits of the unbounded Universe." Manfred calls them forth by using a tyrant-spell which had its birthplace in a condemned star, the burning wreck of a demolished world, a wandering hell in space, and by the strong curse upon his own soul. Byron had been concerned in his earliest verse ("Translation from Horace" and the two Ossian poems) with this particular astronomical phenomenon—a star divorced from the guiding hand of God, certainly not the act of a benevolent deity—and the idea of a personal curse is a motif of such recurrent frequency that it can only be regarded as autobiographical. This is the first time, however, that the two themes have been linked. This coupling appears a second time in the opening scene (ll. 110–131). The seventh Spirit is that of the star of Manfred's destiny. That star was originally a "world as fresh and fair as e'er revolved round sun," but "the hour arrived—and it became a wandering mass of shapeless flame, a pathless comet, and a curse, the menace of the universe. . . ." In the light of all this it is impossible to regard the pantheistic expressions produced in the summer of 1816 as anything other than purely "literary" effusions, the product of a limited literary influence. Certainly they do not express an abiding conviction comparable to the belief which Wordsworth gave to his own similar views.

2

"The beauties of nature are lost on a soul so constituted"

When one comes to an examination of the background of such a divided mind as Byron exhibited in the summer and early fall of 1816, it is interesting to notice first a series of rather explicit statements that the beneficent effects of nature are lost upon the early Byronic heroes. The 1812 addition to the preface of the fourth edition of *Childe Harold* explains that the hero was intended as an example to the extent of showing that "early perversion of mind and morals leads to satiety of past pleasures and disappointment in new ones, and that even the beauties of nature . . . are lost on a soul so constituted." Two passages in the poem[22] suggest the idea in the preface.

> Sweet was the scene, yet soon he thought to flee,
> More restless than the swallow in the skies;
>
> . . . .
>
> To horse! to horse! he quits, for ever quits
> A scene of peace. . . .

For Harold bears with him always a "secret woe,"[23]

> . . . that weariness which springs
> From all I meet, or hear, or see;
> To me no pleasure Beauty brings.

The obvious application of the preface to the poem, of course, lies in the fact that the character of Harold is in no way essentially changed by the many beauties of nature he has contemplated on his travels. He returns the same melancholy, misanthropic, lonely, and guilt-laden pilgrim who originally embarked, without having found in any way the balm and cure for his soul which he sought.

In the Oriental tales, the idea receives greater prominence. The Giaour, guilty of abduction and murder, confesses,[24]

> Shuddering I shrunk from Nature's face,
> Where every hue that charm'd before
> The blackness of my bosom wore.

[22]*Childe Harold*, I, 27–28.
[23]*Ibid.*, I, ll. 849–51.
[24]*The Giaour*, ll. 1197–99.

Lara,[25] wandering one starry night upon his ancestral estate beside a "glassy stream," can no longer contemplate the beauty of the scene:

> . . . nought of evil could delight
> To walk in such a scene, on such a night!
> It was a moment only for the good:
> So Lara deem'd, nor longer there he stood,
> But turn'd in silence to his castle-gate.
> Such scene his soul no more could contemplate;
> . . . a night like this,
> A night of beauty, mock'd such breast as his.

The two guilty lovers in *Parisina*[26] likewise find no pleasure in the beauties of nature:

> And what unto them is the world beside,
> With all its change of time and tide?
> Its living things, its earth and sky,
> Are nothing to their mind and eye.

The explanation of this curious train of thought in Byron's early work is not immediately apparent. It lies deep certainly in the complex roots of his personality and, as I shall shortly indicate, in his reading. If the passages cited have an explanation outside those which Byron appended variously to each one, however, or any deeper significance in Byron's experience, it is best sought perhaps in certain lines in *Lara*.[27] There it is stated that the hero in his eternal seeking had tried "woman, the field, the ocean," all that offered an "escape from thought"

[25]*Lara*, I, 169–80.

[26]*Parisina*, ll. 29–36. Additional indications, less clearly obvious than the instances cited, of this train of thought in Byron's mind are to be noticed in the fact that the troubled and distracted Selim in *The Bride of Abydos* gazes upon sea and strand without seeing them (I, 241–45) and rejects Zuleika's proffered flowers (I, 279–95), even though he formerly cared greatly for them. Similarly, the Corsair, under conditions of tension and danger, is unaware of the beauties of the dawn (III, 396–400).

[27]*Lara*, I, 117–26.

(*i.e.,* remorse) in an excess of feeling, and had failed to find that which he sought. No lines could be more characteristic of the man Byron than these. With him now and always,[28] "the great object of life is sensation—to feel that we exist, even though in pain. It is this 'craving void' which drives us to gaming—to battle—to travel—to intemperate, but keenly felt pursuits of any kind, whose principal attraction is the agitation inseparable from their accomplishment." To forget himself, to lose sight of his own "wretched identity," this was his lifelong quest. He writes for this same purpose, to withdraw himself from himself and keep the mind from recoiling on itself.[29] Violent exercise he sought for the same reason: to lose his consciousness of self in the feeling of languor that followed.[30] He would willingly talk or think of anything besides self.[31] And he went to nature for this same purpose, one for him almost impossible of fulfillment.

The idea that the beauties of nature were lost upon such a soul as Childe Harold's was to grow in intensity in the mind of Byron with the years and to receive an increasingly personal application. The poetry thus far referred to was written before the end of 1815. The note reappears, however, in the autobiographical poems of the first half of 1816, which reveal a succession of passages confessing Byron's inability to achieve the kind of serenity, high pleasure and vision in nature which he believed was there to be found. Early in *Childe Harold,* III, appear two retrospective stanzas which refer back to knowledge gained some time before leaving England in 1816. In the first stanza he is alluding to his first tour. Before that

[28]L. and J., III, 400.
[29]L. and J., II, 351. See also II, 278, 314, 321.
[30]L. and J., II, 410–11.
[31]L. and J., II, 6.

time he had realized that his cup of life "had been quaff'd too quickly,"

> . . . and he found
> The dregs were wormwood; but he fill'd again,
> And from a purer fount, on holier ground,
> And deem'd its spring perpetual—but in vain!
> Still round him clung invisibly a chain
> Which gall'd for ever, fettering though unseen,
> And heavy though it clank'd not . . .
> Entering with every step he took through many
> a scene.
> (stanza 9)

Byron was to use the symbol of the invisible chain even more significantly in *Manfred*, as it will be seen. Similarly, in *Childe Harold*, III,

> Like the Chaldean he could watch the stars,
> Till he had peopled them with beings bright
> As their own beams; and earth, and earth-born jars,
> And human frailties, were forgotten quite.
> *Could* he have kept his spirit to that flight
> He had been happy, but this clay will sink
> Its spark immortal. . . .
> (stanza 14, italics mine)

In much the same fashion, when he bids his adieu to the beauty of the Rhine, he writes,

> Thine is a scene alike where souls united
> Or lonely Contemplation thus might stray;
> And *could* the ceaseless vultures cease to prey
> On self-condemning bosoms, it were here,
> Where Nature . . . .
> (stanza 59; italics mine)

In the "Epistle to Augusta" after reading in lines 57–64 what we might expect about "the Alpine landscapes" which "something worthier do . . . inspire: here to be lonely is not desolate," Byron has written immediately following, these interesting lines:

Oh that thou wert but with me!—but I grow
The fool of my own wishes, and forget
The solitude, which I have vaunted so,
Has lost its praise in this but one regret;
. . . .
I feel an ebb in my philosophy.

Even amid the grandeur of the Alps, where Byron anticipated some kind of intensely moving experience—he failed. In this case the combination of his feelings of self-reproach and the repeated intrusion of insignificant, prosaic details upon his consciousness proved too great for him. The poetry of Wordsworth had lost its power to take him outside himself, if ever it was really able to do so.

The Swiss Journal to Augusta, recording the twelve days between September 17 and September 29, 1816, is the most significant confession Byron ever made for the light it throws on his attitude toward the natural world around him, what he expected of it, and what little it actually had to offer to him. I have attempted to select characteristic passages and to emphasize without destroying the impact of the entire journal. A new paragraph indicates the passage of one or more entire days.

Went to bed at nine—sheets damp: swore and stripped them off and flung them—Heaven knows where. . . .
Stopped at Vevay. . . . Within [the churchyard] General Ludlow's (the Regicide's) monument—black marble—long inscription . . . in which his wife . . . records her long, her tried, and unshaken affection. . . . On our return [from Chillon] met an English party in a carriage; a lady . . . fast . . . asleep in the most anti-narcotic spot in the world—excellent! I remember, at Chamouni, in the very eyes of Mont Blanc, hearing another woman, English also, exclaim to her party

"did you ever see anything more *rural?"*—as if it was High-gate, or Hampstead, or Brompton, or Hayes,—*"Rural!"* quotha!—Rocks, pines, torrents, Glaciers, Clouds, and Summits of eternal snow far above them—and *"Rural!"* .... [At the Château de Clarens] saw on the table of the saloon Blair's sermons and somebody else's (I forget who's) sermons, and a set of noisy children. . . .

Crossed the mountains to Montbovon . . . the whole route beautiful as a Dream. . . . At Mont Davant we breakfasted; afterwards, on a steep ascent dismounted, tumbled down, and cut a finger open; the baggage also got loose and fell down a ravine, till stopped by a large tree: swore. . . . Arrived at a lake in the very nipple of the bosom of the Mountains. . . . In coming down, the Guide tumbled three times; I fell a laugh-ing, and tumbled too. . . . The whole of the Mountain superb. A Shepherd on a very steep and high cliff playing upon his *pipe;* very different from *Arcadia,* (where I saw the pastors with a long Musquet instead of a Crook, and pistols in their Girdles). Our Swiss Shepherd's pipe was sweet, and his tune agreeable. Saw a cow strayed; am told that they often break their necks on and over the crags. . . . The view from the highest points of to-day's journey comprized on one side the greatest part of Lake Leman; on the other, the valleys and mountains of the Canton of Fribourg, and an immense plain, with the Lakes of Neuchâtel and Morat, and all which the borders of these and of the Lake of Geneva inherit: we had both sides of the Jura before us in one point of view. . . . The music of the Cows' bells (for their wealth, like the Patriarchs', is cattle) in the pastures . . . and the Shepherds' shouting to us from crag to crag, and playing on their reeds where the steeps appeared almost inaccessible, with the surrounding scenery, realized all that I have ever heard or imagined of a pastoral existence. . . . I have lately repeopled my mind with Nature. . . .

The people [of the Saarine Valley] looked free, and happy, and *rich* (which last implies neither of the former): the cows superb; a Bull nearly leapt into the Charaban—"agreeable companion in a post-chaise;" Goats and Sheep very thriv-ing. . . .

Entered upon a range of scenes beyond all description or previous conception. Passed a rock; inscription—2 brothers— one murdered the other; just the place for it. After a variety of windings came to an enormous rock. Girl with fruit—very pretty; blue eyes, good teeth, very fair: long but good features —reminded me rather of F^y. Bought some of her pears, and patted her upon the cheek. . . . The torrent [*i.e.*, Staubbach] is in shape curving over the rock, like the *tail* of a white horse streaming in the wind, such as it might be conceived would be that of the *"pale* horse" on which *Death* is mounted in the Apocalypse. . . .

From where we stood, on the *Wengen* Alp . . . the clouds rose from the opposite valley, curling up perpendicular preci- pices like the foam of the Ocean of Hell, during a Springtide. . . . In passing the masses of snow, I made a snowball and pelted H. with it. . . . Glacier . . . very fine . . . like *a frozen hurricane.* . . . Passed *whole woods of withered pines, all withered:* trunks stripped and barkless, branches lifeless; done by a single winter,—their appearance reminded me of me and my family. . . .

Reembarked on the Lake of Thoun; fell asleep part of the way. . . .

From Thoun to Bern, good road, hedges, villages, industry, property, and all sorts of tokens of insipid civilization. . . . Bought a dog. . . . He hath no tail, and is called *"Mutz."* . . .

I am a lover of Nature and an admirer of Beauty. I can bear fatigue and welcome privation, and have seen some of the noblest views in the world. But in all this—the recollections of bitterness, and more especially of recent and more home desolation, which must accompany me through life, have preyed upon me here; and neither the music of the Shepherd, the crash- ing of the Avalanche, nor the torrent, the mountain, the Glacier, the Forest, nor the Cloud, have for one moment light- ened the weight upon my heart, nor enabled me to lose my own wretched identity in the majesty, and the power, and the Glory, around, above, and beneath me.

This is Byron's confession of defeat. The summer and autumn of 1816 produced, poetically, the peak of Byron's enthusiasm for nature, and his finest non-satirical poetry. And although he could never expunge from his soul the memory of the mood of *Childe Harold*, III, and although the Wordsworthian-Rousseauistic note was to reappear twice in later years, he was never again to go to nature with exactly the same kind of fervor that was his on the eve of his Swiss tour.

On September 28, 1816, when Byron summed up the twelve days with the remark that nothing he had seen had "for one moment lightened the weight upon my heart, nor enabled me to lose my own wretched identity in the majesty, and the power, and the Glory, around, above, and beneath me," on this same day Byron's companion and perfect foil, Hobhouse, reached the conclusion that it had been "a very prosperous and beautiful tour."[32] On the preceding day Hobhouse had written, "I lay down in the sun enjoying myself most entirely, and dared to write down in my pocket-book that I was happy."[33] Several days earlier, on September 23, the day upon which Byron "passed *whole woods of withered pines, all withered. . . their appearance reminded me of me and my family*," Hobhouse observed, "Here one's spirits seemed lighter, one's head more clear."[34] Shelley's imagination too had been struck by the withered pines of the Alps,[35] but his more objective specu-

[32]Hobhouse, *Recollections*, II, 24. Compare *La Nouvelle Héloïse* (part 1, letter 23), which may well have influenced Byron. St.-Preux has just completed an eight-days tour in the mountains of Valais, and sums up his impressions as follows: ". . . enfin, le spectacle a je ne sais quoi de magique, de surnaturel qui ravit l'esprit et les sens; on oublie tout, on s'oublie soi-même, on ne sait plus où l'on est."
[33]*Ibid.*, II, 23.
[34]*Ibid.*, II, 21.
[35]*Works*, IX, 186–7. Although many of the images in Byron's poem "Darkness" have been traced to the novel *The Last Man*, it seems possible that it may have been inspired by conversations with Shelley over Buffon's "sublime and gloomy theory." "Darkness," "Prometheus," and *Manfred* reveal similarities, and the passage from Shelley *(loc. cit.)* shows the association in his mind of Buffon and Ahriman. The latter, of course, is the chief spiritual being in *Manfred*. Byron referred to Buffon's *Histoire Naturelle* in 1821 (L. and J., V, 572), and claimed in the list of his reading before 1807, printed in Moore's *Life*, that he had read Buffon.

lations left no room for any purely personal reference to himself.

Manfred was admittedly the product of the tour recorded in the Journal to Augusta—"along with something else"— and thus one may expect to find passages in it which parallel the despairing cry of the Journal. The first two acts may be examined here in detail.

Manfred's request of the assembled spirits of the Universe, like that of Childe Harold, the Byron of the Swiss Journal, and several more of the Byronic heroes is for "forgetfulness" and "self-oblivion," the power to lose the sense of his own wretched identity. Manfred too, of course, fails to achieve this heart-felt wish. Near the end of the opening scene a Voice is heard to cast a spell,

> In the wind there is a voice
> Shall forbid thee to rejoice;
> And to thee shall Night deny
> All the quiet of her sky.

There is then poured upon Manfred's head the potion, *distilled from the qualities of his own being* (ll. 252–61), which binds him, like Childe Harold (III, 9), with a "clankless chain" always upon him. The first scene closes upon this, and the second opens with Manfred alone upon the cliffs. The potion mixed of the elements of his own personality has taken its effect:

> My mother Earth!
> And thou fresh breaking Day, and you, ye Mountains,
> Why are ye beautiful? I cannot love ye.

In spite of Manfred's expressed inability to love "Mother Earth," however, he yearns toward a mystic union with her (I, ii, 313–16) in a way that recalls *Childe Harold*. In the earlier poem (III, 89–90) Byron had written that at the moment when

"all is concentred in a life intense," all having a "part of being,"
"then stirs the feeling infinite," a truth which

> . . . purifies from self: it is a tone,
> The soul and source of music, which makes known
> Eternal harmony,

the great harmony of the universe. Manfred exclaims (I, ii, 313–316),

> Oh, that I were
> The viewless spirit of a lovely sound,
> A living voice, a breathing harmony,
> A bodiless enjoyment. . . .

These lines are followed by two speeches by Manfred upon the fearful destruction of the avalanches. The first act closes as Manfred is led away by the Chamois Hunter.

Thus far the poem contains a rather exact allegory of Byron's own experiences, a creature of contradictions all his life. The opposing tendencies in *Manfred,* from the point of view of this study, are, first, the wish to worship nature, to throw off the "clankless chain," symbol of his humanity and sinfulness, in the act of losing his sense of identity in the great Whole; second, the knowledge that the forces of nature may be harmful; and, finally, the realization embodied in the despairing cry, "Mother Earth . . . I cannot love ye." In the second act, as the poem moves toward Manfred's end and as his quest for forgetfulness and self-oblivion deepens, references to the failure of Nature to afford him peace of mind become more explicit. When at the opening of the second scene Manfred calls up the Witch of the Alps, the "Spirit of the place," the spirit of Nature as she is present to him at that moment, he at first believes (II, ii, 119–23) because of her "calm clear brow, wherein is glass'd serenity of soul," that from her he may gain what he seeks. But it is not to be. His wish (II, ii, 132–36), containing within itself the knowledge of the failure of his first and greater quest, escape from himself, is only

> To look upon thy beauty—nothing further.
> The face of the earth hath madden'd me, and I
> Take refuge in her mysteries, and pierce
> To the abodes of those who govern her—
> But they can nothing aid me.

In the autobiographical "Epistle to Augusta" (ll. 81–86), Byron had made a similar humble request of Nature, as if he had learned that it was possible to expect too much of her healing powers.

> I but ask
> Of Nature that with which she will comply—
> .   .   .   .
> To see her gentle face without a mask,
> And never gaze on it with apathy.

Manfred concludes (II, ii, 224–240) that since the fatal hour his solitude—the great *sine qua non* of courting nature—

> My solitude is solitude no more,
> But peopled with the Furies. . . .
>   Forgetfulness
> I sought in all, save where 'tis to be found.

He never indicates where it is to be found, but for Byron, clearly, it was not in the Swiss Alps.

3

The Literary Tradition:

Sources and Parallels of the Zeluco Theme

The literary background of this strain of thought in Byron is to be found most clearly in the novel,[36] often but not always

---

[36]It has been suggested recently (Bertrand Evans, *Gothic Drama From Walpole to Shelley*, Los Angeles, 1947) that the ancestors of Manfred (and thus by implication the ancestors of Byron's earlier and later heroes

in the Gothic novel. The present section has two purposes: (1) to describe a hitherto disregarded tradition in the novel, one which deeply influenced Byron in the most important way, and (2) to indicate the effects of this influence upon him. The tradition states, in brief, that a villain or any other character with feelings of guilt, misanthropy, or excessive gloom can derive neither pleasure nor spiritual comfort from a contemplation of nature. Because Byron, in his first explicit statement of this idea linked it with John Moore's Zeluco, the villain in the novel of the same name, the theme shall henceforth be referred to in this study as the Zeluco theme. It is the underlying hypothesis of this section that Byron—consciously or otherwise—identified himself and his characters with these variously guilt-laden souls, and so reacted to nature in the time-honored manner prescribed for the guilty by the novel.

---

who share Manfred's characteristics) are to be sought in the Gothic drama, which exhibits, because of conditions peculiar to the theatre, the villain of the Gothic novel being transformed into hero. I have not attempted to read all the plays which Professor Evans describes. Many of them exist only in manuscript. He does not refer to the subject which is one of the particular interests of my own study—that Manfred finds no solace from contemplating the grandeur of nature. I have, however, read a selected group of these plays, and found no references to the strain of thought that I have already described at some length. I list the plays which I examined from the point of view of this study: R. C. Maturin, *Bertram* and *Manuel*; S. T. Coleridge, *Remorse*; Joanna Baillie, *De Montfort*; M. G. Lewis, *Adelmorn* and *The Castle Spectre*; Andrew McDonald, *Vimonda*; Horace Walpole, *The Mysterious Mother*. The explanation may well be that the presence of stage scenery eliminated both exclamations praising the glories of nature as well as those lamenting the fact that nature had no power to comfort a villain. It was noticed long ago, of course, that the descriptive passages typical of Elizabethan plays are no longer to be found in the drama after the introduction of more or less realistic scenery during the Restoration period.

The Zeluco theme is also absent from three other sources of *Manfred* listed by Samuel C. Chew, *The Dramas of Lord Byron* (Göttingen, 1915), pp. 60–66: it does not appear in Beckford's *Vathek* or Shelley's *Queen Mab* or *Alastor*.

In his addition to the preface of the original *Childe Harold,*
following his remark that "even the beauties of nature . . .
are lost" on Harold, Byron stated that the sketch he once intended was that of "a modern Timon, perhaps a poetical Zeluco."
Moore's novel, which appeared in 1789, may be considered
now from the special point of view of this study. Despite the
various opportunities which the plot of *Zeluco* affords, it contains no passages of extended natural description, although an
admiration for "the beauties of nature" is attributed to several
of the characters, and various clichés about nature are scattered
throughout the book. The sentence[37] which Byron had in
mind, though, when he referred to Moore's work, concerns
the deep-dyed though death-bed-repenting villain: "Neither
did the most sublime beauties of nature . . ., to all of which she
[the heroine Laura] was feeling alive, afford any enjoyment
to the mind of Zeluco; although from vanity and affectation
he pretended to admire some of them, and had made himself
master of the common cant of *virtu.*"

Apart from this passage, which Byron remembered, there
are several other qualities attributed to Zeluco which may
very well have caused Byron to see Childe Harold—or himself
—in the portrait.

Zeluco is described[38] as "a self-tormentor" who had "the
daily habit . . . of tormenting himself"; "reflection or retro-
spect on past conduct . . . in him was always attended with
self-condemnation"; "gloom and dissatisfaction attended him
as often as he was not engaged in such pursuits as kill thought
and reflection"; "Zeluco was the greatest of all self-tormentors." He was "fatigued and jaded by a life of comfortless
voluptuousness."

[37]*Zeluco,* ch. 66, p. 379. The novel is reprinted on pp. 345–396 of *The
Republic of Letters; A Weekly Republication of Standard Literature* (New
York, 1834).
[38]*Ibid.,* ch. 14, p. 351; ch. 24, p. 357; ch. 26, p. 358; ch. 69, p. 380;
ch. 18, p. 353.

The novel is actually an account of the travels, amorous adventures, and crimes of the main character, with its scenes placed variously in Palermo, Madrid, Havana, and Naples. Zeluco, who had lost his father at an early age, was "reared by an indulgent mother," and to this fact is traced the wickedness of his later life. When he is first rejected in his suit for the heroine's hand,[39] he "determined on making another tour through Italy, and perhaps through France, in the hopes that a variety of objects would dissipate his vexation." He finally gains Laura for his bride, however, and she bears him a son, but Zeluco shortly afterwards takes a mistress. The mistress, to further her own designs, insinuates that Laura's infant was fathered by Seidlits, and makes much of the fact that Seidlits is only a half brother to Laura. Zeluco, thus imposed upon, strangles the child, thinking it to be the evidence of incest. How much, exactly, of his own life and personality Byron imagined he saw in all this, it is impossible, of course, to say.

That there are not inconsiderable similarities, however, between Child Harold the first and Zeluco is obvious: yet despite this obviousness the novel has never received the credit due it in the various genealogies extant of the Byronic hero. This may be due to its scarcity. Whatever the reason may be, it seems that scholars have accepted perhaps too uncritically the judgment of E. H. Coleridge in his edition of the *Poetry* (II, 8, note 2) that "Zeluco was an unmitigated scoundrel, who led an adventurous life; but the prolix narrative of his villanies does not recall *Childe Harold*." To E. H. Coleridge's citations of Mrs. Radcliffe's novels, too, may perhaps be traced the predisposition to see, too exclusively, Schedoni the Italian in the Byronic hero. Mario Praz in *The Romantic Agony*[40]

[39]*Ibid.*, ch. 34, p. 362.
[40]Praz, *The Romantic Agony* (London, 1933), pp 64–69.

thus denies Zeluco in favor of Schedoni. Sir Walter Raleigh and George Saintsbury take the same position, and agree further in identifying Byron himself with the Radcliffian villain. Samuel C. Chew in *A Literary History of England*[41] also describes Schedoni as "the precursor of Byron's Lara and Manfred." But Zeluco has at least three strong counts in his favor, in addition to the weight of Byron's statement in his preface. Zeluco, as my quotations indicate, suffers from painful feelings of remorse and guilt, Mrs. Radcliffe's villains never. Perhaps even more important from Byron's point of view, is the fact that Zeluco is pictured as a "misanthrope" through no real fault of his own; that is, as Byron read the novel (and as Moore intended it), Zeluco is a man injured, hurt by the world to an extent that determines the very nature of his character. For Zeluco becomes a villain for reasons outside his control—parental neglect and a bad education. Moore's attitude toward his main character is actually one of environmental determinism. This is never true of Mrs. Radcliffe. (In this respect, Moore's novel is similar to the novels of Godwin, which should also have an honorable place in the family tree of the Byronic hero, as shall be seen shortly.) It should be noted too that Byron's addition to his preface mentions Shakespeare's Timon in the same phrase with Zeluco, as if both characters were men essentially of the same stamp: but their only important similarity lies in the fact that each has been rendered misanthropic and villainous through no fault of his own; both become finally what the world has made them. It is not amiss to recall here that Byron had early written of himself (in a letter to Augusta in 1808) that his intercourse with the world had hardened his heart. He had somewhat more reason to think so, of course, in later years. Byron[42]

---

[41]*A Literary History of England*, ed. Baugh (New York, 1948), p. 1194.
[42]*Correspondence*, I, 146-47.

linked the name of Zeluco with his own again in a letter to Lady Melbourne, written on April 7, 1813. "It is rather hard upon me," he writes, "that all my poetical personages must be identified with the writer, and just as fair as if Dr. Moore must be Zeluco, or Milton (begging pardon for mentioning such men in the same sentence with myself) the Devil." The point implied is that Harold, Zeluco, and Satan are all types of the "archangel ruined," beings of a higher order who have fallen from innocence. Mrs. Radcliffe's villains, on the other hand, were presumably villains in their cradles, and never call forth the pathos associated with the character born for a better life than circumstances allowed him.

The Radcliffian villain, finally, is rather completely lacking in psychological subtlety. But Byron recognized[48] in the author of *Zeluco* an "acute and severe . . . observer of mankind." None of this is intended to take away from the honor of Mrs. Radcliffe's creations, whose lineaments are to be seen clearly in the faces of Byron's villains: her own have a Salvator Rosa kind of glamour which Zeluco lacks. But Dr. Moore's careful dissection of motive and the slow hardening of habit was much more likely to appeal to Byron than Mrs. Radcliffe's black and white sketches.

It is not though to any one book, certainly, that one must look for the source of Childe Harold or of any other of Byron's characters. They are too genuinely Byron as Byron saw himself in his own poetic imagination. The books which may be cited are those which nourished a boyish imagination—and those of later date, written within the same tradition. These are the sources of the Byronic hero, along with Byron's own most highly developed feelings of guilt. That the characteristic of guilt is the distinguishing mark of the Byronic hero, Byron himself was ready to admit. In answer to a note

[48]*Poetry*, IV, 334.

in the *Childe Harold's Monitor* of Hodgson, which deplored the effect upon young minds of such heroes as Byron had made popular, he wrote,[44] "I must remark from *Aristotle* and *Rymer*, that the *hero* of tragedy and (I add *meo periculo*) a tragic poem must *be guilty.*" But the point need not be labored. *Childe Harold,* then, describes the early life of a tragic hero whose crimes, like those of Manfred, are not very clearly indicated.

That Byron fed his boyish appetite for romance upon the novel is a fact known. Although on December 6, 1813, he recorded in his journal his distaste for the novel and noted that "it is many a year since I looked into one . . . till I looked yesterday at the worst parts of the *Monk,*" two weeks earlier (November 23) he had referred to a novel of his own writing—one burned because there was too much of himself in it. And in the list of his early reading printed in Moore's *Life* and dated by Byron November 30, 1807, he stated that he had read "novels by the thousand," "the greater part . . . before the age of fifteen." In the next paragraph he returns to the numbers of novels he had read: "I have also read (to my regret at present) about four thousand novels."

Nothing, then, could be more inevitable than that Byron, when his feelings of guilt (deserved or not is no matter) were strongest upon him, should react toward nature in the traditional manner of the guilty as portrayed in the novel.

I have found a form of this tradition in the novel as early as 1763, in Frances Brooke's *Lady Julia Mandeville* (see the appendix for examples of the Zeluco theme in novels which Byron probably had not read). Its earliest appearance, however, among the novels which with certainty or good possibility may be assigned to Byron's reading is in *The Sorrows of Young Werther,* first translated into English in 1779. Byron

[44]L. and J., V, 284.

knew *Werther* well enough in the autumn of 1812 (when he was writing *The Waltz*) to refer in the poem to Werther's opinion of the new dance (ll. 147–150). In later years he was to say to Medwin,[45] "I have a great curiosity about everything relating to Goethe, and please myself with thinking there is some analogy between our characters and writings." Byron recollected[46] in 1821 that he meant to have made Juan "a *Cavalier Servente* in Italy, and a cause for a divorce in England, and a Sentimental 'Werther-faced man' in Germany. . . . " The parallel with Byron's own career is obvious. Byron seems to have read only *Werther* and *Faust,* but may well have been acquainted with the autobiographical basis of the novel. In his intended dedication of *Marino Faliero*[47] to Goethe, he recognized the power of *Werther* when he called it the book which has "put more individuals out of this world than Napoleon himself." Goethe[48] was the "Greatest man of Germany —perhaps of Europe." "I look upon him as a Great Man."[49]

Werther's feelings of guilt, however he rationalized his conduct, are evident, not only from such a slight touch as the pleasure he gains from deliberately allowing himself to be scratched by briars as he wanders through the countryside, but also from a letter[50] he wrote just before his suicide: "And what does it mean, that Albert is your husband . . . and in this

[45]Quoted in L. and J., V, 507.
[46]L. and J., V, 242.
[47]Byron also proposed a dedication of *Sardanapalus* to Goethe. Not until *Werner* was the dedication actually made.
[48]L. and J., V, 36.
[49]L. and J., V, 100.
[50]*The Sorrows of Young Werther,* trans. Rose (London, 1929), p. 118. Byron did not read German. William Rose's translation is from the 1774 edition.

At the risk of monotony, I have quoted at great length in the following pages from novels illustrating the Zeluco theme. The existence of the tradition might be indicated in a manner more concise than that I have chosen, but the novels are often neither well known nor easily accessible. The tradition is also of importance itself, apart from its influence on Byron.

world it is a sin that I love you, that I would like to snatch you from his arms into mine? A sin? Good! I am punishing myself for it." Werther, of course, like Byron, was one of the world's great self-tormentors. This and the fact of Werther's feelings of guilt are alone sufficient to explain why Byron might well have identified himself with Goethe's character.

As Werther loses his sense of innocence and labours increasingly under sensations of guilt and melancholy, his attitude toward nature exhibits four stages: (1) he takes originally a most intense delight in the natural scene, acquiring from nature the blessings of serenity and enjoying at times the ecstasy of the Rousseauistic visionary;[51] (2) once, however, his hopeless and guilty love takes possession of him, the sight of nature becomes a source of misery to him, and a torment: he is haunted by the idea that Nature is an eternally devouring monster, consuming her own; (3) this is followed by a state of apathy in which he has no interest at all in nature; and (4) the last state is one of spiritual dryness, in which the creative faculties are dead, Werther stands self-condemned before his God, and nature seems as lifeless as a varnished picture, incapable of giving rise to a moment of happiness. The pertinent passages[52] follow.

[51]Inasmuch as Rousseau's novels contain no villains, the Zeluco theme does not appear in them. Only the long-suffering husband of Julie, the "sceptic" Wolmar, in La Nouvelle Héloïse (part 5, letter 5) fails to see in nature a beneficent creator: "Imaginez Julie à la promenade avec son mari; l'une admirant dans la riche et brillante parure que la terre étale l'ouvrage et les dons de l'Auteur de l'univers; l'autre ne voyant en tout cela qu'une combinaison fortuite où rien n'est lié que par une force aveugle. . . . Nous ne nous promenons presque jamais Julie et moi, que quelque vue frapante et pittoresque ne lui rappelle ces idées douloureuses. Hélas! dit-elle avec attendrissement; le spectacle de la nature, si vivant si animé pour nous, est mort aux yeux de l'infortuné Wolmar, et dans cette grande harmonie des êtres, où tout parle de Dieu d'une voix si douce, il n'apperçoit qu'un silence éternel."

[52]Werther, pp. 50–53 (letters of August 18 and 22), pp. 86–87 (letter of November 3). The clearest instance of the Zeluco theme in Goethe's

18 August

Was it ordained by Fate that that which renders a man happy becomes later the source of his misery? My heart's full and ardent sympathy with Nature, which flooded me with such bliss and made the world round about

---

Faust (1808) is to be found in the "Wald und Höhle" scene. Faust, realizing that his desire for Gretchen is about to overcome him, goes to nature to strengthen his will to resist. As the scene opens it seems that Faust has been successful (*Faust*, ed. Petsch [Leipzig, 1925]):

> Erhabner Geist, du gabst mir, gabst mir alles,
> Warum ich bat. Du hast mir nicht umsonst
> Dein Angesicht im Feuer zugewendet.
> Gabst mir die herrliche Natur zum Königreich,
> Kraft, sie zu fühlen, zu geniessen.
> (ll. 3217–21)

But the Spirit sublime has also brought to Faust, as he thinks, Mephistopheles, who

> Mich vor mir selbst erniedrigt, und zu nichts,
> Mit einem Worthauch, deine Gaben wandelt.
> Er facht in meiner Brust ein wildes Feuer
> Nach jenem schönen Bild geschäftig an.
> So tauml' ich von Begierde zu Genuss.
> Und im Genuss verschmacht' ich nach Begierde.
> (ll. 3245–50)

At the end of the speech Mephistopheles enters and ridicules Faust's communings with nature. Faust resists throughout the scene; but when he next sees Gretchen in the scene of "Marthens Garten" and explains to her his creed of God's immanence in nature (ll. 3431–58), it is significant that at the very moment he carries in his pocket the sleeping drops for Gretchen's mother and has already planned Gretchen's seduction. The beauties of nature thus are quite lost on Faust.

Byron had heard Monk Lewis translate *Faust* in 1816 when he was still at Diodati: this fact, he said to George Ticknor (*Life, Letters, and Journals of George Ticknor*, October 20, 1817), "accounts for the resemblance between that poem and Manfred," which Ticknor had asked him about.

One more passage from *Faust* may be of interest. On his way through the Harz Mountains to the Walpurgis Night celebration, Faust observes,

> Im Labyrinth der Täler hinzuschleichen,
> Dann diesen Felsen zu ersteigen,
> Von dem der Quell sich ewig sprudelnd stürzt,
> Das ist die Lust, die solche Pfade würzt!
> Der Frühling webt schon in den Birken,
> Und selbst die Fichte fühlt ihn schon;
> Sollt' er nicht auch auf unsre Glieder wirken?
> (ll. 3841–47)

Mephistopheles replies (l. 3848), "Fürwahr, ich spüre nichts davon!"

into a Paradise, has now become an unbearable torment, a
torturing spirit which pursues me everywhere. . . .

It is as though a curtain has been drawn from before my
soul, and the scene of eternal life is being transformed before my eyes into the abyss of the ever open grave. Can you
say *This is,* when everything is transitory, everything rolls past
with the speed of lightning, only rarely endures till its life
force is spent, but is carried away by the current, submerged
and smashed against the rocks? Not a moment but consumes
you and yours, not a moment when you do not yourself destroy something, and inevitably so. The most innocent stroll
costs a myriad tiny creatures their lives, one step annihilates
the laborious constructions of a nation of ants and crushes a
world in little to ignominious ruin. It is not the great occasional catastrophes of the world, the floods that sweep away
your villages, the earthquakes that devour your cities, by which I
am moved. It is the consuming force latent in universal Nature, that has formed nothing that has not destroyed its neigh-
bour and itself, which saps my soul. And so I reel along in
anguish, surrounded by earth and sky and all the weaving
forces of Nature. I see nothing but a monster, eternally devouring, eternally chewing the cud. . . .

22 August

My condition is wretched, Wilhelm! All my energies are
reduced to a restless inactivity. I cannot be idle, and yet I am
unable to take up any task. I have no power of imagination,
no interest in Nature.

3 November

. . . . I am suffering much, because I have lost what was the
sole delight of my life, the holy vivifying power with which
I created worlds around me. It has gone!—When I look out of
my window at the distant hill, as the morning sun pierces the
mist above it and illumines the tranquil meadows in the valley,
and the gentle stream winds toward me between its leafless
willows—oh! when this glorious scene appears before me as
fixed as a varnished picture and all this rapture is incapable of
pumping a single drop of happiness from my heart up into

my brain, and my whole churlish self stands before the face of God like a dried-up spring, like a cracked pitcher!

The Zeluco theme, almost certainly, was an element in the "analogy" which Byron sensed between Goethe's writings and character, and his own.

The Zeluco theme, in various forms, receives great prominence in the novels of Anne Radcliffe.[53] Although it does not appear at all in *A Sicilian Romance* (1790), it is glanced at in one of its forms in her next novel, *The Romance of the Forest* (1791). Here the implication is that a settled and persistent melancholy deprives one of enjoying the restorative powers of nature. Adeline, the heroine,[54] has been kept in a convent by a man she supposes to be her very indifferent father, and recently has been rescued from mysterious ruffians: "With Adeline, the charms of external nature were heightened by those of novelty; she had seldom seen the grandeur of an extensive prospect, or the magnificence of a wide horizon—and not often the picturesque beauties of more confined scenery. Her mind had not lost by long oppression that elastic energy which resists calamity; else, however susceptible might have been her original taste, the beauties of nature would no longer have charmed her thus easily even to temporary repose." The principle is illustrated in a positive fashion by M. Amand,[55] a minor character who suffers from a continued depression of spirits: "Alas! what climate can relieve the sickness of the heart! I go to lose in the varieties of new scenes the remembrance of past happiness; yet the effort is vain; I am everywhere equally restless and unhappy." In spite of this realization, Amand "determined to travel farther into Italy,

[53]Byron had read *The Mysteries of Udolpho* carefully enough to echo phrases from it in *The Giaour, Lara,* and *Childe Harold,* IV. See E. H. Coleridge's notes, *Poetry,* II, 327, 342; III, 88–89, 351.
[54]*The Romance of the Forest* (New York, 1904), ch. 1, p. 13.
[55]*Ibid.,* ch. 18, pp. 342–43.

though he no longer felt any interest in those charming scenes which in happier days . . . would have afforded him the highest degree of mental luxury—now he sought only to escape from himself. . . ." The gloomy melancholy of the Byronic hero, of course, is an obvious point of comparison, as well as Byron's own strenuous efforts to "escape from himself."

The Mysteries of Udolpho (1794) offers the most exact parallels to Byron's idea that the benevolent influences of nature were lost upon him and his heroes. The attiture toward nature of the villain, Montoni, who is sometimes pointed to as an ancestor of Byron's creations, is summed up in a single sentence: he "cared little about views of any kind" (ch. 15), and nothing more is made of the matter. This characteristic in the young hero, Valancourt,[56] however, is treated at some length. The heroine, Emily, is speaking:

"Observe those moonlight woods, and the towers which appear obscurely in the perspective. You used to be a great admirer cf landscape; and I have heard you say that the faculty of deriving consolation under misfortune, from the sublime prospects which neither oppression nor poverty withholds from us, was the peculiar blessing of the innocent." Valancourt was deeply affected. "Yes," replied he; "I had once a taste for innocent and elegant delights—I had once an uncorrupted heart!"

Valancourt in great anguish has just finished declaring himself unworthy of Emily, at that point in the narrative where she has finally escaped from Montoni and has inherited the estates of Madame Montoni. His sins were that he had entered into the social life of Paris and as a result of gambling debts had been thrown into prison. His misery and self-contempt though are very real, and he is convinced that his heart has been at least partially corrupted. The psychology thus glanced

[56]*The Mysteries of Udolpho* (New York, 1931), vol. II, ch. 38, p. 174.

at in the passage above is made explicit elsewhere[57] in the novel. Emily's father is the source of almost all the wisdom, all the correct and proper opinions expressed about the nature of man and the way he should spend his life: "St. Aubert was much pleased with the . . . keen susceptibility to the grandeur of nature which his new acquaintance discovered; and, indeed, he had often been heard to say that without a certain simplicity of heart this taste could not exist in any strong degree." "Virtue and taste," the same character says[58] to himself, echoing Saint-Preux, as he meditates happily upon the sight of Emily and Valancourt enjoying together their delight in natural scenery, "are nearly the same; for virtue is little more than active taste." Obviously, it was impossible for a man of secret crimes or corrupted heart to draw succor from a contemplation of nature, however much needed.

True to this principle, a number of "bad" minor characters in the book are denied a pleasure in nature picturesque or sublime, and not allowed to profit from its effects upon their wicked hearts. Madame Montoni, Emily's cruel aunt, has no taste at all for the grandeur of the Alps, and while Emily is enraptured at her first view of Italy stretching out for miles below her, the older woman is selfishly contemplating in her imagination the splendour of the palaces she believes that she will soon be mistress of. When the party had arrived at Turin, she[59] "was exceedingly rejoiced to be once more on level ground; and . . . added a hope that she should soon be beyond the view of these horrid mountains." "Emily well knew that her aunt had no taste for solitary grandeur."[60]

The Countess of Villefort,[61] who has "a heart, in which even the feelings of ordinary benevolence had long since de-

[57]*Ibid.*, vol. I, ch. 3, p. 34.
[58]*Ibid.*, vol. I, ch. 5, p. 50.
[59]*Ibid.*, vol. I, ch. 14, pp. 172–173.
[60]*Ibid.*, vol. I, ch. 16, p. 215.
[61]*Ibid.*, vol. II, ch. 35, pp. 136, 139, 142.

cayed under the corruptions of luxury," finds no delight at all in a country of "romantic beauty": to her eye it is "only a scene of savage nature." "Reflecting with regret upon the gay parties she had left at Paris, [she] surveyed with disgust what she thought the gloomy woods and solitary wildness of the scene."

And as a final example from *Udolpho*,[62] one reads of Montoni, Quesnel, and their two wives when they are at a villa near the Italian coast on the banks of the Brenta, "Thus the party continued to converse and, as far as civility would permit, to torture each other by mutual boasts, while they reclined on sofas in the portico, and were environed with delights both from nature and art, by which any honest minds would have been tempered to benevolence, and happy imaginations would have been soothed into enchantment."

In *The Italian* (1797) the same ideas are expressed. The following passages are all clear statements of the Zeluco theme and require very little comment. Ellena[63] is the heroine, Schedoni is the villain: "To the harrassed spirits of Ellena the changing scenery was refreshing, and she frequently yielded her cares to the influence of majestic nature. Over the gloom of Schedoni no scenery had, at any moment, power; the shape and paint of external imagery gave neither impression nor colour to his fancy." The next passage[64] refers to the hero's wicked mother and her villa. She connives with Schedoni:

This delightful residence was situated on an airy promontory, that overhung the water, and was nearly embosomed among the woods, that spread far along the heights, and descended with great pomp of foliage and colouring, to the very margin of the waves. It seemed scarcely possible that misery

[62]*Ibid.*, vol. I, ch. 16, p. 215.
[63]*The Italian; or, the Confessional of the Black Penitents* (London, 1844), ch. 21, p. 117.
[64]*Ibid.*, ch. 24, p. 133.

could inhabit so enchanting an abode; yet the Marchesa was wretched amidst all these luxuries of nature and art, which would have perfected the happiness of an innocent mind. Her heart was possessed by evil passions, and all her perceptions were distorted and discoloured by them, which, like a dark magician, had power to change the fairest scenes into those of gloom and desolation.

Another passage[65] uses similar language to refer to the masked ruffians, tools of Schedoni, who are carrying Ellena away by force to be shut up in a convent: "At every step were objects which would have afforded pleasure to a tranquil mind; the beautifully variegated marbles, that formed the cliffs immediately above, their fractured masses embossed with mosses and flowers of every vivid hue that paints the rainbow; the elegance of the shrubs that tufted, and the majestic grace of the palms which waved over them, would have charmed almost any other eye than those of her companions, whose hearts were dead to feeling."

In Matthew Gregory Lewis's *Monk*[66] (1796), the early Childe Harold is described with some completeness. Ambrosio, yet innocent, discovers his temptress Rosario in a grotto of the abbey garden uttering misanthropic sentiments out of unrequited love. Believing her to be what she pretends to be, a member of his order, he promptly delivers to her a brief sermon:

Disgusted at the guilt or absurdity of mankind, the misanthrope flies from it; he resolves to become an hermit, and buries himself in the cavern of some gloomy rock. While hate inflames his bosom, possibly he may feel contented with his situation; but when his passions begin to cool; when Time has mellowed his sorrows, and healed those wounds which he

[65] *Ibid.*, ch. 6, p. 30.
[66] *The Monk* (London, 1796), I, 90–91. Byron had read *The Monk* sometime before December 6, 1813. See L. and J., II, 368.

bore with him to his solitude, think you that Content becomes his companion? Ah! no, Rosario. No longer sustained
by the violence of his passions, he feels all the monotony of
his way of living, and his heart becomes the prey of ennui
and weariness. He looks round, and finds himself alone in
the universe: the love of society revives in his bosom, and
he pants to return to that world which he has abandoned.
Nature loses all her charms in his eyes: no one is near him
to point out her beauties, or share in his admiration of her
excellence and variety. Propped upon the fragment of some
rock, he gazes upon the tumbling waterfall with a vacant eye;
he views, without emotion, the glory of the setting sun.

The novels of Godwin should also occupy an important
place in the list of those which helped to form the mind of
the young Byron. Shelley thought *Mandeville* (1817) "a
Satanic likeness of Childe Harold the first"[67] and sent Byron
a copy in the month of its publication, along with his own
Revolt of Islam. He had written to Byron on September 11,
1816, when Godwin was still urging himself on with difficulty
to finish the novel, that "Northcote the painter, who is an ardent
admirer of all your compositions, had recommended Godwin to
read 'Glenarvon' [Lady Caroline Lamb's portrait of Byron],
affirming that many parts of it exhibited extraordinary
talent."[68] *Mandeville* is too late to have influenced Byron,
but Godwin had been dissecting misanthropic outcasts from
society, ruined by "things as they are," since 1794. The Zeluco theme appears in all of Godwin's novels up through
Mandeville. Byron praised *St. Leon* extravagantly.[69] In reply
to Godwin's remark that the work of writing another novel
would kill him, Byron is reported to have said, "And what
matter? We should have another *St. Leon*." In January, 1816,

[67]*Lord Byron's Correspondence*, II, 62.
[68]*Ibid.*, II, 17.
[69]William Maginn, *A Gallery of Illustrious Literary Characters* (London, 1873), p. 141.

Byron thought well enough of Godwin as a man of letters (he remarked that he had seen him only once in his life) to offer to give to him £600 of the £1050 offered by Murray for *The Siege of Corinth* and *Parisina*. The remaining £450 was to be divided between Coleridge and Maturin. Although Murray objected to this plan and discouraged Byron from carrying it through, Byron did contribute money in 1822 to a fund raised to help Godwin.

The Zeluco theme appears only incidentally in *Caleb Williams* (1794) and *St. Leon* (1799); however, in *Fleetwood: or, The New Man of Feeling* (1805) it is treated at great length. Falkland, Caleb Williams' persecutor, is pictured as spending whole nights in the midst of sublime scenery, but its only effect[70] is to lull him into "a kind of nameless lethargy of despair": his feelings of guilt and misanthropy remain unpurged. Caleb observed[71] that "when I lighted upon him after having sought him among the rocks and precipices, pale, emaciated, solitary, and haggard, the suggestion would continually recur to me . . . surely this man is a murderer!"

St. Leon, who[72] was "destined by nature to wander a solitary outcast on the face of the earth" and who "found a horrible satisfaction in determining to live, and to avenge upon myself the guilt I had incurred" (at this point he has reduced himself and his family to beggary by gambling), is described[73] as too proud to allow the beauties of nature to do their work upon him:

I was wandering, as I had often done, with a gloomy and rebellious spirit, among the rocks, a few miles distant from the place of our habitation. It was the middle of summer. The weather had been remarkably fine; but I disdained to

[70]*Caleb Williams* (London, 1903), vol. II, ch. 4, p. 170.
[71]*Ibid.*, p. 172.
[72]*St. Leon* (London, 1832), ch. 7, pp. 80, 83.
[73]*Ibid.*, ch. 8, p. 87.

allow the gratifications which arise from a pure atmosphere and a serene sky to find entrance in my soul.

The self-torturing, misanthropic, and guilt-laden Fleetwood, however, offers the most exact parallels to Byron and his heroes. He was reared by an indulgent father among scenes of great natural grandeur, and as a solitary child viewed mankind from afar, with fear and disgust. Here he engaged in Rousseauistic reveries, which, he admits, nourished in him a propensity to "depotism." His life as an Oxford undergraduate, however, lessened his love of nature. His four years of dissipation there, furthermore, and a fifth at Paris, where he was deceived by two mistresses, made him a perfect misanthrope, "not of the sterner and more rugged class," but a disillusioned idealist, made miserable by the imperfections of mankind, and haunted by the idea that he is alone in the world. When he travels in the Alps to forget his unhappiness, the image of the faithless countess appears to him in every vista. After the death of his father he returns to England, falls again into a course of dissipation, and repents but is not "made whole." The scenes of nature neither relieve his fits of depression nor afford him any pleasure. He then travels again on the Continent, but carries a secret uneasiness always with him. Thus he spends twenty years in search of contentment, always feeling himself alone in the world, until finally he finds happiness in marriage and views nature again with pleasure. The life and character of Fleetwood are so thoroughly Byronic, and the Zeluco theme is so clearly illustrated by the novel that the following quotations are necessarily of some length. The usually beneficent influences of nature prove to be wholly ineffective in the case of the misanthropic and guilty Fleetwood; indeed, his condition is even aggravated by his life close to nature. I select several illustrative passages from many:[74]

I fell sometimes, for want of an object sufficiently to exercise the passions, into long fits of languor and depression, which were inconceivably wearisome. Exercise and the scenes of nature no longer relieved me. The inactivity which came over me made it very difficult for me to summon the resolution to go out of doors in search of variety. But, when that difficulty was conquered, variety itself afforded me no pleasure. The landscape was as if it had lost the prismatic illusion, which clothes it to the sense of sight in such beautiful colours. The fields were no longer green, nor the skies blue; or at least they afforded no more pleasure to my eyes, than they would have done if the grass had been withered, and the heavens shrouded in pestilence and death. The beautiful and the bold forms of valley and mountain, which had frequently delighted me, seemed to my eye loathsome, and tame, and monotonous. . . .

Thus I spent more than twenty years of my life, continually in search of contentment, which as invariably eluded my pursuit. . . . I wandered among mountains and rivers, through verdant plains, and over immense precipices; but nature had no beauties. . . .

The remarks immediately following are spoken by the good and wise Macneil, who advises Fleetwood to marry, have children, and interest himself even in the lives of his distant relations. Macneil is a reformed Rousseauist, knew the unhappy Frenchman in his youth, and unerringly diagnoses Fleetwood's malady, the Romantic "disease" of a mind preying constantly upon itself:

Fleetwood, you are too much alone. I hear people talk of the raptures of solitude; and with what tenderness of affection

[74]*Fleetwood: or, The New Man of Feeling* (London, 1832), vol. I, ch. 1, pp. 1, 2, 3–5; ch. 3, p. 21; ch. 7, pp. 62, 63–64; ch. 8, p. 65; vol. II, ch. 7, pp. 162–166; ch. 10, p. 175; ch. 11, p. 180; ch. 15, pp. 198–200; ch. 20, pp. 235–236.

they can love a tree, a rivulet, or a mountain. Believe me, they are pretenders; they deceive themselves, or they seek, with their eyes open, to impose upon others. In addition to their trees and their mountains, I will give them the whole brute creation; still it will not do. There is a principle in the heart of man which demands the society of his like.

Fleetwood finally marries Macneil's daughter and becomes a witness to the truth of his father-in-law's remarks. A man reborn, he takes great pleasure again in the scenes of nature:

While we [Fleetwood and his newly acquired wife Mary] resided at Matlock, we visited the beauties and romantic scenery of Derbyshire. . . . But how different were the sensations with which I now visited each charming, or each wonderful scene! Even a bright and spirit-stirring morn did not now stir in me a contemplative and solitary spirit; it turned my eye on my companion, it awakened us to the interchange of cheerful and affectionate looks, it tipped our tongues with many a pleasant sally, and many a tender and sympathetic expression. When we looked down upon the rich and fertile plains, when we hung over the jutting and tremendous precipice, I perceived, with inexpressible pleasure, that mine was no longer a morose and unparticipated sensation, but that another human creature, capable of feeling all my feelings, rejoiced and trembled along with me.

The similarity between *Fleetwood* (1805) and *Mandeville* (1817), which Shelley described to Byron as a "Satanic likeness of Childe Harold the first," is evident even from a single quotation:[75]

But, when these my better angels [his sister Henrietta and her friend Mrs. Willis] left my side, then was the sabbath of my unhallowed cogitations. Then was the tempest and whirlwind of the soul. Then I was wholly delivered up to hatred, disappointment, and remorse, and all those darker emotions that lacerate and tear in pieces the human heart. I looked

[75]*Mandeville* (Edinburgh, 1817), vol. III, ch. 1, pp. 14–15.

round upon my implements of study, I looked from my windows upon the rich and heart-reviving prospects they commanded, and I cast upon them a smile of bitterness and contempt. I said all these meadows, and hedge-rows, and streams, this forest-land, and these woods, as far as the eye can reach, are mine. What matters it? I carry a poison in my bosom, to which they afford no antidote. I bear about with me a blemished reputation, a wound that not all the arts of medicine, and all the incantations of witchcraft, can heal. What avails it then for a man to be rich, who knows that he is destined to be miserable?

E. A. Baker, in the fifth volume of his *History of the English Novel,* remarks of Dr. John Moore's *Mordaunt* (1800) that "at first one seems to be reading Beckford[76] or Byron's letters of travel. . . ." The similarity, even to phrasing, is a striking one. But the impatient, bored, satiated man of the world of

[76]P. 232. Compare the following passages from Beckford's *Dreams (op. cit.,* 123–125 and 157–158), written from the Euganean Hills and Pisa, respectively: "A profusion of aromatic flowers covered the slopes, and exhaled additional perfumes, as the sun declined, and the still hour approached, which was wont to spread over my mind a divine composure, and to restore the tranquillity I might have lost in the day. But now it diffused its reviving coolness in vain, and I remained, if possible, more sad and restless than before."

.   .   .   .

"I lay down in the open turf-walks between the shrubberies, listlessly surveyed the cattle browsing at a distance, and the blue hills that rose above the foliage and bounded the view. During a few minutes I had forgotten every care; but when I began to enquire into my happiness, I found it vanish. I felt myself without those I love most, in situations they would have warmly admired, and without them these pleasant lawns and woodlands were of little avail. On the contrary, they reminded me so strongly of their absence, that my joy was changed into tears. I looked earnestly at the distant hills, and sighed: I scattered the blossoms I had gathered, and cried out incessantly, Let us drive away."
Byron may well have been influenced by the world weariness of the *Dreams.* See *Notes and Queries,* July 4, 1857, and *Quarterly Review,* LI. Beckford may also have taught Byron something of the picturesque technique. See Beckford, *op. cit.,* pp. 21–22, 41, 181, for examples of the very close association which nature and landscape painting had in his mind.

the early pages gives way, in the mind of the author, to a figure who, in the later volumes, is quite a genuine hero: he comes to have less of the "Byronic" about him than any other figure described in the present section of this study. Unless it be granted that Moore was attempting to describe a transformation in his main character, which does not seem probable, it has to be concluded that the figure of Mordaunt was imperfectly conceived.

The younger brother of a noble family, Mordaunt has alternately lived the life of a soldier and that of a man of pleasure. He has gone through a succession of affairs of the heart before the novel opens, lightheartedly casting aside lady after lady, and has a fixed and worldly aversion to marriage. His punishment for all this is a very Byronic sense of *ennui,* which follows him all the way across Europe. The illustrations[77] of the Zeluco theme which immediately follow are all from Mordaunt's first and second letters:

In the country, I became so fond of shooting and hunting, that, in spite of all my past experience, I thought I never should tire of them. When I began to be convinced of my mistake, I was informed that . . . you would accompany me to the continent. . . . The grand tour! Gracious Heaven, what happiness did my imagination anticipate! . . . But when the cup is filled too often, the sparklings on the surface become fewer, and but a poor compensation for the nauseous dregs at the bottom. . . .

I hardly think it possible for any mortal to contemplate the sublime objects of nature, or the beauties of variegated landscape, with more admiration and delight than I have done: yet the Alps, and the Vale of Arno, became, before I left them, Highgate-hill and Turnham-green to me.

That Mordaunt derives absolutely no peace of mind from his contemplations of "the sublime objects of nature" is evident.

[77]*Mordaunt* (London, 1800), I, 11–19, 4–5.

In a later letter (XIV) Mordaunt, like Byron, satirizes[78] romantic descriptions of nature:

Do you insist on a description of the country around Badagòs? I can assure you that it has as strong a resemblance to many other countries you have seen, or of which you have read descriptions, as the foregoing cathedral has to other cathedrals. For example: "the mountains, in general, are lofty and the valleys low: the meadows, particularly after rain, are verdant; not indeed so green as those of England, but still they must be allowed to be of a greenish colour: and most of the rivulets, to the best of my remembrance, flow with a kind of murmuring sound, and in a serpentine direction. . . ."

The similarities between Chateuabriand's *René* (first published apart from *Génie du Christianisme* in 1805) have been pointed out by several scholars but never considered in the light of the present examination. The Zeluco theme is treated at great length in it. Byron names Chateaubriand in *The Age of Bronze* (l. 714) and in his note refers to him with enthusiasm as the author of *Atala*. The two stories were published together in 1805, however, and *René* was always regarded by the author as the sequel to *Atala*. If Byron knew one he probably knew the other. It is probable too that he was familiar with *René* before 1822–23, when he was writing *The Age of Bronze*. Madame de Staël, whom Byron knew in London, was an extravagant admirer of *René*[79] and may well have mentioned the book to him, perhaps even pointing out the similarities between the autobiographical French character and Byron's own creations. But there is no reason to question Byron's knowledge of so famous a book, one which had gone through, in one form or another, nine French editions between 1802 and the end of 1805.

[78]*Ibid.,* I, 175.
[79]*René,* ed. Weil (Paris, 1935), p. lix and notes.

Chateaubriand[80] thought the parallels between his own hero and those of Byron so marked that he felt it necessary to establish his own priority. The silence of Byron, in view of his usual jealous regard for his own originality, may possibly owe something to the incest theme in *René*.

The story is actually the record of René's failure to make his peace with mankind, by reason of his retreating, in progressively greater degrees, into natural solitude. This record is contrasted with that of his sister, who, although she herself is the one who entertains the guilty passion, finds serenity at last in becoming a nun, and wisely advises her brother to leave his solitary retreat at once, "qui ne vous est pas bonne."[81] In his efforts to escape from himself and his *ennui* René first makes the Grand Tour, but profits from neither the scenes of nature nor the crumbling monuments of classic Greece and Rome, and returns home to find himself more alone in the world than ever. He then decides[82] to retire "dans un faubourg pour y vivre totalement ignoré." But this life also palls upon him, and he moves on to a life of absolute natural solitude. Here the spectacle of nature has so little good effect upon his malady that he drives himself to the point of suicide, a fate from which he is saved only by the arrival of his sister. She is[83] "la seule personne au monde" whom he has ever loved; all his "sentiments se venoient confondre en elle, avec la douceur des souvenirs" of his childhood, and he receives her "dans une sorte d'extase de cœur." But when she leaves him to become a nun, he departs for the wilds of Mississippi, lives there even in the depths of the forest an existence melancholy and misanthropic, and dies without ever finding happiness.

[80]*Ibid.*, pp. lx–lxi.
[81]*Ibid.*, p. 55.
[82]*Ibid.*, p. 37.
[83]*Ibid.*, p. 50.

That the beauties of nature are lost upon René is quite clear. For a time, absolute solitude and the spectacle of nature plunged him into a state of ecstacy impossible to describe. But shortly the realization[84] came that,

"Hélas! jétois seul, seul sur la terre! Une langueur secrète s'emparoit de mon corps. Ce dégoût de la vie que j'avois ressenti dès mon enfance, revenoit avec une force nouvelle. Bientôt mon cœur ne fournit plus d'aliment à ma pensée, et je ne m'apercevois de mon existence que par un profond sentiment d'ennui. . . .

"Tout m'échappoit à la fois, l'amitié, le monde, la retraite. J'avois essayé de tout, et tout m'avoit été fatal. Repoussé par la société, abandonné d'Amélie, quand la solitude vint à me manquer, que me restoit-il? C'étoit la dernière planche sur laquelle j'avois espéré me sauver, et je la sentois encore s'enfoncer dans l'abîme!"

Chateaubriand's preface, like that to *Childe Harold,* maintains that the purpose of the story is a moral one, and links René with Werther and with Rousseau,

qui introduisit le premier parmi nous ces rêveries si désastreuses et si coupables. En s'isolant des hommes, en s'abandonnant à ses songes, il a fait croire à une foule de jeunes gens, qu'il est beau de se jeter ainsi dans le vague de la vie. Le roman de *Werther* a développé depuis ce germe de poison. L'auteur du *Génie du Christianisme,* obligé de faire entrer dans le cadre de son apologie quelques tableaux pour l'imagination, a voulu dénoncer cette espèce de vice nouveau, et peindre les funestes conséquences de l'amour outré de la solitude. . . . Il ne faut pas perdre de vue qu'Amélie meurt heureuse et guérie, et que René finit misérablement. Ainsi, le vrai coupable est puni, tandis que sa trop foible victime, remettant son âme blessée entre les mains de *celui qui retourne le malade sur sa couche,* sent renaître une joie ineffable du fond même des tristesses de son cœur. Au reste, le dis-

[84]*Ibid.,* pp. 47–49.

164   BYRON: THE RECORD OF A QUEST

cours du père Souël ne laisse aucun doute sur le but et les moralités religieuses de l'histoire de René.

Father Souël,[85] at the end of René's account, sees not a man to be pitied, but one who has been justly punished,

entêté de chimères, à qui tout déplaît, et qui s'est soustrait aux charges de la société pour se livrer à d'inutiles rêveries. . . . Que faites-vous seul au fond des forêts où vous consumez vos jours, négligeant tous vos devoirs? Des saints, me direz-vous, se sont ensevelis dans les déserts? Ils y étoient avec leurs larmes, et employoient à éteindre leurs passions le temps que vous perdez peut-être à allumer les vôtres. Jeune présomptueux qui avez cru que l'homme se peut suffire à lui-même! La solitude est mauvaise à celui qui n'y vit pas avec Dieu; elle redouble les puissances de l'âme, en même temps qu'elle leur ôte tout sujet pour s'exercer. Quiconque a reçu des forces, doit les consacrer au service de ses semblables; s'il les laisse inutiles, il en est d'abord puni par une secrète misère, et tôt ou tard le ciel lui envoie un châtiment effroyable.

The Zeluco theme is illustrated clearly by two passages[86] in Charlotte Dacre's Zofloya, or The Moor (1806). Victoria has just arrived at the inevitable Gothic castle. She is planning the murder of her husband in order that she may marry his younger brother.

"Here, then," said Victoria, as on the morning after her arrival she gazed from her chamber window upon the beautifully terrific scenery, and the immeasurable waste of endless solitude which composed it—"Here, then, without danger,

[85]Ibid., pp. 77–78.
[86]Zofloya (London, n.d.), ch. 22, p. 160, and ch. 27, p. 196. Montague Summers writes in his introduction (p. xxvi), "With the exception of the great Mrs. Radcliffe and Monk Lewis it is possibly little exaggeration to say that during her hour of success there was no more popular writer of this school than Charlotte Dacre." Zofloya is a source of Shelley's two Gothic romances. Byron refers to Charlotte Dacre in English Bards, ll. 755–758, 927. In his note to the first passage he refers to her "sundry novels in the style of the first edition of The Monk." See also L. and J., III, 68 and note 2; 69, note 2.

may I pursue the path leading to the summit of my wishes; no prying eye can pierce through, here, the secret movements which, to compass my soul's desire, may be requisite. Hail to them, since they perhaps may first witness the rich harvest of my persevering love; and for such a love, perish—perish, al! that may oppose it!''

While thus she continued, her eyes indeed wandering wildly over the world of mountains, but her thoughts far, far beyond them, she was roused by the mild voice of Berenza, who gently seizing her arm, smilingly inquired the subject of her reverie.

A faint blush suffused the guilt-bronzed cheek of Victoria, as in a low voice she merely replied, "I was contemplating the grandeur of the surrounding scenery, my Lord."

. . . .

The stars had all retired, as though shrinking abashed from the view of so much guilt, but louring clouds obscured the face of heaven, the wind sighed hollow among the trees of the forest, and though the lonely solemn grandeur of the scene would have inspired in the breast of virtue deep awe and devotion, directing the soul to inward contemplation, yet was it sad and unwelcome to the evil mind [of Victoria], which bearing within itself an eternal night, feels troubled and appalled in the gloom of nature.

The Zeluco theme is present also in three of Maturin's early novels and in Shelley's two romances. They require, for the most part, very little commentary. Byron had read Maturin's plays *Bertram* and *Manuel*,[87] wrote a highly enthusiastic letter[88] about the former to Maturin, and was instrumental in having it produced at Drury Lane. His plan to divide part of the price paid for *The Siege of Corinth* and *Parisina* between Coleridge and Maturin has already been noted. In 1817 he described Maturin as a "clever man" who "has talent,"

[87]L. and J., IV, 134–136.
[88]*The Correspondence of Sir Walter Scott and Charles Robert Maturin,* ed. Ratchford and McCarthy (Austin, 1939), p. 40.

and in 1821 referred to Maturin's "novels" in a manner indicative of familiarity with them.[89]

In *Fatal Revenge; or, the Family of Montorio* (1807),
Ippolito, at that point in the story where the following passage[90] occurs, has been driven by the malign and seemingly
supernatural influence of Schemoli the monk to believe that
fate has predestined him to commit a murder, and so tries to
escape his self-tormenting thoughts by plunging into a life of
gaming and dissipation. He is finally to murder the man
he thinks to be his father.

Ippolito leant against the casement; it looked into the garden
of the palace: the breeze that breathed over groves of rose and
orange played on his cheek: the setting sun sent his beams
through the twinkling foliage; they tinged with ruddy amber,
they fleckered the waters of a fountain that gurgled among
them, and whose bason, where the waters, that played in
silver showers in the centre, lay still and deep, gave back a
bright and lovely blue of the heavens, without a spot, and
without a shade. Ippolito remained silent long; at length—
"I behold all this," said he, "joyless and unmoved; the
burthen that sits so heavy on my soul has oppressed my senses
too. Or is it that I am already become a disastrous, discordant
atom, amid these elements of harmony and love? And am I
already at war with nature? Oh, how dreadful to be an alien
from our own system and species! not to be able to drink the
evening breeze, or glow with the setting beams of the sun;
not even to know the pleasure those insects are tasting in his
rays; to wish in vain for the quiet life of the fountain that
flows, of the leaf that falls.

[89]L. and J., IV, 134, 136; V, 493.
[90]*Fatal Revenge; or, the Family of Montorio* (London, 1840), ch. 11,
p. 43.

The following passage[91] is from *The Wild Irish Boy* (1808). The speaker is Bethel, "an avowed libertine, a scoffer at religion, and a voluptuary in habit," who "shrunk from the names of sensibility, affection, or worth":

"You pretended a few minutes ago to dislike the wine I pressed you to take: and now you pretend to luxuriate in what you call 'the rich and weeping softness of a watery landscape.' This is all nonsense and self-imposture. Champaigne (when it is good, I mean) has always the same power of stimulating the spirits, though trees and water have not, for they have lost their power of stimulating mine long ago. And it is to be hoped when you come to my years, that is, I mean to my—pshaw!—experience—you will look upon nature with the same disgust that I do."

Wandesford is the villain in *The Milesian Chief* (1812):[92] he is "cold, selfish, unprincipled, and unfeeling," and has already seduced and deserted a beautiful Irish girl.

The following evening Armida and Rosine wandered out on the rocks; Wandesford soon followed them, and Armida, though she saw his approach with reluctance, tried to conceal it, and pointed out some of the striking and original scenery around, perhaps to draw his attention from herself. Wandesford could not help allowing its wild, Salvator beauty, but he spoke the cold, technical language of a man whose claims to taste were derived only from his having been abroad. Armida in vain tried to communicate to him some of the enthusiasm, the dulcia vitia of her mind.

[91]*The Wild Irish Boy* (London, 1808), vol. I, ch. 4, pp. 162–63. Later (vol. III, pp. 14–15) it is observed by Lady Montrevor, who has run through most of the vices, that "He that sacrifices the night to intemperance, will not, cannot in the morning have an eye for nature, or an head for study. The breath of heaven will not smell wooingly to the feverish wretch. . . . .

"This I have experienced myself; so has your father."

[92]*The Milesian Chief* (London, 1812) was published early enough in the year for Byron to have seen it before writing the "Addition to the Preface" of *Childe Harold*. The quotation is from vol. I, ch. 6, pp. 122–23.

Shelley's two imitative romances, *Zastrozzi* (1810) and *St. Irvyne* (1811), also express the Zeluco theme: only those who are free of despair, have a good conscience, and lead a pure life may enjoy the delights of nature. The following quotation[93] from *Zastrozzi* follows a picturesque description of a night scene in a forest: "A scene so fair—a scene so congenial to those who can reflect upon their past lives with pleasure, and anticipate the future with the enthusiasm of innocence, ill accorded with the ferocious soul of Zastrozzi, which at one time agitated by revenge, at another by agonizing remorse, or contending passions, could derive no pleasure from the past— anticipate no happiness in futurity."

Even the mere presence of evil seems to prevent the beneficent influences of nature from having their effect. The hero has allowed himself[94] to remain unresistingly for some time under the roof of the wicked Matilda, although he is fully aware of her designs upon him.

He was sensible of a total distaste of former objects—objects which, perhaps, had formerly forcibly interested him. The terrific grandeur of the Alps, the dashing cataract, as it foamed beneath their feet, ceased to excite those feelings of awe which formerly they were wont to inspire. The lofty pine-groves inspired no additional melancholy, nor did the blooming valleys of Piedmont, or the odoriferous orangeries which scented the air, gladden his deadened soul.

As for Matilda herself, we know[95] long before she stabs the pure Julia that she is a complete villain and a lost soul: "the beauties of nature which surrounded the castella had no . . . power to interest" her.

The kinship of the mind of Shelley at this time with that of Byron is indicated in *St. Irvyne* in another way. In poems

---

[93]Shelley, *op. cit.*, V, 20.
[94]*Ibid.*, V, 54–55.
[95]*Ibid.*, V, 63.

inserted in the romance he twice incorporates lines from *Hours of Idleness,* without acknowledging them. But *St. Irvyne* also expresses the traditional attitude of the villain-hero toward nature. Wolfstein is a member of a band of Alpine banditti, and is shortly to poison his chief (who has saved his life) in order to have the girl Megalena for himself. The following passage from the opening chapter[96] comes immediately after a picturesque description of autumn in the Alps at the hour of twilight.

It was at this dark and silent hour, that Wolfstein, unheeding surrounding objects,—objects which might have touched with awe, or heightened to devotion, any other breast,—wandered alone—pensively he wandered—dark images for futurity possessed his soul: he shuddered when he reflected upon what had passed; nor was his present situation calculated to satisfy a mind eagerly panting for liberty and independence. Conscience too, awakened conscience, upbraided him for the life which he had selected, and, with silent whisperings, stung his soul to madness.

Or apropos of nothing in particular, Shelley indicates[97] that a failure to respond to the delights of nature is caused by the presence of ignoble passions and the demands of selfish appetite.

Lives there, whose soul experiences no degree of delight, is susceptible of no gradations of feelings, at change of scenery? Lives there, who can listen to the cadence of the evening zephyr, and not acknowledge, in his mind, the sensations of celestial melancholy which it awakens? for, if he does, his life were valueless, his death were undeplored. Ambition, avarice, ten thousand mean, ignoble passions, had extinguished within him that soft, but indefinable sensorium of unallayed delight, with which his soul, whose susceptibility is not destroyed by the demands of selfish appetite, thrills exclusively,

96*Ibid.,* V, 114–115.
97*Ibid.,* V, 195–196.

and wants but the union of another, of whom the feelings are in unison with his own, to constitute almost insupportable delight.

The last novel which need be included here is Mary Shelley's *Frankenstein,* which is of particular interest because of the very good possibility that it may have evoked Byron's despairing cry of the Swiss Journal and the parallel passages in *Manfred.* The story of how the idea of *Frankenstein* was born at Byron's suggestion and nourished by a conversation between him and Shelley on "the nature of the principle of life" is told in Mary's preface and is well known. Byron himself had almost certainly seen the early version of it while still at Geneva. Upon its publication he described[98] it as "a wonderful work." It is certainly not impossible that, three months later, Byron remembered the cry of Frankenstein[99] when he was "seized by remorse and the sense of guilt, which hurried [him] away to a hell of intense tortures, such as no language can describe."

Thus not the tenderness of friendship, nor the beauty of earth, nor of heaven, could redeem my soul from woe: the very accents of love were ineffectual. I was encompassed by a cloud which no beneficial influence could penetrate. . . .
Sometimes I could cope with the sullen despair that overwhelmed me: but sometimes the whirlwind passions of my soul drove me to seek, by bodily exercise and by change of place, some relief from my intolerable sensations. It was during an access of this kind that I suddenly left my home, and bending my steps towards the near Alpine valleys, sought in the magnificence, the eternity of such scenes, to forget myself and my ephemeral, because human, sorrows. My wanderings were directed towards the valley of Chamounix. . . .
The immense mountains and precipices that overhung me on every side—the sound of the river raging among the rocks,

[98]L. and J., IV, 298.
[99]*Frankenstein* (New York, 1931), ch. 9, pp. 88–94.

and the dashing of the waterfalls around, spoke of a power mighty as Omnipotence—and I ceased to fear, or to bend before any being less almighty than that which had created and ruled the elements, here displayed in their most terrific guise. . . . Then again the kindly influence ceased to act— I found myself fettered again to grief, and indulging in all the misery of reflection. Then I spurred on my animal, striving so to forget the world, my fears, and, more than all, myself—or, in a more desperate fashion, I alighted, and threw myself on the grass, weighed down by horror and despair.

Frankenstein exhibits the same reactions to nature[100] when he is engaged in the guilty pursuit of forbidden knowledge, at that time when he is creating the monster, and again when he is on his way to consult with English scientists who have information useful in creating the monster's mate: "The summer months passed. . . . It was a most beautiful season; never did the fields bestow a more plentiful harvest, or the vines yield a more luxuriant vintage: but my eyes were insensible to the charms of nature." But after the monster has been completed and Frankenstein joined at the university by his old friend, then ". . . Clerval called forth the better feelings of my heart; he again taught me to love the aspect of nature, and the cheerful faces of children." However, once Frankenstein agrees to create a mate for the monster, he again loses the power to love the innocent face of nature:

Filled with dreary imaginations, I passed through many beautiful and majestic scenes; but my eyes were fixed and unobserving. I could only think of the bourn of my travels, and the work which was to occupy me whilst they endured.

After some days spent in listless indolence, during which I traversed many leagues, I arrived at Strasburgh, where I waited two days for Clerval. He came. Alas! how great was the contrast between us! He was alive to every new scene; joyful when he saw the beauties of the setting sun, and more

[100]*Ibid.*, ch. 4, p. 47; ch. 6, p. 65; ch. 18, p. 162.

happy when he beheld it rise, and recommence a new day. He pointed out to me the shifting colors of the landscape, and the appearances of the sky. "This is what it is to live," he cried, "now I enjoy existence! But you, my dear Frankenstein, wherefore are you desponding and sorrowful!" In truth, I was occupied by gloomy thoughts, and neither saw the descent of the evening star, nor the golden sunrise reflected in the Rhine.—And you, my friend, would be far more amused with the journal of Clerval, who observed the scenery with an eye of feeling and delight, than in listening to my reflections. I, a miserable wretch, haunted by a curse that shut up every avenue to enjoyment.

Even the monster follows the Zeluco pattern. Created benevolent and virtuous, and nourished upon Plutarch's *Lives, Paradise Lost,* and *Werther,* he[101] first takes great pleasure in the beauties of nature: his "spirits were elevated by the enchanting appearance of nature." But once turned misanthrope and villain after he has been beaten and repulsed by men whose love and affection he sought, nature no longer has the power to soothe or please him:[102]

Oh! what a miserable night I passed! the cold stars shone in mockery, and the bare trees waved their branches above me: now and then the sweet voice of a bird burst forth amidst the universal stillness. All, save I, were at rest or in enjoyment: I, like the arch-fiend, bore a hell within me. . . . My daily vows rose for revenge—a deep and deadly revenge such as would alone compensate for the outrages and anguish I had endured.

After some weeks my wound healed, and I continued my journey. The labors I endured were no longer to be alleviated by the bright sun or gentle breezes of spring; all joy was but a mockery, which insulted my desolate state, and made me feel

[101]*Ibid.,* ch. 12, p. 117. See also ch. 13, pp. 118, 120–21, and ch. 15, pp. 135–36.

[102]*Ibid.,* ch. 16, pp. 141, 147–148.

more painfully that I was not made for the enjoyment of pleasure. . . .

I was . . . far too unhappy to enjoy the gentle breezes of evening, or the prospect of the sun setting behind the stupendous mountains of Jura.

Such, then, is the tradition which provided the terms and the pattern of reaction for Byron's feelings of guilt and "misanthropy." It is one of the clearest cases of all, perhaps, of life mirroring literature. One is reminded of the romantic young men and women of the 1920's who believed that they were a lost generation living in a waste land, yet would not have suspected either, probably, if Gertrude Stein and T. S. Eliot had not told them so.

The existence of this tradition also helps to clarify the true implications of Wordsworth's insistent charges of plagiarism[103] —implications quite important for an understanding of Byron, for here Wordsworth revealed a clear insight into Byron's poetry and his personality. The charges center upon the third canto of *Childe Harold,* which represents the period of Byron's most enthusiastic utterances upon nature. Their most important corollary is the implication that Byron's poetry was not the expression of direct and genuine personal experience.

The accusation exists in four forms, some of which have been referred to already. Moore recorded in his diary for October 27, 1820, that Wordsworth had said to him, "The feeling of natural objects which is there expressed [in *Childe Harold,* III] not caught by B[yron] from nature herself, but from him (Wordsworth)." Wordsworth wrote in a letter to Henry Taylor (December 26, 1823) that the "tone . . . of enthusiastic admiration of Nature, and a sensibility to her influences" was one *"assumed* rather than natural" with Byron. To George Ticknor,[104] Wordsworth seemed in early

---

[103]See my section on the picturesque.
[104]*Life, Letters and Journals of George Ticknor,* I, 288.

1819 to feel some "bitterness against him [Byron] for having taken something of his own *lakish* manner lately, and, what is worse, borrowed some of his thoughts." Ticknor added that although Wordsworth admired Byron's talent, he had a "deep-rooted abhorrence of his character." This then is the key to Wordsworth's bitterness. He saw the younger poet assuming a point of view, which he had linked to virtue and made his own, and associating it with a villain-hero, who was also Byron himself.[105] This becomes quite clear from Wordsworth's sonnet on Byron, "Not in the Lucid Intervals of Life," written in 1834. There he again declared that "words, which practiced talent readily affords," do not prove that Nature has actually "touched responsive chords"; for Nature's "gentle beauty [has] power to move" only the innocent. They only are capable of taking to themselves her blessed quiet. Wordsworth was this time right, and his analysis of Byron exposes the fallacy of the Romantic position: for the individual receives from nature only what he brings within him. Byron finally began to realize this, and the realization, imperfect though it may have been, seems enough in itself to explain his greatly decreased interest, during the last three or four years of his life, in the whole idea of a nature benevolent; his failure ever to construct an original or significant creed based upon a vital correspondence between man and the beneficial influences of nature; and the ease and speed with which he threw off the "Wordsworth" manner in late 1816. Byron's *mobilité*, his remarkable chameleon-like ability to assume at once the color of his environment, which explains the presence of the Wordsworthian note (and thus explains a large part of the enthusiasm for nature which Byron expressed in his poetry)—this same quality, then, is also an important source of his failure to discover any deeply satisfying emotional or

[105]It is of no importance here that Wordsworth failed to see the important influence of Rousseau upon all of Byron's poetry of the summer of 1816.

spiritual experience in his communions with nature. The beauties of nature are lost upon such guilty souls as Zeluco, Childe Harold—and Byron. The summer and fall of 1816 represent the turning point in Byron's quest for peace amid the beauties of nature; henceforth the action will follow a descending movement, and the music play in a lower key. Byron was to expect less and less from nature.

4

After Switzerland

The poetry of Byron's exile written in 1816 before his departure from Switzerland had expressed two fundamentally conflicting attitudes toward nature: the high devotion of the Wordsworthian-Rousseauistic note, and the anguished cry of the Zeluco theme. Paralleling these attitudes were two conflicting ideas: the pantheistic notion that love is the great and all-pervading principle of the universe, and the dark suspicion that hate may be the first ruling principle. The various expressions of all these ideas and attitudes were highly charged with the poet's personal feelings, a fact obviously linked with the recent events of Byron's private life. But a great change came over Byron immediately after he left Switzerland: the Zeluco theme and the Wordsworthian note alike disappeared from his poetry, and the emotional tone of the nature passages is at once a quieter one. In short, with the country of Rousseau left behind and Shelley departed for England, there is no longer present any stimulus to urge him toward poetic pantheism; and with his feelings of guilt and remorse temporarily quieted (with the help of Hobhouse and Marianna Segati), the Zeluco theme absents itself. Before the end of the year he was to describe himself as a contented man.

The extremely rapid transformation which Byron had undergone is signalized by the concept and treatment of nature in the third act of *Manfred*. The original form of the act, as Byron admitted, was "damnably bad," and he rewrote it, finishing it at Rome on May 5, 1817. The fact of significance here, however, is not so much its success or failure, as it is the great difference in tone and setting between it and the first two acts. An obvious point of comparison is that nearly all the action takes place within doors. The Swiss Journal to Augusta, so very fruitful in the genesis of the first two acts, both in idea and phrasing, offers not a single parallel to the third act. Lake Leman and the Alps are now at a distance, and with them the peculiar heightened sensitivity to nature which came with the stimulating presence of Shelley. As that poet had cast his shadow over *Childe Harold*, III, so the more down-to-earth Hobhouse had done the same with *Childe Harold*, IV—and it seems, with the last act of *Manfred* as well. At any rate, the hand of Shelley is no longer felt to be present. The Spirits of Nature make no appearance, and there are only two important nature passages in the entire act (III, ii, 180–200 and III, iiii, 261–301). Both passages reflect quite other attitudes toward nature than those present in the opening acts, which were written in Switzerland. The first, Manfred's address to the sun, shows a clear line of descent from James Thomson's "Hymn" to the seasons and is an expression of the Newtonian deism which Byron had put into verse in 1805 and 1806 in his two versions of "Ossian's Address to the Sun" and in "The Prayer of Nature." The sun has become for Manfred "Most glorious Orb," "representative of the Unknown," "chief Star! Centre of many stars," and "Sire of the seasons! Monarch of the climes."

In the second nature passage, that in the last scene of the play (ll. 263–67), Manfred is described on the evening of his death as lingering

> . . . yet with Nature, for the night
> Hath been to me a more familiar face
> Than that of man; and in her starry shade
> Of dim and solitary loveliness,
> I learn'd the language of another world.

This is certainly an innocent Nature, and one to be admired or even loved. The night, furthermore, reminds Manfred (ll. 272–97) of one seen in his youth, when he stood within the Colosseum:

> The trees which grew along the broken arches
> Waved dark in the blue midnight, and the stars
> Shone through the rents of ruin. . . .
> Some cypresses beyond the time-worn breach
> Appear'd to skirt the horizon, yet they stood
> Within a bowshot. . . .
> And thou didst shine, thou rolling moon, upon
> All this, and cast a wide and tender light,
> Which soften'd down the hoar austerity . . .
> Leaving that beautiful which still was so,
> And making that which was not. . . .

This is, of course, pictorial composition with the emphasis on the picturesque as it was understood by Byron. There is no hint of the Zeluco theme.

The explanation of this passage, insofar as it may be traced to the influence of individuals upon Byron, seems to lie, as has been suggested, in the waning influence of Shelley and in the ascendancy of the common-sensical Hobhouse, himself a master of the principles of picturesque composition in prose, as is to be seen from the quotation from his diary given in my introductory chapter. Byron had been with Hobhouse, under conditions favorable for calling forth his picturesque inclinations, from October 6, 1816, when the two left Diodati for Italy, until December 4, when Hobhouse left Byron at Venice for Rome, there to be rejoined by the poet

in late April, 1817. The picturesque treatment of the Colosseum scene, with its famous counterpart in *Childe Harold,*
IV, was the product of course of this trip to Rome.

The other nature passage in the third act of *Manfred,* the
deistic address to the sun, was present in the original draft
and written in Venice before March 9, 1817. At this time
Byron was not only free of the stimulating yet disturbing
presence of Shelley but also had so far suppressed his tormenting memories of Augusta as to be able to consider himself happy and contented in his life with Marianna Segati,
the young wife of a draper in whose house Byron lived for
a time. Claire, too, good "Rousseau man"[106] that she was
("all is love in the universe," she had written, "the silver
showers of the fountain, the quiet life of the leaves, the
flowery path in May, even the deep night of Heaven"),
even Claire had been satisfactorily disposed of, at least for the
time. Add to this that as early as Byron's month in Milan in

[106]From the memoranda Claire kept with her journals. Quoted by
R. G. Grylls, *Claire Clairmont* (London, 1939), p. 257. Claire blended
perfectly with the Rousseauistic-Wordsworthian-Shelleyean mood of the
summer of 1816. Her journals are full of an enthusiasm for the life close
to nature. She records August 17, 1814, in her Journal that she read
As You Like It and "found the wild and romantic touches of this play
very accordant with the scene before me and my feelings. It was indeed
a lovely Evening. How much is lost by those who pass their lives in
cities. They are never visited by those sweet feelings which to recollect
alone is Heaven—It is fortunate for them that they imagine themselves
happy—how boundless and terrific would be their surprise if they could
suddenly become philosophers and view things in their true and beautiful
point of view. We sleep all night by the Kitchen fire—Shelley much
disturbed by the creaking door, the screams of a poor smothered child,
and the *fille* who washes the dishes" (Grylls, *op. cit.,* p. 27). But she
later proved impossible. Claire, however, like Byron, was to realize that
one took from nature only what one brought. After the death of Allegra
she wrote to Mrs. Mason, ". . . I tried the whole journey to follow your
advice and admire the scenery—dearest Lady it was all in vain—I saw
not mountains or valleys, woods or rushing streams, Mrs. K. admired them,
so I suppose they were there—I only saw my lost darling . . ." (*ibid.,*
p. 165).

late 1816, before he moved on to Venice, he was for "at least a third part of the day . . . a dandy," capable in his moments of dandyism of pronouncing "the name of Brummel with a mingled emotion of respect and jealousy,"[107] and it becomes clear how far and how fast Byron had moved away from his prevailing moods in Switzerland. This new-found contentment and his rejection of the part of the inspired, half-maddened poet and metaphysician go far to explain the conventional form of Manfred's address to the sun, half-recollected from Byron's earlier poems or from any number of deistic rhapsodies of the eighteenth century.

The quite remarkable rapidity with which Byron was able to shake off the influence of Shelley and Wordsworth is to be explained negatively by the simple fact of Shelley's absence: there was no longer a pantheist around for Byron's *mobilité* to mirror. But the positive element in the explanation, one feels, is to be sought in Byron's sense of hard fact and actuality, which operated throughout his life against mysticism and "enthusiasm" of all kinds, whether in the form of a fusion of self with external nature or some other. It functioned as a check upon him even during his most "romantic" moments. Thus in *Childe Harold*, III, 6–7, immediately following such enthusiastic lines as,

> Soul of my thought! with whom I traverse earth,
> Invisible but gazing, as I glow
> Mix'd with thy spirit, blended with thy birth,

he pulls himself up short with the remark,

> Yet must I think less wildly:—I *have* thought
> Too long and darkly. . . .

[107]M. H. Beyle, "Lord Byron in Italy," *The Mirror of Literature, Amusement, and Instruction*, XV, 267–68.

In the stanza following the famous seventy-fifth of the third canto ("Are not the mountains, waves, and skies, a part of me . . ."), he recalls himself in a similar fashion:

> But this is not my theme; and I return
> To that which is immediate. . . .

Or in the opening stanzas of *Childe Harold,* IV, speaking of the "beings of the mind" (stanzas six and seven), his conclusion is,

> Yet there are things whose strong reality
> Outshines our fairy-land. . . .
>   . . . for waking Reason deems
> Such over-weening phantasies unsound,
> And other voices speak and other sights surround.

It was this strong sense of fact and actuality in Byron, it may be repeated, which made possible not only the slight duration of the influence of Wordsworth, Shelley, and Rousseau, chiefly operative in the realm of his nature poetry, but also his adverse judgments of the poetry he wrote when under their influence. An associated quality—Byron's strong affinity with the mundane—explains his expressed sense of general well-being immediately following his becoming settled in Venice late in 1816, the very *annus mirabilis* of Shelley's influence. On November 27, 1816, we find him making one of his extremely rare statements that he is happy and contented. The ingredients of that state of mind are instructive in forming an estimate of Byron's needs. He writes,[108]

If I could but remain as I now am, I should not merely be happy, but *contented,* which in my mind is the strangest, and most difficult attainment of the two. . . . I have books—a decent establishment—a fine country—a language which I prefer—most of the amusements and conveniences of life—

[108]*Correspondence,* II, 23–24.

as much of society as I choose to take—and a handsome woman. . . .

Nor was this state of mind, for Byron, a short one. On December 17, he writes[109] that he has been "feeling so much more tranquil, and contented in my present situation. . . . I believe I told you in my last, that I had fallen in love [with Marianna Segati], so that the last month has been one of the pleasantest, and withal the *quietest,* in my recollection." The last time that Byron had written in this vein was from the estate of Lady Oxford at Eywood. In Switzerland, however, he recalls[110] that during the writing of *Childe Harold,* III, from early May until June 27, 1816, "I was half mad . . . between metaphysics, mountains, lakes, love unextinguishable, thoughts unutterable, and the nightmare of my own delinquencies." It is thus not surprising to find him writing of *Manfred,* the first two acts of which were written before he left Switzerland, that it is "a drama as mad as Nat. Lee's Bedlam tragedy,"[111] "a sort of mad drama . . . a Bedlam tragedy," written "for the sake of introducing the Alpine scenery,"[112] or that "I have no great opinion of this piece of phantasy."[113] Quite in this same vein and stemming much from the same common-sensical attitude are his remarks upon the differences between the third and fourth cantos of *Childe Harold.* In comparison with the third, it "treats more of works of art than of Nature."[114] "There are no metaphysics in it. . . ."[115] It is "not a continuation of the Third. I have

[109]*Ibid.,* II, 25.
[110]L. and J., IV, 49.
[111]L. and J., IV, 65–66.
[112]L. and J., IV, 80.
[113]L. and J., IV, 55.
[114]L. and J., IV, 153.
[115]L. and J., IV, 155.

parted company with Shelley and Wordsworth. Subject-matter
and treatment are alike new."[116]

The particular kind of enthusiastic regard for nature which
Byron lost when he parted company with the "metaphysics" of
Shelley and Wordsworth, he never exhibited again. Like
Coleridge, who had come to realize that

> . . . we receive but what we give,
> And in our life alone does Nature live,

Byron had proved[117] on his very pulses the fallacy of the Romantic position:

> No more—no more—Oh! never more on me
> The freshness of the heart can fall like dew,
> Which out of all the lovely things we see
> Extracts emotions beautiful and new,
> Hived in our bosoms like the bag o' the bee:
> Think'st thou the honey with those objects grew?
> Alas! 't was not in them, but in thy power
> To double even the sweetness of a flower.

But unlike the other "Werther-faced men," Byron had moved
cn not to despair, but to the mood of Beppo and Don Juan,[118]
in which

> . . . the sad truth which hovers o'er my desk
> Turns what was once romantic to burlesque.

What he referred to contemptuously in 1821 as "this 'Babble
of green fields' and of bare Nature in general"[119] had ceased,
long before that year, to engage his attention and interest in
the degree that it had in 1816. He decided that the Great

[116]Poetry, II, 311.
[117]Don Juan, I, 214.
[118]Ibid., IV, 3.
[119]L. and J., V, 549. Reviewing two of Maria Edgeworth's novels in
the British Review for February, 1818, C. R. Maturin attributed a similar
satiric application of Shakespeare's phrase to Dr. Johnson, although I
have not been able to trace it: Johnson, according to Maturin, referred to
"the pastoral prosers who 'babble of green fields.' "

Whole was, after all, nothing more than "inanimate nature, unless we adopt the System of Spinosa, that the World is the deity."[120]

Even an inanimate nature, though, has its uses, and one feels Byron most sincere, during the last three highly productive years of his life, when he is viewing the world of nature as a simple and a temporary means of escape from the cares or exhaustions of life. Thus he writes to Isaac Disraeli[121] after referring to the attacks upon him made recently by "the Church, the Chancellor, and all men" that "as long as I retain my feeling and my passion for Nature, I can partly soften or subdue my other passions and resist or endure those of others." He was writing on his balcony overlooking "the islands of Elba and Corsica . . . and my old friend the Mediterranean rolling blue at my feet," and expressed himself, one feels, with a degree of exaggeration no greater than is pardonable. He records a similar soothing effect[122] in a journal he kept in Cephalonia, explaining that after discontinuing it for six weeks he begins it anew, he knows not why, "except that, standing at the window of my apartment in this beautiful village, the calm though cool serenity of a beautiful and transparent Moonlight, showing the Islands, the Mountains, the Sea, with a distant outline of the Morea traced between the double Azure of the waves and skies, has quieted me enough to be able to write." The ninth canto of *Don Juan* is closed with the lines,

> . . . I feel my brain turn round,
> And all my fancies whirling like a mill;

[120]L. and J., V, 547–48.

[121]L. and J., VI, 89.

[122]L. and J., VI, 249. See also *Marino Faliero*, IV, i, 1–111; *Heaven and Earth*, ii, 163, 204; and *Sardanapalus*, V, i, 19, 29–32. Trelawny, *Recollections*, pp. 139–40, and Gamba, *Narrative*, pp. 25–26, record similar instances.

Which is a signal to my nerves and brain,
To take a quiet ride in some green lane.

This certainly is no very high ideal. It seems rather certain, however, that Byron, "admirer of Nature" though he professed himself to be, never actually gained much more than this, if even this always.

The attitude is merely a refinement of a much older one (minus the early heroics) which also derived from the need of Byron's nervous, high-strung temperament to seek a refuge and an escape from the exhausting world of mankind. It was characteristic of him from the first[123] to reason that he or his hero was unfit to herd with man because society is "bad." Thus tainted or thus wounded by society he early sought in the non-human a cure for ills and hurts that were as intimately related to the human as cause and effect. And to the extent that he tried to feed a need for the human with the extra-human he failed, and so eventually put away his Rousseau and his Wordsworth in favor of his own comic muse.

[123]See Byron's "Reply to Blackwood's *Edinburgh Magazine*," L. and J., IV, 479, for a classic expression of this theme in prose. See also *Childe Harold*, III, 12–14; cf. *Manfred*, II, ii, 144–173; *Childe Harold*, III, 15–16, 52, 68–71, 85, 113–114; IV, 32–3, 96, 176–178.

Chapter VI

BYRON AS A PHILOSOPHER OF NATURE

1

The Character of Byron's Deism

Apart from the opinions related to the period of Shelley's and Wordsworth's influence, Byron's "philosophical" views upon nature, the universe, and the relation of Deity to the natural world have not thus far been treated at any length. These views shall be the concern of the present chapter.

Among the more enthusiastic poets of nature during the eighteenth and early nineteenth centuries, it was customary to assume that the order of the universe was purposive, harmonious, and generally benevolent toward man—all these because it was so planned by a good and intelligent Deity. The general concept of nature—there are obvious exceptions, of course—was substantially a compound of the scientific idea of regular and universal laws, and the religious idea of the benevolence and concern of the Deity. Byron was able to accept the scientific basis of this assumption, and did, without undue questionings. He was quite aware, from the time of his youth, of the "myriads of . . . worlds—stars—systems,"[1] and may well have viewed them before 1816 through the

[1] L. and J., III, 408. Marjarum would make Byron's early years (before 1816) the chief period of his deism and the years 1821–1824 a period dominated by Byron's interest in contemporary scientific thought. There seems to be overwhelming evidence, however, that Byron's interest in traditional deism was strongest during the last three years of his life. Marjarum is not concerned with Byron's keen awareness of a nature indifferent or harmful to man, or with the effects of this knowledge upon Byron's deistic assumptions.

same Herschel's telescope which his friend Hobhouse used.[2] Thus he early sang of "suns, which systems now control"[3] and is everywhere generous with astronomical allusions of a general and scientific kind. But Byron's half belief and fear that he somehow bore the curse of Cain, his questionings of a benevolent providence, the general Hebraic tint of his conception of God, indeed, the whole of his life's many-sided rebellion—all these hindered him from giving his whole and unqualified faith to the idea of a universe characterized by any generous amount of benevolence toward man. He is but an atom amid the "myriads . . . of worlds—stars—systems." The solar system itself might be extinguished at any time in "crashing chaos." Attitudes and speculations of this kind, slight as they were before 1816, were to bear splendid and awful fruit in later years.

The prevailing concept of a benevolent nature was, furthermore, most often held by writers, from Shaftesbury to Shelley, who were not orthodox Christians. There can be detected in the cloudy, anguished strains of Byron's thought, however, two persistent elements which worked against such a concept: these were the effects of his early Calvinistic rearing and the tendencies which were later to lead him in the direction of Catholicism. All his life long he proclaimed his "orthodoxy," usually meaning that he believed in a personal God;

[2]In 1821 Byron recalled using Herschel's telescope. It is impossible to establish the date. See Hobhouse, *Recollections*, I, 42–3, for a series of reflections upon man's insignificance in the universe, growing out of his use of this telescope, that Byron himself might have written—all except the amusingly common-sensical and Hobhousian conclusion, that Byron would never have hit upon when in the midst of such a train of thought.

[3]"To M—," l. 27. Indicative of his general distrust of the purposes of providence at this period (1805–06) are his references to "crashing chaos" ("Translation from Horace") and the extinction of the solar system ("Ossian's Address to the Sun," "A Version of Ossian's Address to the Sun").

"the worst of it is, I *do* believe," he said to his wife, and it was often or usually a belief in a God who was "an Avenger, not a Father."[4] These ideas, of course, operated against rather than favored a concept of God as a divine "principle" of love immanent in the universe. For Byron, God is everywhere and repeatedly the Creator, and separate from his works.[5] And so in none of the deliberately phrased pronouncements which he made before 1816 did he ever depart very far from the concept of God as a person who created the world by his fiat and who continues to direct it. Insofar as he did consciously theorize upon the nature of nature he was generally with the deists of the previous century. Thus[6] we find him writing in 1807, for what small comfort it gave him, "I have lived a *Deist*," and in 1811 that,[7]

As to miracles, I agree with Hume that it is more probable men should *lie* or be *deceived,* than that things out of the course of Nature should so happen. . . . I do not believe in any revealed religion . . . I throw myself on the mercy of the *'Great First Cause, least understood,'* . . . God would have made His will known without books . . . had it been His pleasure to ratify any peculiar mode of worship.

This general train of thought, itself the product of a developed literary and philosophical tradition which, given a different cast, produced Wordsworth's line[8] "Thou dost pre-

[4]L. and J., VI, 262, note.

[5]See L. and J., II, 29, 351; III, 403. The sole evidence in the prose of these years, that he was overcoming his Calvinistic-generated distinctions between matter and spirit is his statement, "I am where I was, verging towards Spinoza; and yet it is a gloomy Creed, and I want a better (L. and J., II, 72–3).

[6]L. and J., II, 19, note.

[7]L. and J., II, 35–6. The entire letter constitutes an admirable epitome of almost all the diversified views held at one time or another by the Englishmen who are lumped together usually under the name deists. Most of these are outside the immediate scope of this study.

[8]Wordsworth, "Ode to Duty."

serve the stars from wrong" and in another place[9] enabled
him to refer to "Nature's elemental strife," also produced
Byron's earlier lines in his "Prayer of Nature" (1806),

> Thou who canst guide the wandering star
> Through trackless realms of æther's space;
> Who calm'st the elemental war,
> Whose hand from pole to pole I trace,

and nurtured in him the idea, which he would have been happier without, that is expressed in the lines,

> Father! no prophet's laws I seek,—
> *Thy* laws in Nature's works appear.

And because this is so, God is best worshipped not in "Gothic
domes of mouldering stone" but among his own works, in
"the face of day."

These sentiments, it is hardly necessary to say, are the
commonplaces of an earlier and surviving deism. The poem
is certainly related to Pope's "Universal Prayer," even though
it does not appear to be taken directly from it, as sometimes
has been maintained.[10] We may wonder what the view
expressed in "The Prayer of Nature" and in the prose passages cited actually meant to Byron. Obviously, such thoughts
gave small comfort to him, nor are they at all frequent in his
writings or recorded conversation of his earlier years. In the
places where a record of Byron's "philosophy of nature"
might be expected to appear, there is none. Moore considers

---

[9]Wordsworth, "Composed by the Seashore." Cf. Pope's *Essay on Man,*
I, 169, "But ALL subsists by elemental strife," and *The Rape of the Lock,*
II, 79.

[10]Perhaps this is quibbling. The sentiments expressed in Byron's poem
are all to be found in Pope's work, but the total impact of the "Universal
Prayer" is in no sense anti-Christian as is Byron's piece. The earlier
poem is actually a kind of apology for Pope's treatment of Christianity
in the *Essay on Man.* Byron repeated, substantially, much of what he
says in "The Prayer of Nature" when he wrote "The Adieu," even to
inserting several lines verbatim.

his scepticism but mentions nothing of this. Hobhouse and Polidori are silent. Dallas classes him with the "free-thinkers,"[11] but it is his lack of faith, not his convictions that he is emphasizing. Galt says[12] that "he was deeply imbued with the essence of natural piety," yet this statement occurs in his chapter on Byron's conversations with Kennedy during the last year of his life, a period which Galt had no first hand knowledge of. On the other hand, in his consideration of the earlier years of Byron's life he makes much of the remark-able accuracy and fidelity of Byron's descriptions of natural scenes, and he had been over much the same ground. Here Galt seems to have placed his emphasis where it is properly due. Although the picturesque point of view does not ex-clude the possibility of looking upon the natural world as partaking of something of the divine because the creation of deity, yet evidences of the one do not appear in such gen-erous amounts if the other attitude is habitual. The person-ified abstraction Nature, to be sure, occurs repeatedly in Byron's works before 1816, often as a vaguely considered plastic force, but these passages are so completely poetic and literary as to have almost no bearing upon his serious views.[13] All the indications point again to the conclusion that Byron's early "philosophic" views remained in a limited, literary, and purely intellectual area of his consciousness, and had little effect upon his usual reactions to the natural scene. It was not habitual with him at this time to associate the religious emotion or

[11]*Correspondence of Lord Byron With A Friend* (Philadelphia, 1825), p. 173.
[12]*Life*, 268.
[13]See "Elegy on Newstead Abbey," ll. 101–108; "Translation from Anacreon," ll. 9–10; "To Florence," ll. 5–8; "Translation of the Romaic Song," ll. 9–12; "To M—," ll. 9–16; "Childish Recollections," ll. 309–310; "To a Youthful Friend," ll. 15–16; "One Struggle More, and I Am Free," ll. 39–40; "The Devil's Drive," ll. 181–84. This list of course is by no means complete, nor is there need it should be.

any high and holy enthusiasm with a particular aspect of nature. From these small beginnings, however, was to flow a growing stream of deistic professions, though one is not always impressed with the degree of conviction they imply.

The experience described in the letter by Rousseau to Malesherbes, quoted in my fifth chapter, presupposes after the event and assumes as well at the moment of the experience a pantheistic universe, one in which matter is pervaded with the divine spirit. It presupposes, more or less clearly, a Spinozistic universe in which "the World is the deity."[14] Now although the usual deistic view of the universe, by its rejection of all the evidences of revelation and the man-made traditions of worship, paves the way for pantheistic views, it does not lead inevitably to that end, for it clearly conceives a creator outside his creation and related to it after the time of creation only as a kind of regulator and guardian of the scientific laws which he set in motion in the beginning. It is difficult to believe that these two views may be held simultaneously by one man, and yet Pope seems to have accomplished the feat, and so also did Byron. In the very midst of his pantheistic meditations in *Childe Harold*, III, where he proclaims that there is "not a beam nor air nor leaf. . . . but hath a part of being" (stanza 89) and is engaged in worship of nature—to be clearly distinguished from the pious deist's worship in nature— he turns to write of the early Persians making their altars on the mountain tops, "there to seek the Spirit" (stanza 91), and contrasts those "shrines . . . uprear'd of human hands . . . Goth or Greek" unfavorably with these "unwall'd" temples. It is unprofitable at times to examine too closely the exact meaning of a given line or stanza in Byron, but if here he had in mind even in a general way what he wrote, then he intended to compare two like things, that is, two

[14]L. and J., V, 548.

ways of worshiping a deity who exists apart from his works. How closely his notion of the nature of deity approximated the Christian—a Creator distinct from his works—is to be seen in his note to this stanza, which opens with the statement, "It is to be recollected, that the most beautiful and impressive doctrines of the divine Founder of Christianity were delivered, not in the *Temple,* but on the *Mount.*" He then proceeds to mention the advantages and attractions of outdoor worship among Methodists and Mohammedans. It is a note that any pious and liberal deist of the previous century might have written. The "Nature's realms of worship" of this stanza is to be equated exactly with the position stated in the early "Prayer of Nature" (ll. 17–20) in 1806:

> Shall man confine his Maker's sway
> To Gothic domes of mouldering stone?
> Thy temple is the face of day;
> Earth, ocean, heaven, thy boundless throne.

And in stanza 109, following the lines on Clarens, Rousseau, and a universe whose great principle is Love, we find the old idea expressed,

> But let me quit man's works again to read
> His Maker's, spread around me . . .,

which corresponds exactly with the early lines (37–8) from "The Prayer of Nature,"

> Father! no prophet's laws I seek,—
> *Thy* laws in Nature's works appear.

Or in "The Dream,"[15] written in July, 1816, he observes that the blue sky was so beautiful "that God alone was to be seen in Heaven." Although the pantheistic stanzas written under the guidance of Shelley presuppose philosophically a monistic basis, there is no reason to believe that Byron was aware,

[15]"The Dream," l. 125.

in 1816, of the necessity of refashioning his dualistic universe or that he made any effort to do so. His Calvinistic-generated categories of mind and matter, the Catholic sympathies of his later years, and the deistic beliefs which were produced in part by his inability to accept wholly either one of these two great faiths—all these made for him a dichotomy of spirit and matter the only view which he could consistently maintain. And so, just as he was able to recall that his own religious views in 1814 and 1815 had had much in common with those of his wife, whom he called a Socinian,[16] that is, rejecting revelation and professing a natural religion to the extent of denying the divinity of Christ, the Trinity, and similar Christian doctrines, but still thinking of herself as Christian—so in 1820, Byron, most typically a devout deist— when professing himself to be anything at all—exclaimed to the young Pietro Gamba[17] when they were riding one fine spring day in the pine forest near Ravenna, "How, raising our eyes to heaven, or directing them to earth, can we doubt of the existence of God?"

In spite of—in the very face of—Byron's attacks on nature enthusiasts of all shades, in spite of his talk about the cant of nature, his adoption of Cuvier's theories of a succession of creations, each inferior to the preceding and man degenerating as a result, in spite of his deep consciousness of a nature harmful to man and governed by a capricious and cruel Creator— Byron's most often professed philosophical position during the last years of his life (1821–1824), insofar as it may be determined, was that of deism. The very bulk of the evidence indicates that this is so. This does not mean that he was a consistent deist, nor does it imply that he reduced his other beliefs and attitudes to a consistency with deism. But he did

[16]Kennedy, *Conversations*, p. 196.
[17]*Ibid.*, p. 377.

express deistic views more frequently than any other. Before considering the positive evidence, there is evidence of a negative kind which should be examined—statements indicative of what Byron did not believe. The reference to the fact that "some heathenish philosophers make love the main spring of the universe" has already been noticed. This is a clear reference to his brief discipleship under Shelley and to his own former statement[18] that "love in its most extended and sublime capacity . . . is the great principle of the universe." But he denied Shelley[19] in terms much more explicit than these at several other times: "With his [Shelley's] speculative opinions I have nothing in common, nor desire to have." Elsewhere[20] he writes, "No one knows better than their real author [the author of the notes to *Queen Mab*], that his opinions and mine differ materially upon the metaphysical portion of that work." George Finlay reports his saying[21] that Shelley was "quite mad with his metaphysics, and a bigot in the least pardonable way." Medwin records[22] his remark, "I disowned the other day that I was of Shelley's school of metaphysics." Medwin notes[23] also that he said Shelley was too "mystical"; Trelawny writes[24] he spoke of Shelley's "mystifying metaphysics"; and J. Hamilton Browne states[25] that Byron spoke of Shelley's "unfortunate predilection for metaphysics."

Other negative evidence consistent with deism includes his statement[26] that "Priestley's Christian Materialism always

[18]Note to *Childe Harold*, III, 99. *Poetry*, II, 304–5.
[19]L. and J., VI, 33.
[20]L. and J., VI, 387.
[21]"Reminiscences of Lord Byron," in L. F. C. Stanhope's *Greece in 1823 and 1824*, p. 513.
[22]*Conversations*, p. 51.
[23]*Ibid.*, p. 169.
[24]*Recollections*, p. 26.
[25]*Op. cit.*, XXXVI, 395. The Countess Guiccioli makes this point with emphasis. See *Recollections*, I, 177–78.
[26]L. and J., V, 458.

struck me as deadly," his observation[27] that "a *Creator* is a
more natural imagination than a fortuitous concourse of
atoms," his explicit condemnation[28] of Lucretius and his implied condemnation[29] of "the System of Spinosa, that the
World is the deity," his rejection[30] of Berkeley's denial of the
existence of matter, as Byron misunderstood that philosopher,
and his belief[31] that Coleridge had been "spoilt" by "tran-
scendental philosophy and German metaphysics."

Evidence of a more positive kind pointing to Byron's acceptance of the deistic positions that deity exists apart from
creation and governs it by scientific law and that the natural
world, because it was divinely created, is not only a source of
the religious emotion but evidence as well of the existence of a
creator is to be seen in abundance. This very evidence at
times also contains the seeds of his dissatisfaction with deism.
Thus he requests Murray[32] to send him " 'Leslie's Short and
Easy Method with the Deists,' " but told Kennedy[33] he was
"not perfectly satisfied" with the author's "mode of reasoning." Or arguing to himself in his Detached Thoughts[34] he
reasons from the observable effects of the individual mind
upon the body to the position that "the same Agency, in a
higher and purer degree, may act upon the Stars, etc., ad in-
finitum." The implied doubt here does not seem to be very
strong. He admits,[35] "I am always most religious upon a
sun-shiny day" and goes on to say that "the Night is also a
religious concern; and even more so, when I viewed the Moon

27L. and J., V, 459.
28L. and J., V, 554-55.
29L. and J., V, 548.
30*Don Juan*, XI, 1-2.
31Medwin, *Conversations*, pp. 121-22.
32L. and J., V, 392.
33*Conversations*, p. 231.
34L. and J., V, 458.
35L. and J., V, 458.

and Stars through Herschell's telescope, and saw that they were worlds." With a fine disregard for the literal inspiration of the Bible—which at all times he was not able to command— he writes,[36] "things must have had a beginning, and what matters it *when* or *how?*" To Newton, who provided the principal scientific basis for deism, he gives[27] the very highest praise. In the opening seventeen lines of *Cain,* to consider the poetry, is an expression of the "sun-shiny day" side of Byron's concept of nature: there Adam and his family worship a Creator-God who made earth, ocean, day, night, the other worlds, and "beings to enjoy them, and love both them and thee." In the same play (I, i, 494–504) Byron points out the error of adoring "the symbols of the Invisible" in place of God himself, always a temptation to the too-enthusiastic deist. Cain, in attempting to resist temptation, expresses the deistic commonplace that "the immortal star in its great course must . . . be guided" (II, i, 131–32). This of course echoes his early "Prayer of Nature," where he had written (l. 41) of "Thou who canst guide the wandering star." Similarly, Cain swears (III, i, 128–30) by "all the stars, and all the power which sways them." In *Heaven and Earth,* however (i, 86–8), Byron attributes to the angels the power of "recalling some wandering star" to its course and pictures them (iii, 791–92) "adoring him in his least works display'd; watching this youngest star of his dominions."[38] God, then, or his deputy, is not only "nature's architect,"[39] but also custodian of the laws of physics; and "the myriads of bright worlds . . . pass in worship round him."[40]

[36]L. and J., V, 459.

[37]L. and J., V, 600.

[38]In *The Deformed Transformed,* I, ii, 891–97, it will be recalled, he attributed power over the course of the stars to the devil.

[39]*The Island,* IV, 147.

[40]*The Vision of Judgment,* 40.

Among the authorities several refer explicitly to Byron's deism. Stanhope writes,[41] "he was, as he has often told me, a confirmed deist." The Countess Guiccioli quotes this statement with approval,[42] and elsewhere writes[43] of Byron's "Prayer of Nature" that "though written on the threshold of life, he might, with few modifications, have signed it on the eve of his death." George Finlay, who was a member of the discussion group which Kennedy organized, writes,[44] "I never heard him on any occasion enter the field as a professed deist," but that Kennedy thought he was talking to a group of deists, Byron of course being chief among them and Kennedy's principal target, is indicated by the number of times he refers to deism, usually by name, or addresses his arguments directly against deistic notions. There are at least a dozen such instances in his book.[45]

More valuable as evidence than anybody's contemporary opinion of Byron's position, however, are the individual deistic expressions with which Byron is credited. Thus Lady Blessington writes,[46] "a fine day, a moonlight night, or any other fine object in the phenomena of nature, excites (said Byron) strong feelings of religion in all elevated minds, and an outpouring of the spirit to the Creator." The Countess Guiccioli writes[47] that the more Byron meditated upon nature the more he recognized the hand of the Creator in the works of nature.

---

[41]"Sketch of Lord Byron," *Greece in 1823 and 1824*, p. 534. Stanhope also mentions, p. 542, a conversation in which Byron began "to maintain the principles of deism."

[42]*Recollections*, II, 4.

[43]*Ibid.*, I, 140.

[44]Finlay, *op. cit.*, p. 517.

[45]On pp. 6, 12, 31, 114, 115, 121, 140, 148, 152, 153, 178, 179, 191, 451.

[46]*Conversations*, p. 91. Cf. p. 192, where Byron says "the only time I feel repugnance to it [death] is on a fine day, in solitude, in a beautiful country."

[47]*Recollections*, I, 225.

He told[48] William Parry that "clergymen ought to possess a perfect knowledge of astronomy" and that "all men believe in the great first cause." J. Hamilton Browne records[49] his saying, "no one could be so senseless a brute as to deny the existence of a First Cause," but also notes his "frequently expressed . . . anxiety about attaching himself to some particular creed, as any fixed belief would, he thought, be preferable to the continued state of uncertainty in which he had hitherto existed."

Kennedy, however, who found in Byron so much of his own Calvinistic faith, also records the greatest number of instances of devout deism. Kennedy's book, which Lady Byron thought so true, leads one to think that Byron never more clearly described his position than in "The Prayer of Nature" at the age of nineteen, when thoughts of damnation mingled with those of deism. Thus he told[50] Kennedy that "when I view the wonders of creation, I bow to the Majesty of Heaven," stated[51] as an unquestioned assumption that "the elements of nature follow the respective laws which His will has assigned them," and that[52] "we all admit a Supreme Ruler of the universe." "Since Hume published his celebrated Essay on Miracles," Kennedy states,[53] "it has been the fashion with all real, or would-be Deists, to assert that miracles are incapable of being proved by human testimony, and the sentiment was repeatedly expressed by Lord Byron." But Kennedy emphasizes much more clearly than the deistic strain in Byron's thought the fact of Byron's confessions that he derived no happiness from his beliefs, and makes references to it on six separate oc-

[48]*The Last Days of Lord Byron*, pp. 207, 208.
[49]Browne, *op. cit.*, XXXV, 59.
[50]*Conversations*, p. 135.
[51]*Ibid.*, p. 145.
[52]*Ibid.*, p. 189.
[53]*Ibid.*, p. 445.

casions.[54] Byron's dissatisfaction with his predominantly deistic beliefs is emphasized further, if Kennedy may be trusted
here, by his statements that Byron was the aggressor and
sought him out after he had assembled his discussion group
and was holding meetings.[55] Although it is not part of this
study to investigate thoroughly Byron's Calvinism or his
Catholic tendencies, it would seem that his deism was largely
the product of his inability to accept wholly either of these
two faiths and that it received its intellectual content from
the residue of acceptable ideas left him out of these two
great currents of thought. For Byron's mind of course was
thoroughly Christian, often narrowly Christian, and was
striving, especially in the latter years, to find for itself a
traditional faith. Deism offered solutions neither definite
enough nor particular enough; and, in spite of its attractions,
it never completely captured his mind and heart. There were
also, in the mind of Byron, other competing strains of thought,
which must be considered next.

2

Nature and Nature's God of Wrath and Destruction

A God who made possible and regulated a beautiful spring
day inviting, as Pietro Gamba observed, to "religious medita-
tion" was not the God always present, of course, to Byron's
imagination. Claire Clairmont glances maliciously at this
fact in her Journal for November 18, 1820—as well as at the
ease with which Byron's unsettled opinions were influenced
by immediate surroundings:

Three more [caricatures] to be called Lord Byron's Morning, Noon, & Night. The first he looking at the sky, a sun

---

[54]*Ibid.*, pp. xix, 10, 46, 134–5, 320, 341–2.

[55]Kennedy refers four times to the fact that Byron sought him out;
ibid., pp. xiv-xv, 10–11, 129–30, 211.

brightly shining—saying (come I feel quite bold & cheerful—
there is no God) The second towards evening, a grey tint
spread over the face of Nature, the sun behind a cloud—a
shower of rain falling—a dinner table in the distance covered
with a profusion of dishes, he says—(What a change I feel
in me after dinner; where we see design we suppose a de-
signer; I'll be—I am a Deist) The third—evening—candles
just lighted, all dark without the windows and trees agitated
much by wind beating against the panes, also thunder and
lightning. He says (God bless me!, suppose there should be a
God—it is as well to stand in his good graces. I'll say my
prayers to-night, & write to Murray to put in a touch concerning the blowing of the last Trump.) Pistols are on the
table, also daggers.—bullets, turkish scymitars. . . .

The Hebraic-Calvinistic Jehovah[56] of Byron's childhood, to the
belief in which his letters, poetry, conversations, and the testi-

[56]Byron revealed this side of himself more fully to his wife, probably,
than to any other. She saw in him, of course, what she sought, and
exaggeration must be allowed for in the midst of her truth. I quote from
her notes on Byron's religion written in 1848 for the Reverend Frederick
Robertson as they are selected in E. C. Mayne's Life of Lady Byron,
p. 400: "He was no sceptic"; "conscience was always alive"; "the Bible
was viewed through the fearful medium of Calvinism; God was a God
of Vengeance." "The worst of it is, I do believe!" " 'Too late—too late';
words ever in his mouth."

Lady Byron also recorded an interesting incident which took place on
their honeymoon at Seaham, February 5, 1815 (ibid., p. 172; see also
Byron's account in a letter to Lady Melbourne, Correspondence, I, 301-2):
"He was in the habit of sitting up writing till near one in the morning.
Having been annoyed by a large fire in the small room when he was
thus occupied, he threw a quantity of water on the coals, and some kind
of gas was produced by which he was nearly suffocated. When he came
into the bedroom, he staggered, and was in a state of stupor. I did not
then know the cause, but lost no time in taking him to an open window,
using Eau de Cologne &c to revive him. As soon as he recovered his
consciousness, the idea that he was dying presented itself to his imagination, and he broke forth into the wildest ravings of despair, saying that
he knew he was going to Hell, but that he would defy his Maker to the
last, with other expressions of a revengeful nature."

Claire Clairmont (unpublished Journal, April 15, 1821) shared Lady
Byron's view of Byron's religion: "Religion too with him becomes earthly:

mony of others so liberally attest in every period of his life, is of especial significance in determining his attitudes toward nature during the years of his maturity. For it is a matter of some difficulty for one to become enthusiastic over the creation of a God who placed original sin in the world and then punished men eternally for it—even, it may be, Who unjustly placed the curse of Cain upon oneself.[57] A cruel and capricious Deity is not the most favorable of all starting places for the construction of a philosophy or a religion of nature, and Byron is unique, I believe, among his eminent contemporaries in holding these views of deity. Such a God, possibly, cannot be depended upon always to "guide the wandering star through trackless realms of æther's space," as Byron had sung in "The Prayer of Nature," that remarkable compound of deism and damnation. As has been noticed already, he had been concerned as early as the *Hours of Idleness* period with visions of the crashing chaos of an expiring world and a sun growing cold.[58] Such a view of nature and nature's God, however, received its first mature and fully developed expression in *Manfred.* The views expressed here and the many similar ones expressed later are in no way to be reconciled with the deism already described. Nor did Byron himself apparently attempt any such reconciliation. Once again we see him en-

she bears him not to the heavenly spaces informing them with beneficence & promises of eternal happiness; he turns her into a demon; the fit companion of his savage heroes, bending to all their purposes; the Jack Ketch of the Almighty blowing the last trump as a signal to execute an eternal doom of suffering upon criminal myriads: such are his praise offerings to the Creator of the Beauty & goodness: the possessor of never ending beneficence."

[57]E. H. Coleridge in a note to *Lara*, I, 336, cites a number of passages referring to "Byron's belief or half-persuasion that he was predestined to evil" (*Poetry*, III, 336). Charles du Bos, *Byron et le besoin de la fatalité*, has treated this aspect of Byron's personality.

[58]See "The man of firm and noble soul," and the two versions of Ossian's address to the sun.

tertaining parallel but mutually contradictory strains of thought.

In the last scene of the second act of *Manfred* the assembled Spirits of Nature in their hymn to Arimanes attribute to him control of the natural forces of the universe—"in his hand the sceptre of the elements"—and picture them in their aspects destructive and harmful to man. Manfred refuses to bow to him, and bids Arimanes (II, iiii, 416–17) "bow down to that which is above him, the overruling Infinite, the Maker. . . ." Byron was himself too orthodox to deny Deity— his Calvinism was too strong and he was as well too innately religious a man—but it cannot be overlooked that here to Arimanes is given (II, iiii, 371–86) one of the classic qualities of Deity, that of controlling the physical universe.

> Life is his,
> With all its infinite of agonies—
> And his the spirit of whatever is!

Byron has here described, it is not too fanciful to say, under the name of Arimanes, with conscious intent or otherwise, the same Jehovah whom Cain regarded as unjust and rebelled against, as does Manfred here. The position of Arimanes is in no way analogous to that of Milton's Satan, for the only attempt which Byron makes to justify the ways of God to man—if it may be so dignified—is in the two lines (II, iiii, 416–17) quoted above. Byron has made Arimanes the chief spiritual being in the poem—his superficial resemblances to the Satan type are much less striking than the similarities to Byron's own most deeply felt concept of God—he has given him the control of the physical universe and then rebelled against that authority. The situation here is the very one which Stopford Brooke was first to point out in *Cain*, that of a man rebelling against his own belief. *Manfred* too is at once a record of Byron's faith and of his fear.

The same attitude toward nature and God is also expressed in the famous "Roll on, thou deep and dark blue Ocean" stanzas (179-183) of *Childe Harold*, IV. There Byron extolls the ocean not only because the effects of man's destructive urges stop at its shore but also because upon the face of ocean "the wrecks are all thy deed," and he exults in the fierce power of the ocean to shake from herself a vile mankind, whose fleets are her toys. With this preparation there follows an application of the familiar idea that nature is mirror and symbol of its creator, but here the application is rather startling. This same cruel and capricious Ocean has become (IV, 183)

> Thou glorious mirror, where the Almighty's form
> Glasses itself . . .
> The image of Eternity—the throne
> Of the Invisible . . . .

The difficulties which beset Byron when he tried to reconcile the sentimental deism of his day with his other convictions may be clearly illustrated by an examination of the profession of faith made by Rousseau's Savoyard vicar, which offers a classic and influential statement of the deistic position, and one very probably known to Byron.

The Vicar, like all good deists, deduces from the order of the universe not only God's intelligence, power, and will but also his goodness. The deity of these attributes he perceives in all his works. Byron, as I have pointed out, made a great many professions of this same kind. But the Vicar, when he goes on to trace the history of his faith and to explain it in full, describes a number of assumptions and experiences which it was impossible for Byron to own to. The Vicar explains that his first religious feelings came to him when he was a happy child, and were the product of a sense of contentment with the situation in which God had placed him and of a sense of gratitude toward the author of his being: hence arose his first ideas of the worship due to a beneficent deity. It is a love and reverence inborn; the Vicar had no need to be taught artificial forms of worship. But Byron's boyhood sense of inferiority excluded this and was fed in part by a feeling of his own insignificance before God and the wonders of the heavens. "This," he wrote on June 18, 1813, "and being early disgusted with a Calvinistic Scotch school, where I was cudgelled to Church for the first ten years of my life" afflicted him with a malady, "a disease of the mind," which he identifies with hypochondria. The malady he refers to is his doubt of personal immortality. The Vicar, on the other hand, remarking that happiness is not to be found in this life, longs for the moment when he shall put off the incumbrance of his body. And to anticipate as much as possible this desirable state of happiness, power, and liberty, he exercises his mind in sublime contemplations of the order of the universe and converses with its all-wise Creator, whose beneficent features he traces in his workmanship.

Byron, to be sure, often could agree with the Vicar that the confusion and disorder of man's civilization offered an unhappy contrast to the most perfect harmony and proportion of nature; but he could never agree with the Vicar's third article of faith, that man himself, a free agent, is the author of evil, a fact which frees God from all blame, and that the word *necessity* is one without meaning. Byron's Calvinistic sense of sin and predestination made it impossible for him to believe this.

Such a conflict of ideas as the one described is the soil in which most of Byron's heterodox opinions on nature and nature's God were nourished. It explains many of the nature passages in *Manfred* and *Cain;* it is the source of the "Roll on, thou deep and dark blue Ocean" stanzas; and it made possible, eventually, his treatment of the sea in the second canto of *Don Juan*; that is, it is one of the bases of his realism. In that canto, the sea is in no way identified with its Creator. It is, probably, without his intending it to be, his most original reply to the prevailing attitudes toward nature held by the Lakers and those he designated their tadpoles. His treatment represents not merely a satiric reaction, as do his references to "Wordsworth and Co." Instead it calls forth a great impersonal natural force which man must combat and subdue in order to live, a nature which is for man quite dangerously red in tooth and claw. Nor is this nature merely scenery, a backdrop for the action of man, as is often the case in the earlier Oriental tales: Byron has gone quite out of his way to make of the sea a force which his characters are conscious of at their every waking moment. Here he is more or less at one with the long tradition in English poetry which begins with *Beowulf*.

A summary may not be amiss. In the opening stanzas the note struck is that of the humorous-disgusting (stanza 20); Juan becomes seasick in the midst of his protestations of devotion to Julia. Premonitions of a storm appear a few stanzas later, however, and in stanza 30 one gust lays the ship upon her beam ends. Four stanzas afterwards the masts are gone, some of the ship's company are drunk, some singing psalms: the high wind made the treble and as a bass the hoarse, harsh waves kept time. Wailing blasphemy and devotion clamored in chorus to the roaring ocean. There was "nought but the heavy sea, and coming night." They were "at mercy of the waves, whose mercies are like human beings during civil war" (stanzas 41–2). When they were free of the sinking ship and in the small boats (stanza 49),

> . . . the sunless day went down
> Over the waste of waters; like a veil,

Which, if withdrawn, would but disclose the frown
Of one whose hate is mask'd but to assail,
Thus to their hopeless eyes the night was shown.

This is the hour of twilight, called in the next canto (III, 101) the "heavenliest hour of Heaven," worthiest of the blessed Mary; but here the sea yawns around the sinking ship "like a hell." Then all was hushed, save the wild wind and the remorseless dash of the billows (stanzas 52-3).

After a week in the blistering sun, thoughts of cannibalism arise, Juan's tutor draws the fateful slip, those who eat of his flesh go mad—and we see (stanza 79) the horror and inhumanity which nature, aided by man's folly, may bring man to.

There comes finally as relief, however, a shower, followed by a rainbow and soon after by a beautiful white bird—both regarded by the seamen as good omens and symbols of encouragement. The sight of a turtle is also so interpreted, and finally as if in response to these signs the remaining four men sight the freshness of "growing green" (stanza 103). The stage is set for their deliverance. But Juan alone of the four reaches land. Two are drowned, a third is carried down by a shark. The three symbols of hope had proved false—the rainbow, the bird, and the turtle—and the shower had only lengthened their misery for a few further days. Juan digs his nails into the sand lest the reluctant sea suck him back into its insatiate grave (stanza 108).

This is a nature entirely outside and apart from man, a persisting antagonistic force which must be overcome. Man reads his own mood into her at his peril. Nature is to be subdued, not worshipped. The sea is a "vast—salt—dread—eternal Deep" (stanza 103).

It is interesting to see how Byron treats nature when in the same canto he shows Juan in his prosperity as lover of Haidée, in the episode corresponding to and contrasted with the earlier one depicting his love for Julia in Seville. Although Haidée was "Nature's bride" (stanza 202) and for her it was "enlargement of existence to partake Nature" with Juan (stanza 173), and although "to their young eyes" earth was a paradise (stanza 204), it seems that it is they themselves who make it so. For that side of the island which they made theirs was "bare and rough"; it was a "high and rocky coast" (stanza 100), "wild" (stanza 104), a "barren beach" (stanza 109), and Juan's hiding place, which offered opportunities for highly picturesque description, is termed only a "cliff-worn cave" (stanza 108). There is only one extended description (stanza 177):

> It was a wild and breaker-beaten coast,
> With cliffs above, and a broad sandy shore,
> Guarded by shoals and rocks as by an host,
> With here and there a creek. . . .

The implication would seem to be that nature of itself is neither good, kind, nor necessarily in harmony with the feelings of Juan and Haidée. The romantic episode is enacted against a natural background of severe realism.

During the latter years of Byron's life (1821–1824) a strain of scepticism comes to the fore more clearly than at any time hitherto. It receives full expression in *Saradanapalus* (1821), with the exception of *Manfred* Byron's most autobiographical play as well as his most sceptical.[59] There Byron not only attacks the very basis of deism in its most usual form—the assumption of a benevolent Creator—but also denies that man may ever comprehend the nature of the physical universe. Thus (III, i, 45–53) Sardanapalus, who clearly represents Byron himself, after questioning those gods who

[59]See Samuel C. Chew, *The Dramas of Lord Byron*, pp. 106, 111, 113, the best study of the plays but often inadequate, as it is upon the point under present consideration.

possess the power of all-benevolence and yet do not exert it, goes on to wonder if there would be "air worshippers," that is, "worshippers in the air," as the MS. stands, when the sky is "angry and pelting as even now." After Myrrha has answered that "the Persian prays upon his mountain," Sardanapalus replies, "Yes, when the sun shines." The autobiographical significance of the passage, constituting a complete rejection of an earlier position, becomes clear at once when one recalls *Childe Harold*, III, 91, which begins, "Not vainly did the early Persian make his altar the high places and the peak." Elsewhere in the play (II, i, 248–68), Sardanapalus speaks contemptuously of "all Chaldea's starry mysteries," states he neither knows nor cares about the nature of the heavens, and concludes

> There's something sweet in my uncertainty
> I would not change for your Chaldean lore.

The esthetic pleasure which he derives from the sight of the heavens, he goes on to make clear, is all that concerns him. That the passage is again autobiographical is indicated by *Childe Harold*, III, 14, which opens with the lines, "Like the Chaldean he could watch the stars." Browne records[60] that Byron "spoke frequently of the inane pursuits of mankind, and our limited intelligence, dwelling at some length on . . . the nothingness of all human intellect, when it engages in the ever endless task of endeavouring to explore or solve the hidden and impenetrable mysteries of nature." And Byron had written in *Don Juan* VII, 5, of Socrates' saying that "our only knowledge was 'to know that nothing could be known'" and had alluded to Newton picking up shells on the shore of the great ocean of truth. But that none of these statements imply genuine philosophical scepticism with its refusal to espouse positive and definite ideas of the nature of the physi-

[60]Browne, *op. cit.*, XXXV, 59.

cal universe is rendered quite clear by the existence of such positive views, shortly to be considered. As Trelawny ungraciously expressed it,[61] echoing Johnson on Goldsmith, Byron "had not made up his mind on any subject." The same writer attributes to Shelley[62] almost identical words: "he has not made up his mind, and cannot on any subject whatever." But Byron had his views, irreconcilable though they may have been. Nor was sceptical suspension of belief one of them.

Cain implies or explicitly states several attitudes toward the universe and ideas of its structure, one of these being the most interesting revelation, perhaps, that Byron ever made of his attitude toward the creation. To be noticed first in any consideration of Cain is Byron's repeated linking of the play with Manfred. As early as January 28, 1821, he writes[63] in his diary that he has "pondered the subjects of four tragedies." One of them is "Cain, a metaphysical subject, something in the style of Manfred." When he sends the play to Murray he accompanies it[64] with the remark, "I think that it contains some poetry, being in the style of 'Manfred.' " To Moore he says,[65] "It is in the Manfred metaphysical style." If the play is actually similar to Manfred, we may expect to find evidences of a God and Creator who is not only unjust but capricious in his rule of the physical universe as well. Both of these were implied in

[61]Records, I, 58.
[62]Ibid., I, 78. Trelawny repeats this opinion on pp. 79 and 132, all four instances in almost identical language.
[63]L. and J., V, 189.
[64]L. and J., V, 360.
[65]L. and J., V, 368. Byron also denominated Lara a "metaphysical" poem. Lady Byron writes (Astarte, pp. 20–21), "He often said that 'Lara' was the most metaphysical of his works." Byron thought it was "too metaphysical to please the greatest number of readers" (L. and J., III, 201). The similarities between the three characters are interesting: each has rejected a God of love and each has sought after knowledge forbidden. All three compositions express the Zeluco theme, which may well have been associated in Byron's mind with the term metaphysical. The "autobiographical" element is also strong in all three.

Byron's adaptation of Cuvier's theory of the universe and were made explicit by Byron in the play, as will be pointed out shortly.

Cain has a second important link with an earlier strain of Byron's thought, a strain which has historical origins as old as the discoveries of Copernicus and Galileo. One of the ideas given major expression in the play—the insignificance of the earth and its human inhabitants when compared with the size of the entire universe—had impressed Byron as early as 1813. A letter to William Gifford expressing the idea states quite exactly the text which is illustrated dramatically by the play. Byron wrote[66] in 1813,

I am no Bigot to Infidelity, and did not expect that, because I doubted the immortality of Man, I should be charged with denying the existence of a God. It was the comparative insignificance of ourselves and *our world,* when placed in competition with the mighty whole, of which it is an atom, that first led me to imagine that our pretensions to eternity might be over-rated.

In 1821, Byron described the motivation of Cain's murder of Abel in terms much the same. With the two scenes of the second act in mind—one placed in "the Abyss of Space," the other in "Hades"—he explained[67] concerning Cain that "the object of the Demon is to *depress* him still further in his own estimation than he was before, by showing him infinite things and his own abasement, till he falls into the frame of mind that leads to the Catastrophe, from mere *internal* irritation, *not* premeditation, or envy of *Abel* (which would have made him contemptible), but from the rage and fury against the inadequacy of his state to his conceptions, and which discharges itself rather against Life, and the Author of Life, than the mere living." The depression of Cain "in his own estimation,"

66L. and J., II, 221–22.
67L. and J., V, 470.

which is to drive him on to a "fit of dissatisfaction,"[68] is actually achieved by two separate though related means, both of which are implied in Byron's explanation. The first is by showing Cain his own insignificance and the insignificance of his world when compared in size and importance to all the universe; the second is by means of Lucifer's repeated disadvantageous comparisons of the beauty of Cain's earth with that of the pre-Adamite earth and with the heavenly bodies. These themes as they appear in the play may be summarized here.

At the end of their tour of the universe, when Cain and Lucifer are about to return to the earth, the first objective is stated as a fact realized. Cain exclaims, "Alas! I seem nothing," and Lucifer offers the commentary, "And this should be the human sum of knowledge" (II, ii, 625–27). Byron was to exclaim[69] in similar fashion to Murray, five months after *Cain* had been completed: looking up at the summer sky above him, he had written, "what Nothings we are! before the least of these Stars!" When this statement is read in conjunction with one[70] quite possibly written shortly after the period of *Cain's* composition—"The Night is also a religious concern; and even more so, when I viewed the Moon and Stars through Herschell's telescope, and saw that they were worlds"—it is clear that for Byron the sense of his own insignificance before the wonders of creation was not an altogether unknown aspect of the act of worship or of the religious emotion. These several statements upon man's nothingness in the universe represent in the man Byron the same sense of "abasement" which he was attempting to represent in Cain and are simply further evidences of that twin faith and fear which Stopford Brooke pointed out as the key

[68]L. and J., V, 368.
[69]L. and J., VI, 18.
[70]L. and J., V, 458.

to *Cain,* a record at once of Byron's belief and of his abhorrence. As he wrote in *The Deformed Transformed,* (III, i,
102), men are "themselves alone the real 'Nothings.'"

To return more directly to *Cain,* it is clear that the "infinite
things" of Byron's letter, which were to lead directly to Cain's
"fit of dissatisfaction" and thence to the catastrophe, are
those things seen by Cain on his trip with Lucifer in the second
act: in the first scene, the myriads of worlds and the great
universe which made his own earth seem so insignificant and
inadequate to Cain; and in the second scene, the pre-Adamite
beings so superior to the mankind that Cain knew. This study
of course is concerned principally with the former source of
dissatisfaction, a world decayed and nature running down—
a subject which had interested Englishmen as far back as
Donne in his *Anatomie of the World* and Milton in "Naturam
non pati senium." The trip through space is very skillfully
handled. Lucifer first promises to show Cain "the history of
past, and present, and of future worlds" (II, i, 24–5). As
they travel on through the universe, Cain becomes increasingly
conscious of the littleness of his own world and Lucifer tempts
him with the idea of "worlds greater than thine own" (II, i,
26–49). But Cain is not to yield thus early and, great as are
the sights which he has seen, says that they are "inferior still
to my . . . conceptions" (II, i, 79–83). Still with the purpose of making Cain dissatisfied with his little world, Lucifer
points out the view of the universe with "behold! is it not
glorious?" (II, i, 97–8). Cain expresses his admiration for
these "works, or accidents, or whatsoe'er they may be" with
enthusiasm (II, i, 83–117), and Lucifer takes the opportunity
to tell him to "look back to thine earth" (II, i, 118). Cain
is then forced to admit that he has seen fire-flies "brighter
than yon world" (II, i, 125). Instead of speaking the blas-

phemy that Lucifer wishes him to, however, he proceeds to the conclusion (II, i, 130–32) that

> The little shining fire-fly in its flight,
> And the immortal star in its great course,
> Must both be guided,

and expresses the wish to see Him who guides (II, i, 132–3). It seems as though Lucifer's purpose is not to be accomplished. But by clever verbal maneuvering (II, i, 132–43) Lucifer turns Cain's thoughts at this moment to the mysteries of death. Thus Cain loses his chance to see heaven, and the pair descend to Hades. Lucifer, though, continues to comment on the insignificance of the earth and explains it is but the "wreck" of a former one (II, i, 146–53), and (II, ii, 285–86) that God had destroyed the earlier earth "by a most crushing and inexorable destruction and disorder of the elements." Cain now begins to adopt Lucifer's point of view, and after seeing the superior pre-Adamite race of beings admits (II, ii, 280–83) that the earth as he knows it "is too little and too lowly to sustain such creatures." Lucifer continues to emphasize his point, refers (II, ii, 303–4) to the newly created world as "crush'd into a scarcely-yet shaped planet," states (II, ii, 325–32) that the pre-Adamite world is gone forever, changed completely by its convulsion, and laments, "Oh, what a beautiful world it *was!*" As the play proceeds to its catastrophe Lucifer attacks unremittingly and tempts Cain into unfavorable comparisons of the earth with what he sees. Thus (II, ii, 383–92) Cain sees and admires "the phantasm of an ocean." Lucifer tells him that the ones on earth are "inferior." And so by these means Cain is led on in a "fit of dissatisfaction" to commit his fatal act not against Abel merely but against "Life, and the Author of Life." More truly than of any other of Byron's heroes, it may be said of Cain that "the beauties of nature . . . are lost on a soul so constituted."

Similar uncomplimentary or hostile allusions to the work of the Creator and to his government of the physical universe appear elsewhere in Byron's late poetry. Thus in *Heaven and Earth* (iii, 305–9) the usually orthodox Japhet lapses into a tirade against the injustice of the Almighty and refers to the world after the Flood as

> . . . some emerging world,
> Reeking and dank from out the slime, whose ooze
> Shall slumber o'er the wreck of this until
> The salt morass subside into a sphere
> Beneath the sun. . . .

The Chorus of Spirits refers in the same fashion (iii, 452–56) to the "slime" of the earth after the Flood, "when the hot sun hath baked the reeking soil into a world." In *The Deformed Transformed* (III, i, 138–51) Caesar, like Lucifer, has remarks to make upon man's "little Universe," and observes that sometimes "the System is in peril." And as late as *Don Juan*, IX, (37–40) Cuvier's theory of worlds past and future finds expression, with its corollaries of destruction and a subsequent inferior creation.

> Even worlds miscarry, when too oft they pup,
> And every new creation hath decreased
> In size, from overworking the material.

In a man of Byron's temperament, it is extremely difficult to estimate the degree of conviction with which he held these views. He never deliberately denied them; and when one recalls his infinite capacity for giving expression to self-contradictory opinions, it seems wiser to regard them merely as an additional strain in his thought, taken up late in his life, which never led to anything further. These ideas, furthermore, were much nearer to his Calvinistic concept of deity than to either deism or his Catholic tendencies, and do not represent any serious or major turning to particular scientific theory as a faith.[71] For him Cuvier's theories found added authority because they did not contradict the accounts in Genesis.[72] Sir Walter Scott, who in so many ways had a genuine insight into Byron's character, erred seriously[73] in his letter to Murray when he assumed that Byron might have explained away, if he had wanted to, "the Evil Principle" in *Cain* as inconsistent with "the general benevolence of the Deity." Byron was by no means convinced of the existence of a deity generally benevolent, and for him the evidence of science was just more evidence in favor of a Calvinistically imagined God. This last period of his life reveals more clearly than any other his preoccupation with a God who was not only cruel and unjust but even blood-thirsty.[74] Such a deity, in his government of the physical universe, might be capricious as well. As Byron said[75] to the Countess Guiccioli, "I really do not see why God should be obliged to preserve in the universe the same order which He once established. To whom did He promise that He would never change it . . .?" Or to Medwin[76] he spoke of the time "when a comet shall approach this globe to destroy it, as it often has been and will be destroyed."

One feels that Byron was almost obsessed by the idea of a deity who has the relation of Creator-Destroyer to the physical universe. Thus he makes reference[77] to "Thou who

[71]"I beg leave to observe, that there is no creed nor personal hypothesis of mine in all this" (writing to Murray of *Cain*, L. and J., V, 470).

[72]See letter to Moore, L. and J., V, 368, as well as Byron's preface to the play, *Poetry*, V, 210.

[73]Quoted by E. H. Coleridge, *Poetry*, V, 206.

[74]See *Cain*, III, i, 245–279, 284–5, 292–3; 298–304; *The Deformed Transformed*, I, i, 461–2; L. and J., V, 186, 390, 457; VI, 32 and note, 182, 262 note, 339, 349 note; Lady Blessington, *Conversations*, p. 111; The Countess Guiccioli, *Recollections*, I, 198, 199; Kennedy, *Conversations*, pp. 55–6, 59, 139–40, 172, 189, 227, 228, 235 (cf. 219–22), 325–26 (cf. 335); Medwin, *Conversations*, p. 51.

[75]The Countess Guiccioli, *Recollections*, I, 224.

[76]Medwin, *Conversations*, 129–30.

[77]*Marino Faliero*, V, iii, 734–5.

kindlest and who quenchest suns," has Lucifer speak[78] of a Creator who "makes but to destroy" and maintain[79] that the heavenly bodies have in them the principle of death just as truly as does mankind, uses[80] the words *creation* and *destruction* in reference to the physical world as if they were the twin functions of its Creator, and in *The Island,* incongruously, elevates[81] this process of "eternal change" from creation to destruction and back, to the place where it seems to represent the great principle of the universe. Or in *The Deformed Transformed,* when Byron attributes to Arnold in one place (I, ii, 589) Harold and Manfred's old quest for peace, exhibiting a glaring lack of dramatic propriety, the demon replies (I, ii, 590–601) that the principle of the universe is motion, change, that *"commotion* is the extremest point," and that this "rule of fix'd necessity" governs men, worms, and planets. In the play of *Heaven and Earth,* however, as one might expect, the idea receives its fullest treatment. Even the usually orthodox Japhet swears (iii, 327) by "the Omnipotent who makes and crushes." The idea is expressed fully in the opening lines (266–320) of the third scene and reveals the sharp conflict within Japhet: he loves the beautiful world of nature that God has created but—insofar as his orthodoxy permits—cries out against the Creator for destroying his works. Japhet concludes his long soliloquy with, "All beauteous world! . . . I cannot think upon thy coming doom without a feeling such as—Oh God! and canst thou—." He is saved from the blasphemy he is evidently about to utter by the appearance of the Spirits of Earth.

The idea of a universe which is periodically destroyed and recreated by a deity whose intentions toward man are not

[78]*Cain,* I, 263–4.
[79]*Cain,* I, 275–9.
[80]*The Deformed Transformed,* I, i, 471–3.
[81]*The Island,* II, 155–62.

altogether benevolent is not very far removed from the idea that that creation itself is harmful to man. In all this, of course, Byron has left his old teacher Wordsworth about as far behind as it is possible for one to imagine and, at the same time, reaches forward strikingly in the direction of certain modern attitudes. Professor Raymond Dexter Havens has written[82] of Wordsworth in his *Mind of a Poet* that that poet "ignored sudden, cataclysmic changes, such as floods, fires, and earthquakes, as well as the short life of most plants and animals, and dwelt upon the permanence, moderation, and regularity of nature. One other aspect of his optimistically se-elective conception of the external world merits some attention, his silence about storms." In Byron, on the other hand, the references to a hostile world of nature are so numerous as to constitute one of the major strains of his thought, and exist in the form of both unconsidered and unquestioned assumptions and as explicit statements. Thus he lists[83] comets, droughts, excessively cold winters, and earthquakes along with wars and sickness and asks, "is all this, because Nature is niggard or savage? or Mankind ungrateful?" Or he observes,[84] with Cuvier in mind, that men grow inferior "as the Elements become more inexorable." He writes sceptically[85] that Kennedy "says that the dozen shocks of an Earthquake we had the other day are a sign of his doctrine, or a judgement on his audience," but two weeks later calls[86] Dr. Kennedy "a very good Calvinist, who . . . thinks me . . . a tolerable

[82]*The Mind of a Poet*, p. 114. An extreme example of Byron's failure to appreciate the beauty of a rainy day is to be observed in the first thirty pages of his Ravenna Diary, which contain thirteen separate references to bad weather (L. and J., V, 147, 151, 152, 154, 155, 156, 157, 158, 160, 166, 173–4, 176, 177). Snow and cold weather he disliked equally. See, for humorous examples, *Don Juan*, XIII, 42; X, 21; XIV, 28, 36.
    [83]L. and J., V, 434.
    [84]L. and J., V, 459.
    [85]L. and J., VI, 263.
    [86]L. and J., VI, 271. See also VI, 135, 147.

Christian." Kennedy of course had discovered many points of identity between his own views and those of Byron. In *Sardanapalus,* for example, Byron had seriously denominated thunder and lightning as the symbols of the Divine. In that same play[87] a harmful nature—a swollen river—provides the very turning point of the tragedy and brings about directly the fall of the hero. In *Werner* another swollen river functions as the original cause of the action; because of it the four principal characters meet at the same place, and the action begins. The very theme of *Heaven and Earth,* of course, is destruction—destruction effected by an annihilating sea that is amoral, subject to the will of God and to universal law, which two are one, and sweeping away before it all but the Elect.[88] More remarkable is the way in which the "Spirits of the Earth" are in open opposition to man and he to them. They joy in the universal destruction and breathe the very spirit of annihilation.[89] And the demon in *The Deformed Transformed* remarks (I, ii, 891–7) regarding his "business amongst the stars, which these poor creatures deem were made for them to look at," that it would be a fine "jest now to bring one down amongst them." Even *The Island* contains[90] an extended passage on the horrors of the deep, a kind of *Don Juan,* II, in miniature. "Some heathenish philosophers make love the main spring of the universe,"[91] as he wrote in *Don Juan,* but Byron no longer always does.

[87]*Sardanapalus,* V, i, 189–205.
[88]See especially *Heaven and Earth,* iii, 547–48 and 1095. Compare the "elemental strife" of the latter with "The Prayer of Nature," l. 43, where Byron had written of Him "Who calm'st the elemental war."
[89]See ii, 206–8; iii, 362–3, 379–88, 411–13, 425–28, 486–511, 1044–45, 1129–30.
[90]*The Island,* I, 160–200.
[91]*Don Juan,* IX, 73.

3

The Failure of Byron's Philosophy:
Theory, Fact, and the Observing Personality

If the final function of philosophy is to harmonize all the facts and all man's divergent intuitions as to the nature of things, and refashion these into a consistent scheme, then, without any question, Byron must be denied the name of philosopher: he had neither a philosopher's formal training nor the necessary synthesizing powers of mind. Instead, Byron's "philosophic" mind was a very wonderful grab bag—with everything in it from Plato to Cuvier. The process of emptying it has no justifiable use in the world except insofar as it may illume more fully the figure of a great poet and serve, perhaps, to make us wiser than Byron was.

Because of the way that Byron's mind grew, his thought about the nature of the universe represents not an integration of the thought of the past but a kind of stratification of it, each "layer" retaining something of its original contradictions and conflicting as well, perhaps, with a later "accretion." Intellectually, Byron's failure seems to have been a failure to reconcile finally two broad interests, each deriving historically from essentially different climates of opinion: these were his instinctive interest in facts and his passionate desire to arrive at general principles. The first of these resulted in a realistic depiction of nature: whether he described nature as harmful, comic, picturesque, or indifferent to man, the account is always founded on "fact." The second of these broad interests gave rise to the philosophical position which he espoused most frequently—that represented by the orderly system of deism. This passion for order in Byron, basically a deep need to simplify, is clearly illustrated by his instinctive belief in the demonstrable existence of an order of nature.

Such an order, to be sure, he occasionally questioned, asking how one could know that a cause will always produce the same effect, but his regular and instinctive faith he gave to the rationality of science. This almost unquestioning faith in an order of nature, however, "modern" and scientific though it may seem, is essentially medieval: it was with Byron, as with the medieval thinker, the expression of an ultimate faith in the rationality of God—though Byron questioned that too, at times. Such a Creator, he reasoned, could create only an orderly universe, one in which every event could be related meaningfully (causally) to its antecedent as the exemplification of a general principle. And only when Byron's Hebraic tendencies colored his immediate thought, when the idea of an inscrutable and possibly capricious deity was uppermost in his mind, did he momentarily question the principle of intelligible order in the universe. Thus Byron's concept of nature, whether it expressed itself in terms of sentimental deism, pantheism, or something more realistic than either of these, remained predominantly anti-rationalistic at its base: it was built on faith and faith alone in an intelligible order in things. Byron never systematically examined this foundation of his thought.

The eighteenth-century science which Byron inherited implied that man was helpless before the irresistible forces of natural law. His Calvinism told him even more clearly that existence was predetermined. But Byron made the practical compromise, or attempted to, that the average man has always made: in living from day to day he often had to act as if he himself determined the course of his life. Yet he could not assimilate this radical inconsistency between belief and practice, and it accounts, as such a fundamental split must always, for much that is half-hearted and wavering in him. Byron was familiar with Paley's argument that the watch implies the watch-maker, but he also knew Hume's objection, phrased before Paley gave the argument its final form, that the Creator will be the sort of God who makes the mechanism; that is, the author of a mechanism can be, at best, a mechanic. Byron sensed this difficulty, and rebelled. But the rebellion had in it no more satisfaction for him than the bondage of determination; so, in practice, he tried simply to ignore the difficulty as one too great for him, admitting that he had read more philosophy than he could understand, and concluding finally that action was the proper issue of thought anyway. The only compromise that Byron might have adopted was to allow scientific determinism throughout inanimate nature and deny its validity in some way in living bodies, but his Calvinism was always a much more vital thing to him than his scientific faith, as closely related as the two were, and so he was left with a dilemma. He was unable to achieve the untroubled certainty of Milton, that the ways of God are both just and justifiable to man, for he had too little of the theologian and too much of the limited, fact-respecting scientist in him. Pope's scientific-deistic metaphysics gave him even less comfort than they gave Pope, for Byron had superimposed upon them a concept of deity not indeed necessarily benevolent. Nor was Byron able like Wordsworth to reject the limited scientific assumptions of the eighteenth century; that science and his religion supported one another. Thus the note struck by Byron is much more contemporary than any of these; it is one of distraction and perplexity, which we recognize in Tennyson, Arnold, and many of the poets of the present generation. Byron like these men is often a muddled thinker half-heartedly divided against himself.

Throughout his development, however, with the exception of a few months in 1816, Byron never seriously doubted that the ultimate material fact in the world was an irreducible brute matter spread through space in variously changing forms—

in itself without direction or purpose except that given to it by the Creator. Thus Byron's concept of matter was that of seventeenth and eighteenth century physics: he conceived a passive matter operated on by forces outside it. He objected equally to the monistic extremes of Spinoza's "the world is the Deity" and of Berkeley's "the world is all ideal, all ourselves." For Byron, essentially a dualist who accepted mind and matter on an equal basis, could no more put mind inside matter than he could imagine matter inside mind. Matter is indestructible, and Newton had charted its course. Even in *Childe Harold*, III (27), nature is called "inanimate." In his Journal of 1821, he begins with the unquestioned assumption[92] that "matter is eternal, always changing, but reproduced, and, as far as we can comprehend Eternity, Eternal," and from this assumption goes on to ask, "and why not *Mind?*" Or he writes to Murray[93] in Voltairean phrase, "It is an odd World; but the watch has its mainspring, after all." In this last sentence, interestingly enough, Byron is not referring to the world of physics at all, but to the existence in the world of a moral order which eventually punishes each individual for his crimes. Thus the language of the unambiguous religion of science is applied to the more doubtful religion of the spirit.

Only occasionally[94] did Byron's faith waver:

Nothing more true than *not* to trust your senses;
And yet what are your other evidences?

But even this small doubt is an expression of faith: he is here indulging in a typical tirade against Berkeley (who, like Spinoza, was outside the main line of development of scientific-philosophical thought) and against complex intellectual systems based upon deductive reasoning. Yet Byron, with

[92]L. and J., V, 458.
[93]L. and J., IV, 345.
[94]*Don Juan*, XIV, 2. See also *Don Juan*, I, 214, and *Childe Harold*, IV, 155–158.

his scientist's faith in the senses, resting on his concept of matter as mass located in space and time, and perceived by mind, also inherited and accepted Locke's distinction, so fundamental among the concepts of eighteenth century science, of primary and secondary qualities: color, sound, smell, etc., Byron implies, are qualities in the mind of the observer, not present in the order of nature. This difficulty in seventeenth century thought pushed Byron toward the position of Berkeley and thus toward further confusion in his own thought. But we may safely assume that it worried Byron very little, if at all, except insofar as he realized personally and painfully that the beauties of nature disappeared when the observer's mind was distraught.

The basic assumptions of Byron, then, as to the nature of the universe were essentially those of the science of his time, and contained within themselves the same difficulties. Yet Byron had nothing of Shelley's detailed scientific knowledge. In Byron the earth and moon never converse together, as they do in Shelley, in the accurate language of scientific experiment. But Byron's views were based much more fundamentally than Shelley's finally upon science simply because Byron refused to accept philosophical idealism, whether that of Kant or Berkeley, as a scheme for interpreting the universe. Despite the ever-present Byronic personality, Byron could not consciously interpret the world on a subjectivist basis: his trust of the senses and his faith in the reality of fact precluded this. Yet here again there is a fundamental cleavage in the thought of Byron. He repeatedly realized, with varying degrees of discomfort, that his immediate experience of nature was the outcome of his state of mind at the moment, that is, the outcome of the perceptive peculiarities of the subject enjoying (or not enjoying) the experience. Thus within his own memory he had a very good ground upon which to erect a subjectivist metaphysics and conclude that what is perceived is merely an aspect of the cognitive act. But Byron could never live in a purely conceptual world. There was first of all the naive evidence of the senses: in the same manner exactly in which Dr. Johnson kicked a stone to prove the existence of matter and thus conclude the metaphysical cloudbursts of his opponent, Byron writes[95] that "I once thought myself a philosopher, and talked nonsense with great decorum. . . . At last, a fall from my horse convinced me bodily suffering was an evil. . . ." Thus, then, may the nature of this world be known. In the second place, Byron accepted, above all other scientific hypotheses of his time, the principle of change as operative in a most important way in the history of the universe. The work of Herschel and Cuvier was most influential upon him here, backed up by his understanding of the Old Testament. His historical knowledge then told him of past ages when there were no living beings on earth and of vast star-systems still uninhabited by man. But his common sense told him that things were happening in remote ages, just as they were at the moment on unobserved stars. Thus it was impossible for him to believe that the experienced world was merely an aspect of his own personality. "The lapse of ages," he writes,[96] "*changes all things—time—language—the earth—the bounds of the sea—the stars of the sky, and every thing 'about, around, and underneath' man. . . .*" This sympathy with evolutionary thought was more than a mere whim with him; the appeal to the past was one of the deepest instincts of his personality. Finally, he rejected a subjectivist universe because of his instinct for action. Of all the great Romantic poets Byron put the world of nature to the most consistent *use:* it was thus that he transcended himself, in activity directed to known ends in the known world. A world put to such use is independent of

[95]L. and J., I, 173.
[96]L. and J., V, 161–2. See also *The Deformed Transformed*, I, i, 590–600.

the subject which is cognizant of it. Thus Byron's thought has at least two quite separate focuses, one expressed in *Childe Harold*, III, and another in his life of action. The two were never brought together or reconciled. Byron's difficulty was exactly that of all the more philosophical objectivist thinkers of his day and before who conceded the necessity of accepting the classical scientific doctrines of secondary and primary qualities. Both they and he were forced to deal with the secondary qualities, such as sense-objects, on subjectivist principles because each recognized the evident fact that the individual's apprehension of the external world is determined by the individual.

Byron then inherited the objectivist bias of science, with its contradictions, but along with it he inherited the religious and philosophical traditions which centered their interest on the entity of the self. The church had insisted for centuries on the worth of the individual soul; the Reformation had intensified the emphasis on the individual insight. The Cartesian method had assumed as its primary datum the existence of the soul as a single entity. These traditions strengthened Byron's instinctive egotism; the wonder is that he ever got out of himself. His science, philosophy, and religion then imposed an irreducible dualism upon him. Yet the character of Don Juan in effect questions the unity of the human personality and hints at a concept which denies that the personality is an entity acting consistently or rationally: the personality of Don Juan, romantic at one moment and anti-rómantic the very next, is perilously near being a mere unrelated succession of states of mind. The implication is that the personality is not an immutable entity. What nonsense to talk of soul, Byron once exclaimed, when wine makes it mad and a cloud makes it melancholy. Nor is Juan a completely self-directing personality: he is a contradictory bundle of motives and reactions to stimuli of all kinds—sex, climate, and convention—and he responds almost blindly to each in turn, satisfying his various needs and hungers. The most important of these is sex, and Juan pursues and discards one woman after another, satisfying needs both physical and psychological. But the concept of the self as an undirected succession of states of mind, without any very important rational control, is implied even more clearly by another character than it is by Juan—it is the character of the author. Inconsistency is the essence of the Byron in the poem, and is accurately described in the stanza on mobility (XVI, 97). The idea expressed here seems to be an extension of Byron's concept of his life as a succession of varying roles played with complete sincerity before different audiences. It is essentially the idea of multiple personality, which figures so prominently in the modern novel. But such an idea reduces the consciousness very nearly to a function, and such a reduction of the role of consciousness cuts straight across the fundamental dualism of Byron's thought, which asserted that the two enduring materials of the universe were soul and matter. If the cogitating mind exists in a state of flux (if it exists at all), what then can be known with any certainty about the material universe? It would seem that Byron was dimly aware of these difficulties, but not clearly enough aware of them to state clearly either the problem or its answer. His response was not philosophical scepticism but a jaunty distrust of systems in themselves—a distrust which concealed, imperfectly, his own deep sense of uncertainty. Yet the effect was undeniably to tarnish some of the lustre of the Newtonian universe which he inherited, and to turn him away from philosophy as a serious activity. And paralleling these tendencies to reduce the personality to a succession of mental states was the increasing tendency to emphasize the principle of change as fundamental in the universe, an idea which tended to overshadow (although not inconsistent with) Byron's earlier notion of matter as the fundamental fact of the universe. Thus did his ideas result in greater and greater uncertainty, and his comfortable deistic universe become increasingly untenable. But none of these problems was the one which vitiated Byron's philosophy of nature from the first and which was enough in itself, probably, to wreck it finally. An order in nature he accepted from first to last. The question he could never answer with any lasting satisfaction to himself, however, was this: what is the exact status of the enduring natural order? He successfully made the jump, on the strength of faith alone, from the conviction of the existence of such an order to the conviction of some greater reality behind it. The idea of a Creator was always a more "natural" supposition to him than that of a fortuitous concourse of atoms. Nature was never self-explanatory for Byron. But he never found the necessary faith to believe, consistently, that the natural order was essentially benevolent to man; and if not, what is then to be said of its Creator? This is the fundamental question which Byron finally stumbled over, and his failure to answer it was a failure in faith. Nothing was more evident to him than that things changed, but was it for good or for ill? And if for ill, what, again, is to be said of the Creator?

Byron, like Aristotle, found it necessary to complete his metaphysics by the introduction of a Prime Mover, and as long as Byron's deistic universe held tightly together, with its ideas of a benevolent Creator and creation, all was seemingly well. But like Aristotle's, Byron's metaphysical thought did not lead him very far towards the production of a God available for religious purposes, if such speculation, alone, ever may. And when the emphasis of Byron's thought began to shift toward change, not always for the better, as a fundamental law of creation, the uncertainties began to cloud fast upon him. The Prime Mover became increasingly identified with the idea of motion, change; and the future, as a result, became increasingly doubtful. But unlike Aristotle, Byron began not with a metaphysics, to follow wherever it led him, but with Calvinistic Christianity, which retained vestiges of a God of wrath and vengeance. A vengeful Prime Mover of a universe whose great principle was change thus had increased opportunities to be vengeful. Byron realized this, and the realization removed him a further step from peace of mind. Thus the medley of metaphysics and religion in Byron's mind caught him in the trap many another mind has fallen into: if God is conceived as the ultimate metaphysical reality, creator and sustainer of the universe, then he is author of it all—and creates and sustains the harmful along with the helpful. Byron sought to escape this ancient problem in the Manichaean doctrine of the Two Principles, which he seems not to have fully understood. *Cain,* which is the principal statement of Byron's Manichaean tendencies, is a record of Byron's struggle to reject a disturbing idea, just as *Manfred* is.

Thus it was that the very essence of Byron's thought was conflict. That conflict, however, and it should be made very clear, was not a simple one between science and religion. Newton himself had expressed the hope that his clear formulation would strengthen men in their faith, and was himself presumably a very good Christian. The lack of harmony among Byron's beliefs is explained in part by the fact that he was not a trained philosopher. In part it is explained by his refusal to throw out half the factual evidence. Wordsworth seems to have been able to do this. With the clear, logical intellect that Byron did not have, he constructed a satisfying religion of nature out of an understanding of his own experience among natural surroundings peculiar to a small area of the earth, elaborated a scheme of thought which fitted more or less exactly the experiences which claimed his interest, and ignored the evidence which confused the scheme with contradictory instances. Byron, with his painful determination to take into account the whole evidence, and lacking the limited interests of Wordsworth, was not able to do this. But the failure of Byron's religious thought, however, was finally something psychological. Byron's failure to find a faith wholly acceptable to him deepened the sense of conflict and uncertainty within him, to be sure, but it is more meaningful to recall that the psychological conflict hindered his arriving at the certainty of any one congenial faith. For religion, finally, answers the deep need of the human spirit for assimilation. It has been seen how this need within Byron became most urgent during his tour of the Alps in 1816, only to fail of fulfillment. The act of worship, essentially, is one of surrender. But the mark of the guilty Byronic hero is domination, assertion of self. He must prove that he has been misjudged, that the law was wrong, or that he is superior to the law. Manfred has risen above laws and creeds, even above the power of Arimanes himself. The man who so labors under the necessity of proving himself innocent, however, may well believe in his secret self that he is guilty: if so, the crime must be punished. And so Manfred, after scourging himself variously with remorse and doubt, attempts finally to destroy himself. In rising above the gods without leaving beneath him his sense of justice, he is forced to assume himself the role of judge, and so sentences and punishes himself, and never allows himself much peace, for he who has passed judgment against the gods must take double care that he is not too lenient with himself. So Byron lashed away at himself.

Chapter VII

THE CONTEMPORANEOUSNESS OF BYRON: A CRITICAL POSTSCRIPT

Byron in perspective is Byron at a distance, the distance between our present and his. Byron seen thus is Byron reduced but, more important, Byron seen whole, not fragmentarily—Byron still, with all his contradictions and conflicts, but these shrunken to their proper proportions. The foregoing chapters have attempted to throw a strong and clear light on certain closely defined aspects of the man and his work. Such a necessary limitation inevitably distorts. But it may also produce a clean cross section, one quite useful in recreating the whole. That whole—and its present significance—is the concern of this chapter, an essay on what Byron, poet, thinker, and personality, writing about the world he lived in, thinking about it, and living in it, may mean to this generation. For he, among the great English poets, was the first of our true contemporaries, and although he has provided us with no great number of very clear answers, the questions he asked and the confusions which were his, are still ours. It is no mere accident that the poet awarded a recent Pulitzer prize, the author of *The Age of Anxiety*, should also have written (in his *Letters from Iceland*) a long "Letter to Lord Byron": the ease with which Auden's "Letter" assumed the *Don Juan* manner is less a tribute to Auden's powers than a proof of the strong and congenial bond between his mind[1] and Byron's. Like Auden ("Letter to Lord Byron") Byron had

> Come only to the rather tame conclusion
> That no man by himself has life's solution.

[1] See especially "Letter to Lord Byron. Part III," stanzas 4–21.

One of the major sources of Byron's failure to work out for himself an integrated view of human life and its relation to the universe is also peculiarly modern: it is his refusal (or inability) to look through blinkers at the problems of man and his relation to his civilization and the created universe. All Byron's talk about cant—and I know of no other English poet before him who hated it so much—is the genuine preface to the twentieth century reaction in disgust against slogans and attitudes too falsely idealistic, and to the resulting attitudes and techniques of realism and naturalism. Hemingway, for example, speaking of his early years, once defined his "greatest difficulty" (and hence by implication one of his chief aims) as that of "knowing truly what you really felt, rather than what you were supposed to feel, and had been taught to feel." Robinson Jeffers writes similarly of his own development in the introduction to his *Selected Poetry* of 1937: ". . . I decided not to tell lies in verse. Not to feign any emotion that I did not feel; . . . not to say anything because it was popular, or generally accepted, or fashionable in intellectual circles, unless I myself believed it; and not to believe easily." The valid emotion was also one of Byron's chief aims,[2] and like Hemingway he sought to base it upon an accurate reporting of the facts. The Byron of *Don Juan* and the letters was no less painfully honest when describing himself than when describing the visible world around him. This respect —even reverence—for fact is essentially that of modern science.

The effect of such extreme and basic honesty in thinking about men and things may be to form a man simply disillusioned, but Byron was more than that. He was a genuine rebel in art and life, a critic, and hence a man with faith in his way as a better one—in short, an optimist, with some kind

[2]See, for example, L. and J., II, 351.

of faith that things may be improved. Even beneath the anguished cries of *Childe Harold,* one hears the optimistic buoyancy of the movement of the lines; the same buoyancy is just beneath the surface of *Don Juan's* cynicism. F. Scott Fitzgerald's prose sometimes reveals the same contradiction. And so Byron examined the facts, questioned and rejected many a myth still with us, always trying to write out of himself honestly what he really felt, rather than what he was supposed to feel, inventing a new idiom to express himself—and was sustained, however imperfectly, through it all by the faith that he would make new discoveries, would by himself find "life's solution." It was essentially modern man's uncertain faith in himself, and Byron never found a better.

Byron's rejection, however, of the whole complex of ideas clustered about the prevailing romantic concept of nature represents much more than a mere negative achievement: for in attaining to the state of mind which enabled him to view nature in the cool light of the comic vision, he had also attained—if fitfully and incompletely—the kind of detachment indispensable to the creation of enduring art. It was in thus escaping, at least temporarily, from his own "wretched identity," that he achieved the style which P. E. More could describe as "the only epic manner left for a poet of the nineteenth century to adopt with power of conviction." But *Don Juan* is epic not only in scope: it has also the epic's impersonal quality. The subject of *Childe Harold,* finally, is Byron himself; consciousness of his own ego is with him in every scene. The scenery of "Donny Johnny," on the other hand, is scenery as it affects Juan—a much less autogenous figure than Harold—and a few other characters essentially dramatic. Thus Byron finally learned to translate his sea-storm memories, for example (and the several accounts which he read), not into the rhetoric or lyricism of *Childe Harold,* but into the vivid and objective descriptions of the second canto of *Don Juan*. He has, in short, become master of the scene; it no longer determines his feelings or thoughts at random. And so it should be, as he indicated in the last paragraph he wrote to the Reverend Mr. Bowles: "You see the man of education, the gentleman, and the scholar, sporting with his subject,—its master, not its slave."[3]

It is this kind of easy mastery over his materials, this detachment from his art, which makes possible the characteristic verbal irony of *Don Juan*—an unexpected incongruity following fast upon lines either pathetic, sublime, or in some other way serious. The process is classical in its simplicity: making good use of his strong sense of fact, Byron matched together the actual and the ideal, held them up to the light, and then described clearly the sharply silhouetted incongruities. The abundance of such humor in *Don Juan*, appealing as it does to the critical faculties and using the common-sensical and normal as standards, necessarily links the poem with the productions of reason and with classic art. It is this kind of "dry mock" which replaced, in Byron's mind, an earlier attitude toward nature which was often accompanied with impassioned sighs and wild declamations—and resulted, at its worst, in sentimentalism beyond defense.

Yet because of the generally satiric impact of *Don Juan*, the poem often has been denied high imaginative qualities. "A creator in the highest sense," it has been said, "Byron is not."[4] Just exactly what criticism of this kind may mean is to be seen, perhaps, in a statement of Carlyle's: "Unconsciousness is the sign of creation; consciousness at best that of manufacture."[5] "Conscious thought expresses itself readily

---

[3]L. and J., V, 592.

[4]C. H. Herford, *Age of Wordsworth* (London, 1897), p. 236.

[5]Carlyle's *Essays*, "Characteristics." Quoted by Professor Prescott in *The Poetic Mind* (New York, 1922), p. 97.

in words," writes Professor F. C. Prescott, "and is voluble." The deeper, poetic mind expresses itself "only in symbols—in significant pictures."[6] In *Don Juan*, to be sure, metaphors have disappeared almost altogether in favor of similes— similes which emphasize the similarity of the two things compared, which put the illustration in its clearest light. Such a use of figures, appealing to the reason and bringing out points of likeness clearly, is often said to be, by older as well as contemporary criticism, "altogether remote and alien from poetic usage."[7] Such criticism, of course, will place the highest premium on the misty metaphors of a Shelley or, in another context, on the obscure complexities of a Wallace Stevens. Yet if poetry is to continue to be read, let it once more be said, then poetic figures, however functional, must also communicate: communication is also among the functions of metaphor and simile. This was a major article in Byron's faith.

Undoubtedly, however, a preponderance of simile over metaphor does indicate a type of poetic mind differing in some basic way from one in which the ratio is reversed. In the words of William James,[8]

There are two stages in reasoned thought, one where similarity merely operates to call up cognate thoughts, and another farther stage, where the bond of identity between cognate thoughts is *noticed.* So minds of genius may be divided into two main sorts, those who *notice* the bond and those who merely *obey* it. The former are the abstract reasoners, the men of science; the latter are the poets, the men of intuition.

In *Don Juan* I have counted twelve instances in which Byron used the nature simile deliberately and self-consciously for a humorous effect: it is as if the self-conscious clarity of the Augustan poets had come out from behind its mask of im-

[6]*Ibid.,* p. 99.
[7]J. G. Jennings, *An Essay on Metaphor in Poetry* (London, 1915), p. 37.
[8]William James, *Psychology*, II, 361, quoted by Prescott, *op. cit.*, p. 218.

personality. The lines following are from the famous harem scene of *Don Juan* (VI, 68) and describe one of the sleeping beauties:

> A fourth as marble, statue-like and still,
> Lay in a breathless, hush'd, and stony sleep;
> White, cold, and pure, as looks a frozen rill,
> Or the snow minaret on an Alpine steep,
> Or Lot's wife done in salt,—or what you will;—
> My similes are gather'd in a heap,
> So pick and choose—perhaps you'll be content
> With a carved lady on a monument.

Another[9] of Juan's loves is described in the same manner:

> But Adeline was not indifferent: for
> (*Now* for a common-place!) beneath the snow,
> As a volcano holds the lava more
> Within—*et cetera.* Shall I go on?—No!
> I hate to hunt down a tired metaphor,
> So let the often-used volcano go.
> Poor thing! How frequently, by me and others,
> It hath been stirr'd up till its smoke quite smothers!

> I'll have another figure in a trice:—
> What say you to a bottle of champagne?
> Frozen into a very vinous ice,
> Which leaves few drops of that immortal rain,
> Yet in the very centre, past all price,
> About a liquid glassful will remain;
> And this is stronger than the strongest grape
> Could e'er express in its expanded shape:

> 'Tis the whole spirit brought to a quintessence;
> And thus the chilliest aspects may concentre
> A hidden nectar under a cold presence.

Rather than deny such passages the name of poetry, it is more discreet, perhaps, to observe that the figures appeal to the

---

[9]*Don Juan*, XIII, 36–38. For other figures of this kind in *Don Juan*, see the "Dedication," 2; I, 55; II, 5–6; V, 132; VI, 33–34, 57; VIII, 29; IX, 26–27; XII, 41.

reason as well as the imagination. They are essentially classical in the clarity of their conception. But they are also peculiarly modern: if such a style is one which may be adopted
by a poet "with power of conviction," it is only because it can
convey the poet's *absence* of conviction. On the level of poetic
diction, it is simply a matter of refusing to use the tired metaphor, as Byron says. But on another, it is—in both the figures
—his rejection of the feigned emotion, his refusal to tell lies
in verse, whether talking about country landscapes, modern
cities, or the contradictions of women.

This state of mind, pointing in one way as it does toward
classical art, also paves the way, paradoxically, for the kind
of ambiguity characteristic of contemporary verse. Nowhere
is Byron so modern as here, where he sets up a state of
tension between the complexities of several points of view.
This deliberate use of ambiguity saves him, as it does many
a modern poet, from sentimentalism; it also allows him to
project successfully a state of mind, to project it honestly,
without "cant," and without the falseness of oversimplification. The Daniel Boone stanzas in the eighth canto are a case
in point: Byron knew that the life of the noble savage is
actually an unattainable ideal, and the figure of Boone the
child of nature is used as a symbolic device to satirize man's
inhumanity to man. But health, happiness, long life, a realiz-
able sort of Roman utilitarian virtue, freedom from care,
gain, corruption, lust, and ignoble splendor (all of which
Boone symbolizes) are desirable, and it is to these that Byron
gives his faith, not to the myth of the noble savage, to a
belief that life spent treading "wilds of deepest maze" is
necessarily characterized by these qualities. Byron no more
wished to become a Daniel Boone than Swift wished to become a Houyhnhnm. Yet the concept of Eden is an ancient
one and the desire for a life of simplicity one of the strongest

desires of all: it is difficult to reject the old gods without re-gret. That regret is also present in Byron's lines, in a linger-ing half-wish that the life of the noble savage could still be believed in as a thing real and possible. Thus the ironic epithet stands in the same stanza beside another used without irony to convey subtly a state of mind far from simple. And so by this means, Byron is enabled to qualify his attitude, pro-tect himself from the simple and sentimental, mingle attitudes of approval and disapproval, and thus by means of a symbol to attack with great effectiveness the horrors of civilized war-fare without being forced to embrace the fallacies of the con-cept set up as its opposite, the peaceful life of Boone.

The formal vehicles of Byron's humor in *Don Juan* thus deny, in effect, many of the articles in the nineteenth century poetic credo and point forward toward certain critical posi-tions typical of the present generation, and implicit as well in much good verse written in any period. Byron's reaction against a sentimentalized concept of nature and the merely pretty not only made it possible for him to include references to a nature "ugly" and harmful to man (or "ugly" but useful, as in the tenth canto's parody of the picturesque tour); his complete rejection of "the cant of nature" also allowed him to reveal the apparently irrelevant or warring elements within his total consciousness of nature. A successful reconciliation Byron did not always achieve, but his effort to do so represents an important far step along the way toward the recognition that things in themselves are neither poetic nor unpoetic. And like that of the contemporary poet, too, Byron's effort in *Don Juan* to fuse and thus reconcile what in ordinary experience is inharmonious is essentially an effort to discover order in the universe without oversimplifying the world-picture. Byron, in brief, with his immense and essentially modern conscious-ness of self, was unwilling to ignore the immense complexity of his experience. The result, in the poetry, is often a view of nature or civilization which may be flatly contradicted elsewhere, but it is also one which is cruelly inclusive in its method, refusing to achieve its unity by the mere exclusion of the "unpoetic," one which often expresses a lively awareness that the obvious attitude is not the only possible attitude, and thus one which can still speak directly, conversationally, and with force and good humor to the mind of the present century.

Sunset and twilight time, for example, as Byron knew, have always been loved by lovers of the picturesque; but as he knew quite as well, the hour may be one "less liked by husbands than by lovers." So also the warm sun of the South may create a beautiful natural paradise, but[10]

> What men call gallantry, and gods adultery,
> Is much more common where the climate's sultry.

Now the effect of irony—it is true of many a poet of the recent past—may be one which implies more clearly than anything else an absence of strong and single-minded conviction in the poet, a deep-rooted uncertainty of mind; that is, the diverse elements of experience gathered together may seem to defy the poet's powers of reconciliation. Such an effect may be deliberately intended; the mood of uncertainty is a very real and characteristic one of the present century. But the effect may also be unintentional: the state of mind which wavers, off balance, between two points of view may smack less of integration than of fragmentation, and may produce the effect simply of a mind open at both ends. Both, one feels, are typical enough of the twentieth century poetic mind. As Eliot has expressed it, "When a poet's mind is perfectly

[10]*Don Juan*, I, 63. For similar expressions of the effect of climate upon the passions and lives of men see *Don Juan*, V, 157; VIII, 128; X, 33; I, 69; IV, 56; X, 37, 44; X, 58.

equipped for its work, it is constantly amalgamating disparate experience; the ordinary man's experience is chaotic, irregular, fragmentary. The latter falls in love, or reads Spinoza, and these two experiences have nothing to do with each other, or with the noise of the typewriter or the smell of cooking; in the mind of the poet these experiences are always forming new wholes." In Eliot's sense, it must be admitted, the mind of Byron did not always form new wholes. At its occasional best, Byron's comic vision suggests that the physical, the ludicrous, the vulgar, or prosaic are necessarily at the very center of the sublime or the spiritual; but its usual implication is the simpler one that life is merely a comic mixture, and man had best laugh to keep from weeping. On the other hand, neither did Byron suppress nine-tenths of his awareness of the world around him: this was his great service to English poetry in the nineteenth century. This too explains in part his enduring and immense popularity, even when poets who synthesized their experience more successfully are at hand. If the experience of the ordinary man is fragmentary, then he must recognize his fellow in the remarkable combination of genuis and John Doe which is Byron. A picturesque starlit night, as a matter of literal fact, *is* put to its several uses.

Yet to notice those several conflicting uses one after another in two lines of verse is not necessarily to reconcile them. The reasons are not far to seek. Successful non-dramatic irony probably always demands an integrated personality which has won through to an integrated world-view; reconciliation would seem otherwise to be impossible. As MacNeice wrote of his own *Autumn Journal,* in the foreword to his *Poems 1925–1940,* it is

in a sense a failure; it fails in depth. I had foreseen that failure. We shall not be capable of depth—of tragedy or *great* poetry—until we have made sense of our world.

"Autumn Journal" remains a journal—topical, personal, rambling, but, failing other things, honest.

Much of this description fits rather exactly Byron's *Don Juan*. Byron's failure was also a failure to make sense of his world. One is left finally with the impression of a man containing within himself tremendous unresolved conflicts, both personal and philosophical. But this too the modern mind can respond to. For Byron, before Pound, was the type of the wanderer, a wanderer over the face of the earth, a wanderer among conflicting creeds, the "wandering outlaw of his own dark mind." And insofar as this century is at the same time the century of the common man and the century of homeless men and lost generations, Byron can speak to them all, for his problems are still theirs.

However chaotic and unintegrated oftentimes the elements in the ordinary man's experience may be, he does not confuse nature with art, nor assume that they are fundamentally similar: this is the error of the bookish mentality, and of many of the nineteenth century poets. But it was almost never Byron's error, and for this too we may still read him. "The weather is still muggy as a London May," he writes,[11] "—mist, mizzle, the air replete with Scotticisms, which, though fine in the descriptions of Ossian, are somewhat tiresome in real, prosaic perspective." A mind of this kind recognizes without reconciling the disparate elements of experience. This is Byron's regular way; it is his firm grip on reality which is speaking, and his limited power of synthesis. He never believed, as Arnold wrote to Clough, that one of the offices of poetry is "to compose and elevate the mind by a sustained tone, numerous allusions, and a grand style." *Don Juan* denies all these: when Byron's poem achieves unity of tone it is one progressive, not static, one shifting easily from pathos to

[11] L. and J., V, 176.

bathos to the sublime, but attempting always to give Byron's whole thought and to give it honestly and without self-deception. If the twilight hour is put to both esthetic and immoral uses, we may rely on Byron to say so, and so deny, in effect, that poetry should be limited to fine feelings or moral uplift.

If the net product of all Byron's serious and deliberately considered "philosophical" thought is confusion, what then is its present use? That confusion itself, first of all, has its use; it is the voice of a kindred spirit speaking, and the subject, finally, is the problem of unbelief. That voice, whether indifferent or proudly defiant, more than often expresses an anguished sense of vacancy. It is one concerned with the personal consequences of irreligion, the voice of unbelief faithfully describing the consequences of unbelief. Thus it speaks in a language that may be understood still, the language of discontent, blank misgiving, and spiritual desolation. The words are those of a man in quest of a faith.

But this is not enough, of course; the same voice, conveying the same frustration and intellectual confusion, speaks, in an idiom even more contemporary, out of a hundred pages printed today. Byron's final contribution is not here. It is to be sought, instead, in certain basic attitudes and assumptions about nature and civilization which are, at least on the surface, neither religious nor philosophical. They are all, in the best sense, realistic, conservative, and stoical—Byron's ability to look facts squarely in the face, see them clearly, and accept the implications of their existence. These fundamental attitudes represent, together, Byron's refusal to accept flight as a way out— in a word, his anti-primitivism. He refused to escape into a Wordsworthian asylum of natural solitude, into Chateaubriand's land of the happy savage, or into anybody's dream of the Middle Ages or a future Utopia. Egocentric as Byron was, he never once accepted the myth of man's perfectibility, which said that man's beautiful soul, once free of all the "artificial" burdens of existing civilization, would then rise its own master, "free from guilt and pain." This for Byron was the blind sin of pride, if nothing worse. Man was a compound of good and evil, requiring both restraint and support from a source completely without him, and Byron had only to look within himself to see that this was so. "My good and evil are at perpetual war," he writes[12] after a visit with a craniologist. Man's soul was a moral battleground, and the forces of light and darkness fought over it. This pervasive idea about the nature of human nature colored all that Byron ever wrote and is the root of what is best in him; it accounts for the harmony he sensed between himself and things as they are, and at the same time allowed him to see things clearly as they are, imperfect. It did not, of course, provide him to any degree with a sense of inner harmony; the idea itself, although it has been used by religion, is not essentially religious; it belongs quite as much to psychology, that is, to science, and need not have religious overtones.

Byron had all the temptation that unhappy people always have had to blame their unhappiness on the structure of their civilization—to blame even the principle of civilization—and so turn for comfort to some Golden Age of the past or the future where there was or would be a society without arts, sciences, or crafts, and men lived, or would live, happily together without money, trade, private property, or strife of any kind. But Byron's view of the world made this impossible for him. The sources of virtue and happiness are always, for him, within the individual. During his moments of clearest insight he saw that both nature and civilization were things indifferent in themselves to both good and ill, happiness

[12]L. and J., III, 137.

or unhappiness, though they might be used for either. In his speech against the Framework Bill of 1812, for example, although he pleaded for the rioting workers, he never implied at any time that the new machines should be outlawed as things evil in themselves, or that their use be circumscribed. Instead, his whole argument is based on the assumption[13] that the new machines are things indifferent, and may be used as men will: ". . . the adoption of the enlarged machinery in that state of our commerce which the country once boasted might have been beneficial . . .; yet, in the present situation of our manufacturers . . ., frames of this description tend materially to aggravate the distress and discontent of the disappointed sufferers." The real cause of these distresses, he goes on to say, lies deeper—in the government's destructive policy of the past eighteen years. Or in his speech for Catholic emancipation in 1812, as a climax to his damnation of the Protestant Charter Schools, he says,[14] "Better would it be to send them [the children] any where than teach them such doctrines; better send them to those islands in the South Seas, where they might more humanely learn to become cannibals . . . ." Byron never once seriously glorified a state of things as they are not and cannot even be, nor ever once seriously attacked, even by implication, the principle of civilization as it is in its best broad outlines.

> I mean to show things really as they are,
> Not as they ought to be. . . .[15]

Particular evil there was of course, and he rebelled against it, and sometimes sought to escape from it. His long-contemplated South American project of becoming a planter remains (after the element of purely personal dissatisfaction

[13]L. and J., II, 426.
[14]L. and J., II, 436–437.
[15]*Don Juan*, XII, 40.

has been subtracted) the most serious criticism he ever passed upon the two forms of Western civilization which he knew at first hand. Italy seemed to him in 1819 to be unbearably effeminate; England had just had the Peterloo Massacre, which had been preceded by the suspension of the Habeas Corpus Act and the restriction of the press. In 1815–1816 it had denied him the right, in effect, to establish a home and a family there. But what Byron hoped to find in South America was actually more civilization, not less. As he wrote to Hobhouse,[16] he wanted only a free country which would allow him to be a "decent Citizen" and give him the opportunity to occupy himself rationally. But Byron for once did not have the facts, and Hobhouse made the appropriate comment[17] in a letter to Murray:

But our poet is too good for a planter—too good to sit down before a fire made of mare's legs, to a dinner of beef without salt and bread. It is the wildest of all his meditations—pray tell him. The plague and Yellow Jack, and famine and free quarter, besides a thousand other ills, will stare him in the face. No tooth-brushes, no corn-rubbers, no *Quarterly Reviews*. In short, plenty of all he abominates and nothing of all he loves.

Byron did not go, of course, and his refusal represents his final comment. This is his contribution. He is the rebel within the accepted order of things, the loyal and realistic opposition.

This is the attitude behind his poetic treatment of London, Newstead, and the life of the noble savage. London is described in *Don Juan* (X, 83; XI, 8, 21–23) as smokey, crowded, confused and wicked; but it remains the center of the world and the symbol of the present best that man has achieved. It even has a beauty of its own, and in describing

---

[16]L. and J., IV, 357–358.

[17]*Memoir and Correspondence of John Murray*, ed. Smiles (London, 1891), I, 409.

it[18] Byron extended the normally prescribed limits of picturesque composition, and reached that point which was a few
years ago the boast of "modern" poetry—the beauty of indus-
trial civilization:

> A mighty mass of brick, and smoke, and shipping,
> Dirty and dusky, but as wide as eye
> Could reach, with here and there a sail just skipping
> In sight, then lost amidst the forestry
> Of masts; a wilderness of steeples peeping
> On tiptoe through their sea-coal canopy;
> A huge, dun cupola, like a foolscap crown
> On a fool's head—and there is London Town!

This is the poetry of a man who is trying to come to grips
with the world as it is, not as he imagines it should be. Byron
likes the sounds and hurry of the city, and he spoke out of
a knowledge of the facts, for he had proved experimentally
all that the essentially provincial Dr. Johnson had ever said
about London. Except in the limited literal sense imposed
upon him by society, Byron's world was never beyond the
horizon:[19]

> . . . The man who has stood on the Acropolis,
> And look'd down over Attica; or he
> Who has sail'd where picturesque Constantinople is,
> Or seen Timbuctoo, or hath taken tea
> In small-eyed China's crockery-ware metropolis,
> Or sat amidst the bricks of Nineveh,
> May not think much of London's first appearance—
> But ask him what he thinks of it a year hence!

Byron's satire is that of the true-born Englishman, that of a
man who had walked the streets of London and remembered
what he saw because it pleased him.

[18]*Don Juan*, X, 82.
[19]*Ibid.*, XI, 7.

But the Londoner has always had his week end in the country when he could afford it. Such a man, though, does not of course deny civilization; he takes it along with him into the country—and the heavy baggage may be of quantities sufficient enough to be quite amusing. The Newstead cantos of *Don Juan* (XIII–XVII) have, of course, a general satirical import. That satire is aimed chiefly, not at the idea of nature itself or at a life close to nature, but at the city-bred man out of his accustomed environment. There are bores and fools enough assembled at Newstead but, all in all, no more of them than Juan meets anywhere else. The guests and their hosts, in short, represent the average humanity encountered in *Don Juan;* they are the world as Byron saw it. Their reaction to country life is left in no doubt. To a man and a woman they are utterly bored, and spend most of their hours trying to escape that boredom. The elderly walk in the library or in the gardens, others play billiards and cards, go boating, fishing, or ride to the hounds, and meet again in the evening for dinner and duets, from which they retire as early as possible to their beds. Of the country gentleman's chief recreation, Juan (XIV, 35) thought at heart,

> . . . like courtly Chesterfield,
> Who, after a long chase o'er hills, dales, bushes,
> And what not, though he rode beyond all price,
> Ask'd next day, 'If men ever hunted *twice?*'

In brief,

> . . . of all nature's discrepancies, none
> Upon the whole is greater than the difference
> Beheld between the country and the town,
> Of which the latter merits every preference.

But life at an English country estate is hardly a life of natural solitude; it is an aspect, a single aspect of English civilization, and this accounts for the similarity between parts of the Newstead cantos and the estate poem of the eighteenth century. The long passage (XIII, 55–72) descriptive of Newstead and its grounds, for example, is wholly without satiric overtones, and differs from the typical estate poem of the eighteenth century only in that it was written by a former owner of the estate instead of the usual flattering applicant for a position. An old monastery, now a mansion of "huge halls, long galleries, spacious chambers," "stood embosm'd in a happy valley, crown'd by high woodlands" and reflected in a "lucid lake."

> Amidst the court a Gothic fountain play'd
> Symmetrical, but deck'd with carvings quaint.

Newstead, in short, offers the perfect setting for a gracious and highly civilized life; whether it is actually lived depends on the people in it. The sources of virtue and happiness are within the individual. The lines on the autumn harvest (XIII, 75–77) which follow are also out of the eighteenth century, and recall nothing so much as the tradition of Philips' *Cider* (1708). It is a mellow season of gathered corn, a manor full of nut-brown partridges and brilliant pheasants, a cellar stocked with wine—a season with as many indoor comforts as outdoor attractions, and all for the purpose of enabling man to live a life more gracious. Nothing reveals the centrality of man in the thought of Byron more clearly than his attitude toward the season of autumn: it is primarily the season of productiveness, the time when nature is of most *use* to man. This age-old attitude has nothing in common with the romantic nostalgia which glorifies the sadness of the season as a prelude to the death and decay of winter.

Byron's contemporaneousness is revealed once more by his attitude toward the simple life close to nature. In the June, 1932, issue of *Harper's Magazine*, George Boas, arguing "In Defense of Machines" and things as they are generally in the present century, distinguished two kinds of pastoralists:

"The pastoralist is usually either a genuine lover of rural things or a city dweller to whom the country means the spring gardens, the old swimming hole, barn dances, and corn husking, rather than winter, weeding and 'cultivating,' hauling water, the wood pile, drought, and insect pests." This is exactly the distinction that Byron made betwen the "Lakers" and their "Under-sect," and the knowledge contained in it explains why Byron never glorified the hard life of the peasant. There are two sorts of "Naturals," Byron explained,[20]

the Lakers, who whine about Nature because they live in Cumberland; and their *under-sect* (which some one has maliciously called the 'Cockney School'), who are enthusiastical for the country because they live in London. It is to be observed, that the rustical founders are rather anxious to disclaim any connexion with their metropolitan followers, whom they ungraciously review, and call cockneys, atheists, foolish fellows, bad writers, and other hard names not less ungrateful than unjust. I can understand the pretensions of the aquatic gentlemen of Windermere to what Mr. Braham terms '*entusymusy,*' for lakes, and mountains, and daffodils, and buttercups; but I should be glad to be apprized of the foundation of the London propensities of their imitative brethren to the same 'high argument.' Southey, Wordsworth, and Coleridge have rambled over half Europe, and seen Nature in most of her varieties (although I think that they have occasionally not used her very well) ; but what on earth—of earth, and sea, and Nature—have the others seen?

It all goes back to one of the main facets of Byron's mind— his respect for fact. The knowledge of what he had seen in England and Europe kept him from ever sketching a sentimental picture of the Happy Peasant. The same respect for fact, if nothing else, saved him from subscribing to the myth of the noble savage, created benevolent and kept that way by his simple life close to nature. It is sometimes maintained

[20]L. and J., V, 587–588.

that the heroes of the early Oriental tales are akin to the noble savage, but nothing could be wider of the mark. They prefer a life apart from civilization, to be sure, and feel hemmed in by cities, which they sometimes feel to be centers of corruption; but each one is a man of violence and lacks the benevolence of the noble savage; and many of them, as I have pointed out at some length, labor under a burden of guilt which flatly excludes the essential innocence and purity of soul that the noble savage has always. Byron would have agreed without qualification to the sentiments expressed by MacNeice in his *Autumn Journal* of 1939 (section XII):

> Not that I would rather be a peasant; the Happy
>   Peasant
> Like the Noble Savage is a myth;
> I do not envy the self-possession of an elm-tree
> Nor the aplomb of a granite monolith.
> All that I would like to be is human, having a share
> In a civilised, articulate and well-adjusted
> Community where the mind is given its due
> But the body is not distrusted.

Haidée represents the nearest approach that Byron ever made to drawing the noble savage type. She is "Nature's bride,"[21] essentially benevolent and innocent. But for a number of reasons she raises no question of Byron's serious belief in the idea. The prevailing romantic tone of the Haidée episode, first of all, is completely dissipated after the death of Haidée and the desolation of the island, and Juan moves on to other conquests of the same kind. This perhaps is the most important point. Juan's relations with women are all alike. Haidée was "Nature's bride," but in the next line[22] she is described as "Passion's child." And so are they all. Byron's application of the phrase "a child of Nature" to the voluptuous

[21]*Don Juan*, II, 202.
[22]*Loc. cit.*

Dudù of harem fame[23] seems to indicate beyond any question that he was using the old words in a new way. Although Dudù is treated with quite the same degree of seriousness by Byron that Haidée receives, their only other similarity is a lack of inhibitions. The question of environment does not enter into the matter; both finally are symbols of the other sex for Juan to conquer. In this sense, in their lack of a restraining sexual morality, all of Juan's conquests are brides and children of nature, and Byron is laughing again.

The question of Byron's serious belief in the idea of the noble savage is answered further by the comic episodes surrounding that of Haidée, which tend to shed their own light upon it, and also by numerous references[24] within the Haidée episode itself which are not of a serious kind. And there is finally the fact of Haidée's father, which throws a comic light necessarily over the daughter. Lambro has the same "love . . . of scenes sublime" that his daughter has; he takes "a pleasure in the gentle stream" and shows "a joy in flowers." But Lambro is a pirate and slaver, and remains quite unaffected by the beauty of his natural surroundings. Taste and virtue for Byron are not the same, and in sensing this Byron withdrew, in a single movement, the ethical content from nature, upon which the entire Return to Nature Movement depended. Insofar as Lambro is the complete man of feeling who unfortunately lacks a conscience, he may be regarded as a kind of parody of the noble savage. But he is actually nearer to Byron's early heroes than to the noble savage type, and provides the most superb example of all, perhaps, of Byron's ability to turn and mock himself. For Lambro is a

[23] *Ibid.*, VI, 60. This interpretation is borne out further by Byron's application of the humorous phrase "Nature's good old college" (II, 136) to Zoe, Haidée's more experienced companion.

[24] *Ibid.*, II, 136, 142, 144–45, 148, 189–190, 193–194. For Lambro, see III, 56.

strange and wonderful mixture of Byron and the Byronic hero grown old, and become (of all things) the outraged father of an erring daughter. Like Byron himself he has become miserly and acquired a menagerie. But he also has most of the distinguishing marks of the early heroes: "of mild demeanor though of savage mood," he was "meant for something better"; a man more sinned against than sinning, he had taken to the sea originally out of patriotic motives, had seen his mercy abused, and allowed his heart to become hardened. Now he shows only "hate to the world," and in his daughter finds "his only shrine of feeling undefiled." He is the old mixture of good and ill unbelievably heightened, but this time comically stripped of the old romantic mystery and mastery.

In *Cain* Byron even attacked Adam's paradise of innocence:

> The snake spoke truth: it was the tree of knowledge,
> It was the tree of life; knowledge is good,
> And life is good; and how can both be evil?

To attack Adam, the man of virtue happy because of his ignorance, is manifestly to attack the first assumption of the noble savage idea, the assumption that innocence based upon ignorance represents man's highest good. Whether the Biblical account was to be taken as literal truth or fable, the fallen state of man was always a fact for Byron. In an age which had long been talking about innate goodness and uncorrupted virtue in a state of nature, Byron held consistently to a belief in the existence of sin and the humanistic ideal of virtue as self-discipline. The fall of man—however he resented the injustice of its consequences—is the all-shadowing fact for him.[25] *The Island* exhibits the most remarkable collision of these two traditions of thought. In part, a large part, it captures the pastoral's spirit and mood of innocence to a surprising degree.

[25]For humorous references in *Don Juan*, see I, 127; II, 193; V, 49, 109; IX, 19; XIV, 23, 78.

But its ending is that of tragedy, which satisfies the forces of the existing moral order. E. K. Chamber's definition[26] of the pastoral form also provides a pretty good description of important elements in Byron's poem:

Pastoral is not the poetry of country life, but the poetry of the townsman's dream of country life. . . . Three spiritual notes characterize the pastoral. One is the exaltation of content, connecting itself on the one side with the longing for a renewed simplicity of manners, on the other with a vivid sense of the uncertainty of all human advantages. . . . Then there is the note of love; the one serious preoccupation of the pastoral life. . . . And finally there is the note of delight in, and refreshment from, natural beauty.

To illustrate the obvious presence of each one of these characteristics in *The Island* would be tedious. They are there in large measure; but the structure of the poem emphasizes, if anything, the moral responsibility which attaches to human actions. In Byron's treatment of the mutineers, there is nothing of the dishonesty or confusion which may result from a belief in man's natural goodness. The end can never, of itself, justify the means. But even the end does not receive Byron's approval. The purpose of the mutiny is to satisfy

The wish—which ages have not yet subdued
In man—to have no master save his mood.

This is the language of the moralist, and moral Byron always is, as he himself maintained. The mutineers achieve a masterless condition for a short time, of course; but the forces of law and order, convention and restraint, are finally satisfied in the death of Christian. The tragic flaw in his character is his tendency to flout the moral order.

If Byron failed to achieve integration and harmony in almost every way—in his personality, thought, and poetry—it

[26]*English Pastorals*, ed. Chambers (London, 1895), pp. xxxix-xli.

seems absurd to link his name with that of the Greeks. Yet the fact that he made his earliest and his latest pilgrimage to Greece is one of the most revealing biographical facts about him, and therein, in a very real way, lies the unity of his life. From its focal point in Greece the best of Byron emerges for the contemporary world, the Greek way translated, not always well, but more meaningfully for us by his essentially modern mind. I do not mean here to enter into the old classical-romantic argument or to imply that the qualities of proportion, balance, harmony, coherence and the like were predominant in either Byron's thought or poetry. It is not a fine sense of form or structure which links Byron with classical Greece. Both his long works are without form in the usual sense, and he realized it. The first *Childe Harold,* he admitted before its publication,[27] "was intended to be a poem on *Ariosto's plan,* that *is* to *say* on *no plan* at all. . . ." He said the same thing about *Don Juan* on numerous occasions, both in and out of the poem. If Byron must be pigeonholed, he is best called realist. Certainly the term romantic is unsatisfactory, even for *Childe Harold,* earth-bound as it is. Byron inherited certain ideas, to be sure, from the early eighteenth century and before, and a poetic vocabularly which he used as late as *The Island,* but it is not to these that I refer.

The meaning and value of Byron's relations with Greece are in part to be sought in what he tried to be, not necessarily in what he achieved. He was, briefly, one of the last of the English poets to try to make himself a complete man—poet, scholar, lover, sportsman, world traveller, statesman, soldier, and administrator. It is the Greek idea of wholeness, modified of course by the European Renaissance. Byron's ideal, expressed by word and deed from first to last, was to make of himself a man equally at ease on horseback, swimming in the

27L. and J., I, 320.

sea, admiring a picturesque view, writing at his desk, or directing the affairs of a nation fighting for its freedom. He hated specialists, and none more than the mere speculator about this existence, these dreamers, he called them. Action before philosophy every time. So it was with the active Greeks, who had no time for the issueless contemplation of their Eastern neighbors, which left life behind it in successive stages of abstract thought or symbolic art. The world was a place to modify, not something to contemplate or forget in contemplation. But the poets have always been associated with the philosophers and mystics, and so they were in Byron's mind. The result is again something peculiarly modern: the poet's distrust of his own profession, a feeling of insecurity which reveals itself on one level by the ridicule of things "poetic," on another by the attempt to say more in a poem than can ever be communicated. But the modern poet's distrust of his own calling is most clearly revealed by his desertion to the sphere of action. Witness the recent Spanish War or the successful writers who have taken jobs in the government. As Stephen Spender explained it in *The Still Centre* (1942), "The violence of the times we are living in, the necessity of sweeping and general and immediate action, tend to dwarf the experience of the individual, and to make his immediate environment and occupations perhaps something that he is even ashamed of." Byron asks, "Who would write, who had any thing better to do? 'Action—action—action'—said Demosthenes: 'Action*s*—action*s*,' I say, and not writing,—least of all rhyme."[28] "I prefer the talents of action—of war, or the senate, or even of science,—to all the speculations of those mere dreamers of another existence (I don't mean religiously but fancifully) and spectators of this apathy."[29]

[28]L. and J., II, 345.
[29]L. and J., III, 405.

The emphasis is everywhere in Byron on life. After an amusing account of watching a group of prostitutes at Covent Garden he exclaims, "How I do delight in observing life as it really is!—and myself, after all, the worst of any."[30] Hazlitt has said that Byron in *Childe Harold* turned the world into a great mausoleum. Two observations need to be made upon this statement. First, the stately and magnificent tombs which Byron described were always those of great and daring men. No poet has ever sung more gloriously the sentiment of history in landscape than Byron did. Greece was a land hallowed because of its human memories. He could never agree with Coleridge, who wrote,[31] "I believe I should walk over the plain of Marathon without taking more interest in it than in any other plain of similar features." Instead, Byron stood again with Dr. Johnson, who believed that "That man is little to be envied, whose patriotism would not gain force upon the plain of Marathon, or whose piety would not grow warmer among the ruins of Iona." In the second place, it must be admitted, to be sure, that Byron early enrolled in the Graveyard School of poetry, and he is one of the great masters of the language of desolation and black melancholy. Through the fourth canto of *Childe Harold,* the skull, the worm, the bat, the owl, the cypress, the tomb in a midnight graveyard— these are recurrent themes, and the grave shall bear the chiefest prize away. This sort of thing disappears with *Beppo,* of course. But before this, in life or poetry, it was never Byron's way to recoil instinctively from the world of outside fact, or deny its importance. The reality for him was so obviously based on the present *fact* that he sometimes used the word interchangeably with *truth.* His was an affirmative spirit, and

[30]L. and J., II, 378.
[31]This, and following statement by Johnson are quoted from F. L. Lucas's *The Decline and Fall of the Romantic Ideal* (New York, 1936), p. 234.

the facts of life were never black or bitter enough to force him to turn away, and seek refuge in a Word which had no dealings with the World. A kind of Greek joy in life is ever pulsing beneath these midnight meditations, and for this reason some of it is very bad poetry. We are not convinced. But neither do we despair. The leaden weight and despairing movement of line evident in certain modern poems is not here. Byron was not a defeated man. Aging Antony in his last years though he was, his tremendous energy carried him on, and his last major works, the latter cantos of *Don Juan,* and *The Island,* show no falling off: the natural world is described with the same enthusiasm as in *Childe Harold,* III; the delight in men and women as they are has diminished no whit. The waste land of the spirit Byron knew, but he refused to give himself up a willing victim to depression or to a philosophy which denied the world. The world for him, bitter and brief though he realized life to be, remained for him a place of reasonable wonder and delight, and finally, a place of meaningful action among men. It is in this that Byron has earned his place among the most completely civilized of the poets: seeing the world with less illusions than many of his contemporaries, he yet delighted in it, nevertheless; and dedicating himself to the things of the mind, he yet retained unimpaired his power to act.

APPENDIX

The earliest form of the Zeluco theme which I have come upon appears in *Lady Julia Mandeville* (1763) by Frances Brooke. It is probable, I should think, that the idea may be traced to an even earlier date. The implication of the passage,[1] as in most novels employing the theme, is that a corrupted mind can take no pleasure in the beauties of nature. The hero is writing to a friend:

. . . my Lord leading us into the garden, an unexpected scene opened on my view, which recalled the idea of the fabulous pleasures of the golden age, and could not but be infinitely pleasing to every mind uncorrupted by the false glare of tinsel pomp, and awake to the genuine charms of simplicity and nature.

On a spacious lawn, bounded on every side by a profusion of the most odoriferous flowering shrubs, a joyous band of villagers were assembled. . . .

The Zeluco theme assumes several forms in a later novel by Mrs. Brooke, *The History of Emily Montague* (1769), which is said to be the first Canadian novel. It contains elaborate and enthusiastic natural descriptions. In the passage[2] following, the hero is describing Sir George Clayton, who "with a splendid income, is avaricious, selfish, proud, vain, and profuse; lavish to every caprice of vanity and ostentation which regards himself, coldly inattentive to the real wants of others":

I study my fellow traveller closely; his character, indeed, is not difficult to ascertain; his feelings are dull, nothing makes the least impression on him; he is as insensible to the various beauties of the charming country through which we have travelled, as the very Canadian peasants themselves who in-

[1]Frances Brooke, *Lady Julia Mandeville*, ed. Poole (London, 1930), p. 47.
[2]Frances Brooke, *The History of Emily Montague*, ed. Burpee (Ottawa, 1931), p. 66 (letter 30) and p. 48 (letter 17).

habit it. I watched his eyes at some of the most beautiful prospects, and saw not the least gleam of pleasure there. . . .

In the passage[3] below, the implication is that a love of nature and a gloomy disposition are incompatible: the first lesson taught by the Book of Nature (for those who can read it) is that man should be happy. The heroine is writing to her closest friend:

> You say true, my dear Bell: Heaven doubtless formed us to be happy even in this world; and we obey its dictates in being so, when we can without encroaching on the happiness of others.
> This lesson is, I think, plain from the book Providence has spread before us: the whole universe smiles, the earth is clothed in lively colors, the animals are playful, the birds sing: in being chearful with innocence, we seem to conform to the order of nature, and the will of that Beneficent Power to whom we owe our being.
> If the Supreme Creator had meant us to be gloomy, he would, it seems to me, have clothed the earth in black, not in that lively green, which is the livery of chearfulness and joy.

The friend to whom the above letter is addressed, the witty and attractive Arabella Fermor,[4] handles the theme with a somewhat lighter touch: "I believe I shall set about writing a system of ethics myself, which shall be short, clear, and comprehensive; nearer the Epicurean perhaps than the Stoic; but rural, refined, and sentimental; rural by all means; for who does not know that virtue is a country gentlewoman? all the good mammas will tell you, there is no such being heard of in town."

Clara Reeve's *The Exiles; or, Memoirs of the Count de Cronstadt* (1788) states the Zeluco theme[5] clearly and suc-

---

[3]*Ibid.*, pp. 270–271 (letter 196).
[4]*Ibid.*, p. 44 (letter 15).
[5]Clara Reeve, *The Exiles* (London, 1788), I, 4, 12, 14.

cinctly. The hero is forced by circumstances into a bigamous marriage and so wears "the veil of melancholy drawn over his countenance." He admits in a letter to his friend, ". . . yes, I am indeed unhappy—a secret grief preys on my heart . . ." and shortly afterwards is forced to confess, ". . . alas! I have lost my relish for the spring and the country; nature holds out all her charms to me in vain."

The scene of most of the first volume of Charlotte Smith's *Ethelinde, or the Recluse of the Lake* (1789) is laid at Grasmere Abbey on Grasmere Water. There the virtuous Lord Newenden takes his dissolute wife, as he later explains[6] after she has eloped with another man, in the "hope that such a journey might yield her a salutary respite from perpetual company, late hours, and deep play, and a foolish idea that the scenes of sublime and beautiful nature might awaken in her mind a taste for simple and domestic pleasures." But the beauties of nature are lost upon a soul so constituted, even from the first. In the following passage,[7] the unfortunate pair are approaching Grasmere:

"Look, my love," continued he, "at the wild grandeur of that varied and bold outline; observe the effects of the sun's rays on the summits of the crags, while the large and swelling clouds that pass over seem almost to touch them, and give them numberless shades in their progress."

"I see but little beauty in those dreary looking mountains," answered Lady Newenden, with a cold and disdainful smile.

The heroine,[8] who is persecuted by Lady Newenden, "had learned to see the face of nature with the taste of a painter, and the enthusiasm of a poet: while to Lady Newenden all was a blank, which offered nothing to gratify either her per-

---

[6]Charlotte Smith, *Ethelinde* (London, 1790), IV, x, 243.
[7]*Ibid.*, I, ii, 31.
[8]*Ibid.*, I, ii, 33–34.

sonal vanity, or the consequence she assumed from her splendid fortune."

The Zeluco theme is glanced at again in Charlotte Smith's *The Young Philosopher* (1798). The hero George, who is the young philosopher, is an ardent devotee, but his older brother, who attempts to seduce the heroine and is described as entirely devoid of principle of any kind, cares nothing for the face of nature. At the time of the passage following,[9] the elder brother is making the grand tour: ". . . George was envying his brother the delights that he was incapable of tasting, sighing with boyish enthusiasm for the scenes of simple hospitality in the Pais de Vaud, and languishing to wander among Alpine rocks and torrents, and to gaze on an imaginary Clarens from the rocks of Meillerie."

Three passages[10] in *The Children of the Abbey* (1796) by Regina Maria Roche state the Zeluco theme by implication—a villain can take no delight in nature. Amanda is the heroine:

'Oh, how sweet, how lovely is the dewy landscape!' exclaimed Amanda, with that delight which scenes of calm and vernal nature never fail of raising in minds of piety and tenderness.

.   .   .   .

Amanda, in spite of sadness, beheld the charming scene with admiration, and Fitzalan contemplated it with delight. 'All nature,' he exclaimed, 'points out to man the gratitude due to the divine Dispenser of good; hardened must that heart be against the feelings of sensibility, which the harmony and fragrance of this early hour awaken not to a perfect sense of it!'

.   .   .   .

Spontaneous praise burst from the lips of Amanda, and she felt all that calm and sweet delight which ever pervades a mind of religion and sensibility, on viewing the rural beauties of nature.

[9]Charlotte Smith, *The Young Philosopher* (London, 1798), I, iii, 61.

[10]Regina Maria Roche, *The Children of the Abbey* (London, no date; sixth edition), vii, 80; ix, 101; xli, 574.

The last novel that need be included here is Charles Robert Maturin's *Melmoth the Wanderer* (1820), which is interesting not only because of its late date but also because of the prominence it gives to the Zeluco theme, and the other close resemblances between its main character and the Byronic hero. Melmoth has sold his soul to the devil in return for a prolonged life on earth, but has found nothing but bitterness in his bargain, from which he can escape only by finding another soul who will accept it. The Zeluco theme is most prominent in the episode of Immalee, a child of nature whom Melmoth meets in an island paradise and eventually marries. Of course the beauties of nature (as well as those of the innocent mind of Immalee) are lost[11] upon him:

. . . he sunk down beside her, passed his hand over his livid brow, and, wiping off some cold drops, thought for a moment he was not the Cain of the moral world, and that the brand was effaced,—at least for a moment. The habitual and impervious gloom of his soul soon returned. He felt again the gnawings of the worm that never dies, and the scorchings of the fire that is never to be quenched. He turned the fatal light of his dark eyes on the only being who never shrunk from their expression, for her innocence made her fearless. He looked intensely at her, while rage, despair, and pity, convulsed his heart; and as he beheld the confiding and conciliating smile with which this gentle being met a look that might have withered the heart of the boldest within him,—a Semele gazing in supplicating love on the lightnings that were to blast her,—one human drop dimmed their portentous lustre, as its softened rays fell on her. Turning fiercely away, he flung his view on the ocean, as if to find, in the sight of human life, some fuel for the fire that was consuming his vitals. The ocean, that lay calm and bright before them as a sea of jasper, never reflected two more different countenances, or sent more opposite feelings to two hearts. Over Immalee's, it breathed that

[11]Charles Robert Maturin, *Melmoth the Wanderer* (London, 1892), II, xvii, 225–226.

deep and delicious reverie, which those forms of nature that unite tranquility and profundity diffuse over souls whose innocence gives them a right to an unmingled and exclusive enjoyment of nature. None but crimeless and unimpassioned minds ever truly enjoyed earth, ocean, and heaven. At our first transgression, nature expels us, as it did our first parents, from her paradise for ever.

To the stranger the view was fraught with far different visions. He viewed it as a tiger views a forest abounding with prey; there might be the storm and the wreck; or, if the elements were obstinately calm, there might be the gaudy and gilded pleasure barge, in which a Rajah and the beautiful women of his harem were inhaling the sea breeze under canopies of silk and gold, overturned by the unskilfullness of their rowers, and their plunge, and struggle, and dying agony, amid the smile and beauty of the calm ocean, produce one of those contrasts in which his fierce spirit delighted. Or, were even this denied, he could watch the vessels as they floated by, and from the skiff to the huge trader, be sure that every one bore its freight of woe and crime.

Melmoth[12] is possessed by a demon of "superhuman misanthropy," and a "union of inward despair and outward levity" characterize him. A "tone of ruthless irony" and an attitude of "sarcastic levity" are employed by him whenever the finer sensibilities of man are discussed.[13] "Such was the overflowing acrimony of this being, that he could not speak of the beneficence of nature, or the luxuries of art, without interweaving something that seemed like a satire on, or a scorn of both."[14]

As Melmoth's baleful influence begins to take effect upon the pure Immalee, even she begins to lose her love of the beauties of nature. At the point in the narrative where the

12*Ibid.*, II, xvii, 233, 243.
13*Ibid.*, II, xx, 321.
14*Ibid.*, II, xx, 305.

following passage occurs,[15] Melmoth has already rejected the simple plea of Immalee that he remain with her forever on her island, has departed for a time, and now returns to the enamoured child of nature:

When he found her, she was leaning against a rock; the ocean was pouring its eternal murmur of waters at her feet; she had chosen the most desolate spot she could find;—there was neither flower or shrub near her;—the calcined rocks, the off-spring of volcano—the restless roar of the sea, whose waves almost touched her small foot, that seemed by its heedless protrusion at once to court and neglect danger—these objects were all that surrounded her. The first time he had beheld her, she was embowered amid flowers and odours, amid all the glorious luxuries of vegetable and animal nature. . . . Now she stood as if deserted even by nature, whose child she was; the rock was her resting-place, and the ocean seemed the bed where she purposed to rest; she had no shells on her bosom, no roses in her hair—her character seemed to have changed with her feelings; she no longer loved all that is beautiful in nature; she seemed, by an anticipation of her destiny, to make alliance with all that is awful and ominous. She had begun to love the rocks and the ocean, the thunder of the wave, and the sterility of the sand,—awful objects, the incessant recurrence of whose very sound seems intended to remind us of grief and of eternity. Their restless monotony of repetition, corresponds with the beatings of a heart which asks its destiny from the phenomena of nature, and feels the answer is—'Misery.'

.   .   .   .

"When we first met, my bosom was covered with roses—now it is shaded with the dark leaves of the ocymum. When he saw me first, the living things all loved me—now I care not whether they love me or not—I have forgot to love them. When he came to the isle every night, I hoped the moon would be bright—now I care not whether she is clouded or bright.

[15]*Ibid*, II, xviii, 248–249, 255–256. See also II, xx, 301–302.

Before he came, every thing loved me, and I had more things to love than I could reckon by the hairs of my head—now I feel I can love but one, and that one has deserted me. Since I have seen him all things have changed. The flowers have not the colours they once had—there is no music in the flow of the waters—the stars do not smile on me from heaven as they did,—and I myself begin to love the storm better than the calm."

BIBLIOGRAPHY

EDITIONS OF BYRON'S WORKS

Letters and Journals of Lord Byron. Edited by Rowland E. Prothero (Lord Ernle). London, 1898–1901. 6 vols.

Lord Byron's Correspondence. Edited by John Murray. London, 1922. 2 vols.

The Poetical Works of Lord Byron. Edited by Ernest Hartley Coleridge. London, 1898–1904. 7 vols.

The Complete Poetical Works of Lord Byron. Edited by Paul Elmer More. Cambridge edition. New York, 1905.

N.B. Quotations of Byron's poetry are normally from the Cambridge edition. MS. readings and Byron's notes are taken from the E. H. Coleridge edition. The terms L. and J. and *Correspondence* have been used in footnotes to refer to the first two editions listed above.

SELECTED LIST OF WORKS CITED AND OTHER PERTINENT STUDIES

Aubin, Robert Arnold. *Topographical Poetry in XVIII-Century England.* New York, 1936.

Beach, Joseph Warren. *The Concept of Nature in Nineteenth-Century English Poetry.* New York, 1936.

Beyle, Marie Henri ("De Stendhal"). "Reminiscences of Lord Byron in Italy," *The Mirror of Literature, Amusement, and Instruction,* XV (1830). 266–68.

Bisson, L. A. "Rousseau and the Romantic Experience," *Modern Language Review,* XXXVII (1942). 37–49.

Blake, William. *Poetry and Prose.* Edited by Geoffrey Keynes. Bloomsbury, 1927.

Blessington, The Countess of (Marguerite P. F. Gardiner). *A Journal of the Conversations of Lord Byron.* London, 1893.

Boyd, E. F. *Byron's Don Juan.* New Brunswick, 1945.

Brown, Wallace C. "Byron and English Interest in the Near East," *Studies in Philology,* XXXIV (1937). 55–64.

Browne, J. Hamilton. "Voyage from Leghorn to Cephalonia with Lord Byron," *Blackwood's Edinburgh Magazine,* XXXV (1834). 56–67; XXXVI (1834). 392–407.

Bush, Mary D. "Rational Proof of a Deity from the Order of Nature," *ELH,* IX (1942). 288–319.

Calvert, William J. *Byron: Romantic Paradox.* Chapel Hill, 1935.

Chew, Samuel C. *Byron in England.* New York, 1924.

————. *The Dramas of Lord Byron.* Göttingen, 1915.

Dallas, R. C. *Correspondence of Lord Byron with a Friend.* Philadelphia, 1825.

Deane, C. V. *Aspects of Eighteenth Century Nature Poetry.* Oxford, 1935.

Evans, Bertrand. *Gothic Drama From Walpole to Shelley.* Los Angeles, 1947.

Fairchild, Hoxie Neale. *The Noble Savage.* New York, 1928.

Finlay, George. "Reminiscences of Lord Byron." In L. F. C. Stanhope's *Greece in 1823 and 1824.* London, 1825.

Frere, John Hookham. *The Monks and the Giants.* Edited by R. D. Waller. Manchester, 1926.

Fuess, Claude M. *Lord Byron as a Satirist in Verse.* New York, 1912.

Galt, John. *The Life of Lord Byron.* New York, 1830.

Gamba, Peter. *A Narrative of Lord Byron's Last Journey to Greece.* London, 1825.

Gilpin, William. *Remarks on Forest Scenery and Other Woodland Views.* Edited by Sir Thomas Dick Lauder. Two volumes in one. Edinburgh, 1834.

————. *Three Essays: On Picturesque Beauty; On Picturesque Travel; and On Sketching Landscape: To which is added a poem. On Landscape Painting.* London, 1792.

Goode, Clement Tyson. *Byron As Critic.* Weimar, 1923.

Grylls, R. Glynn. *Claire Clairmont.* London, 1939.

Guiccioli, Teresa G. *My Recollections of Lord Byron.* Translated by Hubert E. H. Jerningham. London, 1869. 2 vols.

Haas, C. E. De. *Nature and the Country in English Poetry of the First Half of the Eighteenth Century.* Amsterdam, 1928.

Havens, Raymond Dexter. *The Mind of a Poet*. Baltimore, 1941.
————. "Romantic Aspects of the Age of Pope," *PMLA*, XXVII (1912). 297–324.
Hobhouse, John Cam (Lord Broughton). "Lord Byron in Greece," *The Westminster Review*, II (1824). 225–62.
————. *Recollections of a Long Life*. London, 1909–1911. Vols. 1–3 only.
Hodgson, J. and Laird, F. C. *The Beauties of England and Wales*. London, 1813. Vol. 12, part 1, only. Two volumes in one, "Northumberland" and "Nottinghamshire."
Hunt, Leigh. *Lord Byron and Some of His Contemporaries*. Philadelphia, 1828.
Hussey, Christopher. *The Picturesque: Studies in a Point of View*. London, 1927.
Kennedy, James. *Conversations on Religion with Lord Byron*. London, 1830.
Lovejoy, Arthur O. "The Parallel of Deism and Classicism," *Modern Philology*, XXIX (1932). 281–99.
Manwaring, Elizabeth Wheeler. *Italian Landscape in Eighteenth Century England*. New York, 1925.
Marjarum, Edward Wayne. *Byron as Skeptic and Believer*. Princeton, 1938.
Martin, Abbott C. "The Love of Solitude in Eighteenth Century Poetry," *South Atlantic Quarterly*, XXIX (1930). 48–59.
Maurois, André. *Byron*. Translated by Hamish Miles. New York, 1930.
————. "The Ethics of Biography," *English Institute Annual* for 1942 (1943). 6–28.
Mayne, Ethel Colburn. *Byron*. London, 1912. 2 vols.
————. *The Life and Letters of Anne Isabella, Lady Noel Byron*. London, 1929.
Medwin, Thomas. *Journal of the Conversations of Lord Byron*. New York, 1824.
Milbanke, Ralph (Earl of Lovelace). *Astarte*. London, 1921.
Monk, Samuel H. *The Sublime: A Study of Critical Theories in XVIII-Century England*. New York, 1935.

Moore, C. A. "The Return to Nature in English Poetry of the Eighteenth Century," *Studies in Philology*, XIV (1917). 243–91.

Moore, Thomas. *The Life of Lord Byron*. London, 1851.

————. *Memoirs, Journal and Correspondence*. Edited by Lord John Russell. London, 1853. Vol. 3 only.

Murray, John. *Memoir and Correspondence of John Murray*. Edited by Samuel Smiles. London, 1891. 2 vols.

Parry, William. *The Last Days of Lord Byron*. London, 1825.

Polidori, John William. *The Diary of Dr. John William Polidori*. Edited by William Michael Rossetti. London, 1911.

Radcliffe, Anne. *Gaston de Blondeville. To which is prefixed a Memoir of the Author, with Extracts from her Journals*. London, 1826. 4 vols.

————. *Journey Through Holland and Germany*. London, 1795. 2 vols.

Richter, Helene. *Lord Byron: Persönlichkeit und Werk*. Halle, 1929.

Robinson, Henry Crabb. *Diary, Reminiscences, and Correspondence*. Edited by Thomas Sadler. London, 1869. Vol. 2 only.

Shelley, Percy Bysshe. *Complete Works*. Edited by Roger Ingpen and Walter E. Peck. London, 1928–1929. Vols. 5–10 only.

Sickels, Eleanor M. *The Gloomy Egoist: Moods and Themes of Melancholy from Gray to Keats*. New York, 1932.

Stanhope, L. F. C. *Greece in 1823 and 1824 . . . to which are added, Reminiscences of Lord Byron*. London, 1825. (Contains "Reminiscences of Lord Byron" by George Finlay and "Sketch of Lord Byron" by Stanhope).

Templeman, William D. *The Life and Works of William Gilpin*. Urbana, Illinois, 1939.

Ticknor, Anna. *Life, Letters, and Journals of George Ticknor*. Boston, 1909. 2 vols.

Trelawny, Edward John. *Recollections of the Last Days of Shelley and Byron*. London, 1906.

————. *Records of Shelley, Byron, and the Author*. London 1878.

Trueblood, P. G. *The Flowering of Byron's Genius: Studies in Byron's Don Juan.* Stanford, 1945.

White, Newman I. "The Development, Use and Abuse of Interpretation in Biography," *English Institute Annual* for 1942 (1943). 29–57.

————. *Shelley.* New York, 1940. 2 vols.

Willey, Basil. *The Eighteenth Century Background: Studies in the Idea of Nature.* London, 1940.

Williams, Edward Ellerker. *Journal of Edward Ellerker Williams.* London, 1902.

Williams, George G. "The Beginnings of Nature Poetry in the Eighteenth Century," *Studies in Philology,* XXVII (1930). 583–608.

Wordsworth, William and Dorothy. *Letters, 1821–1830.* Edited by Ernest De Selincourt. Oxford, 1939.

LIST OF NOVELS CITED

Barrett, Eaton Stannard. *The Heroine.* Edited by Michael Sadleir. New York, 1927.

Brooke, Frances. *Lady Julia Mandeville.* Edited by E. Phillips Poole. London, 1930.

————. *The History of Emily Montague.* Edited by Lawrence J. Burpee. Ottawa, 1931.

Chateaubriand, François René, Vicomte de. *René.* Edited by Armand Weil. Paris, 1935.

Dacre, Charlotte. *Zofloya, or The Moor.* Edited by Montague Summers. London, n.d.

Godwin, William. *Caleb Williams, or Things As They Are.* London, 1903.

————. *Fleetwood: or, The New Man of Feeling.* London, 1832.

————. *Mandeville.* Edinburgh, 1817. 3 vols.

————. *St. Leon.* London, 1832.

Goethe, Johann Wolfgang von. *The Sorrows of Young Werther.* Translated by William Rose. London, 1929.

Lewis, Matthew Gregory. *The Monk.* London, 1796. 3 vols.

Maturin, Charles Robert. *Fatal Revenge; or, the Family of Montorio.* London, 1840.

————. *Melmoth the Wanderer*. London, 1892. 4 vols.

————. *The Milesian Chief*. London, 1812. 4 vols.

————. *The Wild Irish Boy*. London, 1808. 3 vols.

Moore, John. *Mordaunt*. London, 1800. 3 vols.

————. *Zeluco*. In vol. 1 of *The Republic of Letters*. New York, 1834.

Radcliffe, Anne. *The Italian*. London, 1844.

————. *The Mysteries of Udolpho*. New York, 1931. 2 vols.

————. *The Romance of the Forest*. New York, 1904.

Reeve, Clara. *The Exiles; or, Memoirs of the Count de Cronstadt*. London, 1788. 3 vols.

Roche, Regina Maria. *The Children of the Abbey*. London, n.d., sixth edition.

Rousseau, Jean-Jacques. *La Nouvelle Héloïse*. Edited by Daniel Mornet. Paris, 1925. 4 vols.

Shelley, Mary. *Frankenstein*. New York, 1931.

Shelley, Percy Bysshe. *St. Irvyne*. Edited by Roger Ingpen and Walter E. Peck in vol. 5 of the *Complete Works*. London, 1929.

————. *Zastrozzi*. Edited by Roger Ingpen and Walter E. Peck in vol. 5 of the *Complete Works*. London, 1929.

Smith, Charlotte. *Ethelinde, or the Recluse of the Lake*. London, 1790. 5 vols.

————. *The Young Philosopher*. London, 1798. 4 vols.